Political Writings, 1953–1993

Maurice Blanchot

Political Writings, 1953–1993

Translated, with an Introduction, by Zakir Paul

FORDHAM UNIVERSITY PRESS

New York 2010

The core of this book was published in French as Maurice Blanchot, *Écrits politiques: 1958–1993* in 2003 by Éditions Léo Scheer, © *Éditions Lignes & Manifestes*, 2003. The texts translated as "An Approach to Communism (Needs, Values)," "[Interrogation with the judge]," "[Questioned by the judge]," "The Course of the World," "Letter to Ilija Bojovic," "Paranoia in Power (The Dialectics of Repression: A Small Contribution to Research)," and "Yes, Silence Is Necessary for Writing" appear in French in Maurice Blanchot, *Écrits politiques: 1953–1993*, © Éditions Gallimard, 2008.

FRENCH VOICES

Cet ourvrage, publié dans le cadre d'un programme d'aide à la publication, bénéficie du soutien financier du ministère des Affaires étrangères, du Service culturel de l'ambassade de France aux Etats-Unis, ainsi que de l'appui de FACE (French American Cultural Exchange).

This work, published as part of a program providing publication assistance, received financial support from the French Ministry of Foreign Affairs, from the Cultural Services of the French Embassy in the United States, and from FACE (French American Cultural Exchange).

For Library of Congress Cataloging-in-Publication Data, see page 201.

12 11 10 5 4 3 2 1

CONTENTS

TRANSLATOR'S NOTE

Most of the texts in this volume were collected in *Écrits politiques: 1958–1993*, assembled by Michel Surya and published by *Lignes & Manifestes* and Éditions Léo Scheer in 2003. According to the editor's acknowledgments, this volume was largely made possible by the issues of *Lignes* devoted to Blanchot, Dionys Mascolo, and Robert Antelme, respectively, in addition to the help of Daniel Dobbels, Christophe Bident, Jean-Luc Nancy, and Monique Antelme. An expanded version of this edition, with additional texts and variants, was published by Gallimard in 2008. The additional texts included both here and in the Gallimard volume are: "An Approach to Communism (Needs, Values)," "[Interrogation with the judge]," "[Questioned by the judge]," "The Course of the World," "Letter to Ilija Bojovic," "Paranoia in Power (The Dialectics of Repression: A Small Contribution to Research)," and "Yes, Silence Is Necessary for Writing."

The following texts included here have not been published in either book version in French. The "Letters from the *Revue internationale*" were published in *Lignes*, no. 11 (1990). "For Friendship" was published as *Pour l'amitié* by Fourbis in 1996. "Our Clandestine Companion" appeared as "Notre compagne clandestine" in Maurice Blanchot et al., *Textes pour Emmanuel Levinas* (Paris: Jean-Michel Place, 1980), 79–87. "The Ascendent Word; or, Are We Still Worthy of Poetry?" appeared as "La parole ascendante, ou Sommes-nous toujours digne de la poésie? (notes éparses)," an afterword to Vadim Kozovoï, *Hors de la colline* (Paris: Hermann, 1984), 119–27. "Encounters (On the Resistance and May 68)" appeared as "Les rencontres" in *Le nouvel observateur*, no. 1045 (November 1984): 84. "Peace, Peace Far and Near" appeared as "Paix, paix au lointain et au proche," in *De la Bible à nos jours*, catalog of a show of the Independent Artists' Society, Paris, Grand Palais, 1985. The "Letter to Blandine Jeanson" took the place of the author's photograph in *Photographies en quête d'auteur* (Paris: Agence Vu, 1986). "Our Responsibility (On Nelson Mandela)" was published as 'Notre responsabilité" in Jacques Derrida et al.,

Pour Nelson Mandela (Paris: Gallimard, 1986), 213–17. "What Is Closest to Me" was published as "Ce qui m'est le plus proche," in *Globe*, no. 30 (July-August 1988): 56. "[I think it suits a writer better] (On Nationalism and Internationalism)" appeared as "Je crois qu'il convient mieux à un écrivain" in *La règle du jeu*, no 3. (January 1991): 221–22.

Translations of some of these texts have previously appeared in Michael Holland, ed., *The Blanchot Reader* (Cambridge: Blackwell, 1995); Maurice Blanchot, *Friendship*, trans. Elizabeth Rottenberg (Stanford: Stanford University Press, 2003), and special issues of *The Oxford Literary Review* (no. 22, *Disastrous Blanchot*, ed. Timothy Clark, Leslie Hill, and Nicholas Royle, 2000) and *Paragraph* (no. 30, *Blanchot's Epoch*, ed. Leslie Hill and Michael Holland, 2007). The essays on Levinas and Antelme were translated in *Face to Face with Levinas*, ed. Richard A. Cohen (Albany: State University of New York Press, 2007), and in *On Robert Antelme's Human Race*, ed. Daniel Dobbels (Evanston, Ill.: Northwestern University Press, 2003), respectively. They have all been retranslated for the present volume.

Throughout the text author's footnotes are indicated in the asterisk-dagger sequence, while translator's notes appear with Arabic numerals.

This translation would not have been possible without the unflagging support of Helen Tartar and the editorial team at Fordham University Press. Christophe Bident, Michael Holland, Jean-Michel Rabaté, and Samuel Weber were invaluable sources of expertise and encouragement. Jeff Fort generously read the manuscript, made countless corrections, and offered suggestions for improvement throughout. Any remaining errors are my own. I would also like to thank Eduardo Cadava, Daniel Heller-Roazen, Geneviève Rousselière, Thomas Trezise, and Arnd Wedemeyer for their incisive comments on the introduction.

Foreword

The Friendship of the No

KEVIN HART

"the irreducible refusal, the friendship
of this sure, unshakable, rigorous No"

BLANCHOT, "Refusal"

Maurice Blanchot was always a political writer, and although over his lifetime his politics changed radically, from the far right to the far left and then to the side of the far left, he remained constant in his rejection of party and in his affirmation of dissidence. When in 1986 Emmanuel Levinas was reminiscing with François Poiré about his close friend, the first thing he said about Blanchot is that when they met as undergraduates at Strasbourg "I had the impression of an extreme intelligence, of an aristocratic cast of mind." The second is that Blanchot was "Very distanced politically from me during that epoch, he was monarchist."[1] Extreme intelligence and, as we shall see, extreme politics: the combination is volatile, regardless of whether the politics are on the right or on the left. Levinas goes on to say of his friend that "He experienced the occupation in an extremely heightened and painful way . . . he also experienced 1968 in an extraordinary manner."[2] Levinas and Blanchot vowed friendship shortly after they met, a vow that was never broken on either side. Nor was the vow of friendship that Blanchot must have made early on to the "No," for it sustained him throughout his political itinerary, in the grim years leading up to the Vichy régime and the occupation of France by the *Wehrmacht*, as well as when the Fourth Republic was dissolved in 1958, when *les événements* of May 1968 irrupted, and when, not so very long after the student-worker uprising, some members of the French far left upset Blanchot by supporting Palestine over Israel.

As an author, the young Blanchot begins to come into focus for us as a journalist committed to the far right. He reached adulthood during what

Emmanuel Mounier ironically called the time of *le désordre établi*, the established disorder, in which fascism and communism were both vying for supremacy in a world in which France seemed weak and impotent, threatened by an impending war it could not win. Only a spiritual, national revolution, it seemed, could save France. In one of Blanchot's first pieces, "Les pensées politiques de M. Paul Valéry" ("The Political Thinking of Paul Valéry"), published in *La revue française* in August 1931, he reviewed the great poet's *Regards sur le monde actuel* (*Reflections on the World Today*, 1931). Blanchot noted how, for Valéry, the word *political* is seductive and "excites considerable scruples and distaste in the author's mind," and that history "is nothing but a *horrible mélange*."[3] Blanchot takes exception to what he sees as Valéry's endorsement of amnesia as a political virtue and views his image of Europe as a monster—a Hippogryph or a Siren, or, indeed, a horror with many heads, like Cerberus or the Hydra, each with its own thoughts. "Europe will never have had the policy [*la politique*] which its thought demands," writes Valéry.[4] To which Blanchot says yes and no, for some European countries have no policies at all. What frightens Blanchot is the specter of *Homo Europaeus*, a creature like Aristide Briand, who risks having no politics or thought and attaining only mediocrity. Valéry's elegant, weary reflections on the world today remain too fuzzy for the young Blanchot, too unaware of the need to remember what has happened, and too unconcerned with saving France in a world in which Europe is not so much "a balance of weaknesses" as a tragic play of weakness (France) and growing strengths nearby.[5]

Blanchot's own political views are more readily seen in another of his first pieces, "Comment s'emparer du pouvoir?" ("How to Seize Power?") also published in August 1931, in *Journal des débats*. There he reviewed the Italian Curzio Malaparte's much-discussed *Technique du coup d'état* (1931).[6] Malaparte argued that "the problem of the conquest and defense of the State is not a political one . . . it is a technical problem"—a matter of knowing when and how to occupy the telephone exchanges, control the water reserves and the electricity generators, and so on—and also taught the hard lesson that a revolution can wear itself out in strategy.[7] Critical of Hitler and Mussolini, Malaparte was removed from the National Fascist Party and exiled, first in Lipari and then, more comfortably, in Ischia. Blanchot argued against Malaparte in his review that revolution is not always or entirely a matter of technique. Some revolutions are embedded in a prior politics, as was the case with the 1917 Russian overthrow of Czarist autocracy. Yet there is also the possibility of a revolution that comes about through "the bad politics of governments," and then the revolution must presumably itself create a new politics.[8]

The latter had been, more or less, the situation in France since World War I, Blanchot judged, pointing disparagingly to the premiership of Aristide Briand and the presidency of Raymond Poincaré.[9] Things did not improve over the years between the two wars. For all their policy differences, the governments of Pierre Laval and Edouard Daladier, as well as the Popular Front alliance of Léon Blum, could merely form pacts and sign treaties with nearby countries, doing nothing decisive to strengthen France.[10] Far from helping to secure France, Blum's government was infiltrated by agents from Moscow.[11] Not that anticommunists were especially needed: those people were insufficiently radical. In general, the young Blanchot thought, a government is only as good as its ability to enforce the rule of law, and accordingly a weak government in unstable times must be overthrown for the good of the country. Besides, Blanchot asked himself, why pay taxes to a coterie of private interests pretending to govern the country?[12] Certainly the League of Nations was no help; its muzzy internationalism could bring no clarity to the situation in France, since only force and the willingness to use it when needed create clarity in politics. A revolution must come, and it must come from French dissidents. Only "national ideas" give youth the hope it needs, he said in 1933, and each day, he surmised, events brought the national, spiritual revolution closer "and make it more necessary."[13]

On the far right wing though he surely was, at no time was Blanchot attracted to fascism. His nonconformism was absolute. His preoccupation was protecting France against the threats of German rearmament and Soviet expansionism, against liberal ineffectiveness and the encroachments of international socialism. There was no point in looking to Hitler: all he could give German youth was "a new religion" that was a "perverted nationalism," namely, that of a superior race.[14] Fascism promoted an affirmative sense of "neither-nor" ("neither right nor left"), a fusion of elements from each side of politics achieved in a supposedly higher synthesis; but Blanchot took "neither-nor" in a negative sense, criticizing both the left and the right as pungently as he could.[15] He communicated his message in diverse, scattered, and at times irreconcilable ways. He wrote for the then generally respectable conservative paper *Journal des débats*, as well as (and usually more fiercely) for short-lived nonconformist organs, which ventured much further out on the right wing of politics than the readers of that venerable paper were easy with. Some of these organs were Catholic nationalist papers, which attracted young intellectuals who had broken with the royalist movement Action Française (condemned by Pius XI in 1926) and who formed La Jeune Droite: *Réaction*, *La revue du siècle* (*The Review of the Century*, renamed *La revue du XXe siècle*, *The Review of the Twentieth Century*, in 1934) and *La revue universelle*. Other papers to which he contributed were even more extreme in their nationalist fervor: *Le rempart*, *Combat*, and *L'Insurgé*. His pieces for these ephemeral publications are striking, at once independent and inflammatory. If at times Blanchot may be found supporting the parliament, at other times he calls for its overthrow; he looks to democracy only to the extent that diplomacy can still save France.[16] His faith in parliament is intermittent, at best. In June 1933, when he expresses hope in diplomacy he also asserts, in another place, that national revolution is France's only chance of salvation.[17] In 1936, he is to be heard insisting that public salvation can be achieved only through terrorism.[18]

It is important to point out that Blanchot denounces what he calls, in no uncertain terms, "the barbaric persecutions of the Jews" and that he does so as early as May 1, 1933.[19] Did the young Blanchot publish reviews and commentaries in papers that ran articles with anti-Semitic leanings? Yes, he did. Would it have been possible at the time to write for a right-wing paper, broadsheet, or periodical without appearing near such material? No, it would not: a certain level of anti-Semitism was everywhere and widely tolerated. Blanchot himself says that when *L'Insurgé* ran a foully anti-Semitic article he immediately worked with Thierry Maulnier to have the paper closed down.[20] Did Blanchot himself make anti-Semitic remarks? Not as such, although, to be sure, he included Jews in his tirades against all people whose influence threatened France, namely the "holy alliance" of "Soviet, Jewish, Capitalist interests," a coalition that he deemed to be "antinational" and "antisocial."[21] Did Blanchot publish in the anti-Semitic, fascistic paper *Je suis partout*? No, he did not, and in fact that horrid paper denounced him to the Gestapo, as well as finding his first novel, *Thomas l'obscur* (*Thomas the Obscure*, 1941), objectionably Jewish.[22] In the interview from which I have already quoted, Levinas says, "I must mention especially that he saved my wife during the war while I was in captivity."[23] At considerable personal risk, Blanchot had hidden Raïssa Levinas in his apartment in Paris. It is also worth mentioning that Marguerite Blanchot, the author's sister, helped his friend Paul Lévy, owner of *Le rempart* and then *Aux écoutes*, avoid being caught by the Gestapo.[24] It is difficult to imagine that Blanchot himself was not involved in this good work. Given that the Germans would have known Lévy's direct and sustained criticisms of Nazism, including an editorial for *Le rempart* entitled "La peste hitlérienne" ("The Hitlerian Plague"), they were looking for him for one reason, and for one reason only.[25]

If we listen to Blanchot's political rhetoric in 1937, toward the end of his time as a right-wing journalist, we can hear one politics that fades away and another that will remain, albeit transformed. In *L'Insurgé* he repeats the refrain that to be French now is to be against France from within its borders.[26] His last pieces appear in *Combat*, the monthly directed by Jean de Fabrègues and Thierry Maulnier (not the later clandestine paper of the same title associated with Albert Camus). In "La France, nation à venir" ("France, a Nation to Come"), published in *Combat* in November 1937, he laments that "The spiritual mission of France is not to be France but to assure the triumph of Marxism or Fascism in Spain."[27] And in "On demande des dissidents" ("Dissidents Wanted"), his final piece for *Combat*, published in December 1937, he provides his last word on how energies can best be mobilized in France. He begins by deploring the fact that once there were dissidents in the country but they cannot be found any longer, and he concludes by outlining what a true dissident is and why we need them:

> In reality what counts is not being above parties but being against them. It is not to take that vulgar slogan "neither right nor left," but to be really against the right and against the left. One can see in these conditions that the true form of dissidence is abandoning a position without ceasing to maintain the same hostility with regard to the contrary position or, rather, abandoning the position in order to accentuate this hostility. The true communist dissident is someone who leaves communism not in order to find common ground with capitalism but in order to define the true conditions of the struggle against capitalism. In the same way, the true nationalist dissident is someone who neglects traditional formulas of nationalism, not in order to seek reconciliation with internationalism but in order to fight internationalism in all of its forms, including the economy and the nation itself. These two examples of dissidence seem to us each as useful as the other. But they seem equally rare. We need dissidents.[28]

Combat continued publishing until July 1939, but without the help of Blanchot, who, so far as we can tell, stopped writing political journalism. Or, to put the matter more exactly, he stopped *signing* political journalism. He continued as editor of the *Journal des débats* and *Aux écoutes* until 1940 and presumably wrote unsigned editorials.

What Blanchot stopped expressing, then presumably dropped, though neither simply nor all at once, were a nationalist fervor for securing France by way of a revolution and a distaste for international solutions to national political problems.[29] And what remained was the negative cast of the neither-nor attitude: not just neither Marxism nor fascism (a matter of indifference to him, it would seem, in the November essay) but a principled and sustained critique of all parties and all positions. To be sure, in "Dissidents Wanted" this relentless critique is needed in order to save France from almost certain peril. Later, however, the style of critique he calls on dissidents to embody will be put to other ends. It would be a mistake to infer that Blanchot simply stopped writing about politics in order to write literature and write about it: he had been reviewing literary books since June 1931, writing a novel since 1932, and composing short stories since 1935. Yet in 1938 he stopped writing about current political events; indeed, in 1939 he published only one article, a piece on Gérard de Nerval.[30] He wrote a column, "Chronique de la vie intellectuelle" ("A Chronicle of Intellectual Life"), for the then Pétainist *Journal des débats* from April 1941 to August 1944, and he published a second novel, *Aminadab*, in 1942.[31]

Does *L'Arrêt de mort* (*Death Sentence*, 1948), his fourth narrative, indirectly tell us what Blanchot was doing in 1938? "These things happened to me in 1938," he says in the opening sentence, "I feel the greatest uneasiness in speaking of them."[32] We too should have the greatest uneasiness when reading Blanchot's narratives, especially when being invited to identify first-person narration and autobiography. For Blanchot misaligns facts and narratives at the very moments when we are most likely to anticipate personal revelations. "The only date I can be sure of is the 13th of October—Wednesday, the 13th of October," the narrator tells us, but, as Christophe Bident points out, there was no such day in 1938 (the thirteenth fell on a Thursday that year), although there was in 1937.[33] Perhaps the personal events described in *Death Sentence* took place in 1937 and run parallel to the political events of 1938, above all the Munich agreement about the Sudetenland, dated September 29 and signed the following day. ("Since September I had been living in Arcachon. It was during the Munich crisis," we are told in *Death Sentence*.[34]) We know that Blanchot was in a sanitarium at Cambo-les-Bains, near the Spanish border, being treated for tuberculosis sometime in the late 1930s; perhaps it was over the summer and early autumn of 1937, giving him an opportunity to reflect on his life and political commitments and perhaps also to work on *Thomas the Obscure*. On September 22, 1937, he would have turned thirty: a time to take stock of things.

At any rate, at some point before, during, or just after the war Blanchot moved from the far right toward the left. The first definite sign of this change was his involvement in *Actualité* (1946), which he edited with Georges Bataille and Pierre Prévost. In late 1937 he had been against the Spanish Republic, and certainly against Blum's ineffectual support for it.[35] Now, though, he was for *L'Éspagne libre*. In his contribution to the journal, a belated review of Malraux's novel about how the Republicans fought the Fascists in Spain, *L'Espoir* (*Days of Hope*, 1937), Blanchot affirms that "hope always has the same name: liberty."[36] This change in political allegiance was by no means publicly known or even well known in the French intellectual world. For one thing, Blanchot retreated to the village of Èze in the south of France from the end of 1946 to 1957, almost the whole time of the Fourth Republic, making only sporadic trips to Paris, and it was in Èze that he wrote some of his finest narrative and critical work, including the *récit* version of *Thomas the Obscure* (1950), *Au moment voulu* (*When the Time Comes*, 1951), *Celui qui ne m'accompagnait pas* (*The One Who Was Standing Apart from Me*, 1953), *L'Espace littéraire* (*The Space of Literature*, 1955), *Le dernier homme* (*The Last Man*, 1957), along with major essays later to appear in *L'Entretien infini* (*The Infinite Conversation*, 1969) and *L'Amitié* (*Friendship*, 1971). The essays he published just after the war were placed in journals with quite different political associations from those he favored before the war: *L'Arche*, *Cahiers de la Pléiade*, *Critique*, *Les temps modernes*. Yet it was only in 1958, when Dionys Mascolo founded the anti-Gaullist journal *Le 14 juillet* that he received a letter from Blanchot in which the former right-winger announced what then must have seemed to be a complete about-face. "After the publication of the first number," Mascolo says in an interview, "Maurice Blanchot, who had not said a word about politics since the war, sent me a letter that bowled me over: 'I want to tell you that I agree with you. I refuse all the past and accept nothing of the present.'"[37] It is not quite true to say that Blanchot had not uttered a political word since the war. In December 1953 he had favorably reviewed Mascolo's *Le communisme* (1953) in *La nouvelle nouvelle revue française*.[38] Yet there is no denying the directness of Blanchot's comment in his letter of 1958.

What made Blanchot change his political position so radically? Was it the events of 1937–38? Were there other events? Did it happen all at once or over a period of years?

We know that on July 20, 1944, he narrowly avoided being executed by the Vlassov army.[39] As he faced the firing squad, the young Blanchot (as remembered by the older writer) "experienced then a feeling of extraordinary lightness, a sort of beatitude (nothing happy, however)—sovereign elation?"[40] The soldiers allowed him to escape while their lieutenant was distracted. Only later, when he returned to the scene, did he discover that three young men had been slaughtered, presumably in vengeance for his escape. "No doubt what then began for the young man was the torment of injustice. No more ecstasy; the feeling that he was only living because, even in the eyes of the Russians, he belonged to a noble class."[41] One might see Blanchot's change of political allegiance occurring in the very moment in which he *feels* the full force of injustice. And yet it must have been enmeshed in a prior decision, for he speaks of being himself in the Maquis and of his comrades managing to distract the lieutenant, the very event that allowed him to escape summary execution. It was on July 10, 1940, he tells us, when he was present at the sitting of the National Assembly in which power was handed over to Marshall Pétain and the Third Republic ended, that he made a decision: "At that moment, I realized that Europe and perhaps the world were surrendering to the worst. My decision was immediate. Come what may, our duty was to keep alive centers of resistance in France, intellectual ones if nothing else. That was how I met Georges Bataille, and also became involved in clandestine activity which I have never spoken about, and shall not speak about here."[42] Is this decision what effects Blanchot's passage from the right to the left of politics? Not if one takes him at his word in a letter written to Maurice Nadeau on April 17, 1977. Then he says about his early right-wing journalism:

> I shall not defend the texts that I saw fit to publish at that time. There can be no doubt that I have changed. As far as I can tell, I changed under the influence of writing (at the time, I was writing *Thomas the Obscure* and *Aminadab*), and also through my knowledge of events (at the time I was working on a paper whose proprietor was a Jew, and we were visited by many German-Jewish émigrés).[43]

Blanchot recalls here his days of working for Paul Lévy, for the weekly paper *Aux écoutes*. That was between 1933 and 1940. In 1941 he was involved with the Vichyite group Young France, as well as engaged in talks with Pierre Drieu La Rochelle concerning the possibility of becoming the editor of an entirely literary *Nouvelle revue française*, which came to nothing. "Let me be frank," he reports himself as saying to Drieu, "I cannot invite people to contribute to a journal in which I would not myself want to be published."[44] Does this indicate a political change of view on Blanchot's part? Not necessarily: the right-wing Blanchot was always firmly against collaboration in any form. What is striking in the letter to Maurice Nadeau from which I have quoted is not only that Blanchot attributes his political change to *writing*, along with "knowledge of events," but also that he mentions writing *before* mentioning Lévy or the émigrés. As we have seen, Blanchot started writing *Thomas the Obscure* in 1932, interrupted his work on it to write two stories, "Le dernier mot" ("The Last Word," 1935) and "L'Idyll" ("The Idylle," 1936), and stopped writing right-wing journalism in 1938.[45] Recalling his experience of writing in the 1930s, he tells us that composing "The Last Word" was "an attempt to short-circuit the other book that was being written [*Thomas the Obscure*], in order to overcome that endlessness and reach a silent decision."[46] The writing of *Thomas the Obscure*, he says, led him to encounter "in the search for annihilation (absence) the impossibility of escaping being (presence)—which was not even a contradiction in fact, but the demand of an endlessness that is unhappy even in dying." The silent decision, I take it, is "the renunciation of the roles of Teacher and Judge—a renunciation that is itself futile."[47]

None of these reflections on writing—*Thomas the Obscure*, *Aminadab*, "The Idyll," or "The Last Word"—quite explains how the experience of writing narrative fiction can precipitate a shift from the right wing to the left wing of politics. It could happen only for a singular personality. (It plainly did not happen with Brasillach or Céline.) Only in later texts by Blanchot does it become clear. Consider, for example, his proposal in May 1993 to intervene in the *fatwa* declared against Salman Rushdie by the Ayatollah Khomeini: "To write is, through passivity, to place oneself already beyond death—a death which fleetingly establishes a search for the Other [*l'Autre*], a relation without relation to others [*autrui*]."[48] In writing, then, two things become apparent. The first is that there is no substantial "I": the sense of a deep self is revealed to be an illusion by the "demand of an endlessness" that comes with writing.[49] And the second is that one becomes aware of the other person in the strangeness of a relation without relation. I am related to the other person not by way of dialectical engagement or by way of fusion but solely by a relation that exceeds both of those possibilities.[50] There may not be an "I" in a metaphysical sense, but there is one in a moral and political sense: individuals have responsibility. Blanchot makes the point even more clearly in his "Note" to *The Infinite Conversation*. He says there:

> Writing passes through the advent of communism, recognized as the ultimate affirmation—communism being still always beyond communism.

> Writing thus becomes a terrible responsibility. Invisibly, writing is called upon to undo the discourse in which, however unhappy we believe ourselves to be, we who have it at our disposal remain comfortably installed. From this point of view writing is the greatest violence, for it transgresses the law, every law, and also its own.[51]

How can one's act of writing point to a communism that exceeds any government and warms our desire for greater justice? Because writing, not speech

> seems to devote itself solely to itself as something that remains without identity, and little by little brings forth possibilities that are entirely other: an anonymous, distracted, deferred, and dispersed way of being in relation, by which everything is brought into question—and first of all the idea of God, of the Self, of the Subject, then of Truth and the One, then finally the idea of the Book and the Work."[52]

It is doubtful that these formulations were in Blanchot's mind in the mid to late 1930s, although he was already beginning to work toward them. There is no doubt that he changed his vocabulary over the years, giving more prominence to writing over speech in the 1960s, for example.[53] The extent to which his meetings with German-Jewish émigrés while working for Paul Lévy gave him a sense of the moral elevation of the other person is also hard to say. We are looking back in hindsight with lenses ground by Blanchot, Derrida, and Levinas. Certainly in 1960, in the one interview that Blanchot ever gave, on the "Déclaration sur le droit à l'insoumission dans la Guerre d'Algérie" ("Declaration of the Right to Insubordination in the Algerian War"), he says that he signed the declaration "as a writer" and then goes on to specify "not as a political writer or as a citizen involved in political struggles, but as a nonpolitical writer led to comment on problems that essentially involve him" ("[First I would like to say]"). This is not what one would expect of a major act of political defiance, but it makes sense if one understands that, for Blanchot, the act of writing places one in relation with other people, a relation without relation or, as he sometimes says, a neutral relation. One does not have to be an engaged or committed writer to be political, as Sartre taught in *Qu'est-ce que la littérature?* (*What Is Literature*, 1948). One simply has to be a *writer* who is aware of being in relation with others and therefore of being responsible for what happens to them.[54] As early as 1946, Blanchot was speaking of the hyper-responsibility of the writer in terms that resonate with the "Note" of 1969: the writer is responsible, he says, "to the laws he recognizes, before those he does not recognize, before others that he is alone in recognizing, and also before that absence of law which his work [*oeuvre*], where imposture necessarily predominates, deludes him into considering essential."[55] Transgression of the law may be essential to the writer, but so too is responsibility to the law.

In *Le pas au-delà* (*The Step Not Beyond*, 1973), Blanchot writes, "Tout doit s'effacer, tout s'effacera [Everything must efface itself, everything will efface itself]."[56] In the margin to a letter to Roger Laporte about his early political life, he writes, "Tout s'efface, tout doit s'effacer." What has passed, he says to Laporte, is without importance. And yet, if we look elsewhere in Blanchot, we find another wisdom. In a comment on automatic writing in *The Space of Literature*, Blanchot sympathetically puts the surrealists' position as follows: "Everything must become public. The secret must be violated. The dark must enter into the day, it must dawn. What cannot be said must nevertheless be heard: *Quidquid latet apparebit.* Everything hidden: *that* is what must appear. And not with the anxiety of a guilty conscience, but with the insouciance of happy lips."[57] Blanchot quotes here from the Requium Mass, where we hear, "Judex ergo cum sedebit, quidquid latet, apparebit, nil inultum remanebit [When the judge sits, what is hidden will be revealed, nothing will remain unavenged]." In 1986, Mascolo wrote to Blanchot about a letter from Robert Antelme that he had discovered; it had been written shortly after their mutual friend's return from Dachau. Should it be published? he asked Blanchot. And Blanchot replied by quoting his own view, *quidquid latet apparebit*, adding, in his own words, "Rien ne doit, rien ne restera caché [Nothing must, nothing will, remain hidden]."[58] Blanchot's reflections on his early political life run between two limits: his conviction that he should have no public role as a writer and his understanding that all decisions and acts will come to light and be judged.

In his letter to Laporte, Blanchot alludes to his principle of letting each express himself according to his responsibility. Yet responsibility is linked to memory. After speaking of the injustice of apartheid, he writes, "I do not recall the awful facts only so that they will not be erased from memory, but also so that memory of them should make us more aware of our responsibility" ("Our Responsibility [On Nelson Mandela]"). We must remember in order to be fully responsible. Most of all, we must remember the Shoah. "Once again I transcribe what was written at Birkenau and escapes memory as it escapes thought, by way of a warning from which no thoughts and no memories are free: 'Know what happened here. Do not forget. And yet you will never know'" ("Writing Committed to Silence"). It is the transmission of that injunction to know, and for those who have not known horror to know only within limits, that is important. One must live within that memory and forge one's own sense of responsibility for it. "It comes down to each one to remain (or to fall) in the face of the event: the event beyond answer, beyond questions. That is the pact" (ibid.). It is a covenant made with those murdered in the death camps, and a covenant made with his friend Levinas and with all Jews.

If infinite responsibility marks Blanchot's later political life, so does infinite contestation. He keeps the idea of infinite contestation, the relentless questioning of positions, from his early days, but rather than leading to national revolution, as he believed at the time of writing his last piece for *Combat*, he comes to think of it as indicating a communism beyond communism: a demand for justice that is (and always shall be) beyond the declarations and actions of the French Communist Party, for example. Readers of Blanchot's literary criticism will be familiar with his insistence that art too is endless contestation.[59] Consider this remark from "The Great Reducers" (1965):

> Literature is perhaps essentially (I am not saying uniquely or manifestly) a power of contestation: contestation of the established power, contestation of what is (and of the fact of being), contestation of language and of the forms of literary language, finally contestation of itself as power. It constantly works against the limits that it helps fix, and when these limits, pushed back indefinitely, finally disappear in the knowledge and happiness of a truly or ideally accomplished totality, then its force of transgression becomes more denunciatory, for it is the unlimited itself, having become its limit, that it denounces by the neuter affirmation that speaks in it, which always speaks beyond.[60]

And when he lays out the grounds for the *Revue internationale*, a few years before writing "The Great Reducers," he tells us much the same thing: "art is infinite contestation, contestation of itself and contestation of other forms of power—and this not only in simple anarchy, but in the free quest for original power that art and literature represent (*power without power*)" ("[The gravity of the project]"). And before writing either of these pieces, in 1953, he had already recognized that political and artistic contestations derive from a single source: "It is undoubtedly the task of our time to move toward an affirmation that is entirely other. A difficult and essentially risky task. It is to this task that communism recalls us with a rigor that it itself often shirks, and it is also to this task that 'artistic experience,' in the realm that is proper to it, recalls us. A remarkable coincidence" ("An Approach to Communism [Needs, Values]"). Indeed, criticism and "inner experience" are also forms of infinite contestation, and they too mark out "our time" as one that is seeking to affirm the "entirely *other*."[61] That irreducible otherness, experienced by the writer as "the demand of an endlessness," is what he will increasingly call the Outside or the Neutral. Its approach will be his main concern in the years to follow, whether it be in literature, fostering international communication in the *Revue internationale*, or in walking the streets in May 1968.

As should be apparent by now, the book I am prefacing, *Political Writings*, is nothing like a complete collection of Blanchot's political writings. Such an edition would have to include, first, all the right-wing journalism of the 1930s. It would also have to include *La communauté inavouable* (*The Unavowable Community*, 1983) and a fair number of additional texts, some of them substantial essays ("Intellectuals under Scrutiny," for example), some of them quite short, and some of them letters to journals.[62] Should one include his reflections on Foucault and his reviews of books on communism? Should one include essays in *The Infinite Conversation* that arise from May 1968 and fragments from *The Writing of the Disaster* that discuss Auschwitz? Should one include *Death Sentence*, *Le Très-Haut* (*The Most High*), "La folie du jour" ("The Madness of the Day"), and perhaps other narrative writings? Doubtless, and doubtless there are more writings of political interest, some of which are visible—letters to Kozovoï and Mascolo, for example—and others that may one day come to light, including letters to Derrida, Jabès, and Levinas. (There is a brief, unpublished correspondence about the "de Man affair" and, as already indicated, a long, fascinating letter to Laporte about Blanchot's early political life, also unpublished.) Blanchot seldom appeared "on the street" in demonstrations; not every cause moved him to act. And he never drew attention to himself on the street when protesting against the war in Algeria or in May 1968. "When a number of us took part in the May 1968 movement," he writes:

> they hoped to be preserved from any ambition in the singular, and in a way they succeeded, through not being singled out for attention, but treated in the same way as everyone else, the strength of the anti-authoritarian movement making it almost easy to forget all particularity, and impossible to

> distinguish between young and old, the unknown and the too well known, as if, despite the differences and the incessant disputes, each person recognized himself in the anonymous words inscribed on the walls, which, in the end, even when on occasion they were the result of a collective effort, never declared themselves the words of an author, being of all and for all, in their contradictory formulation.[63]

Yet from his last home on the Place des Pensées in Le Mesnil Saint-Denis, just outside Paris, he was constantly involved in the affairs of his day. He was, as Christophe Bident puts it so well in the subtitle of his biography of Blanchot, our "invisible partner."

Political Writings begins with Blanchot in 1953, already seasoned in his leftist views, protesting against France's involvement in Algeria and shortly thereafter hoping that a new journal, the *Revue internationale*, can bring writers together in a project of intense political and literary significance. It also includes the tracts that Blanchot wrote, and left unsigned, during May 1968, as well as reflections relating to them. And it gives us a number of texts dealing with the "Heidegger affair," Judaism, and other political concerns of the eighties and nineties.[64] Some of these late political texts speak for themselves: they are expressions of solidarity, cries for justice, warnings not to forget the horror of the Shoah. Others are highly nuanced pieces: "Reading Marx," for instance, which is surely the best short essay ever written on the father of communism. In many of these pieces, Blanchot's thoughts about anonymous speech and fragmentary writing come to the fore, and I will say something about these before commenting on a couple of specific issues.

The "Manifesto of the 121," Blanchot tells us, "was never a question of stylistic research, but on the contrary of speaking as if anonymously in order to attain the simplicity of a just conclusion" ("Update"), and in his letter to Sartre of December 2, 1960, he evokes "a certain anonymous community of names" ("[Maurice Blanchot to Jean-Paul Sartre]"). He insists that *Comité*, the organ of The Students' and Writers' Action Committee, will feature only anonymous texts. "Anonymity aims not to remove the author's right of possession over what he writes, nor even to make him impersonal by freeing him from himself (his history, his person, the suspicion attached to his particularity), but to constitute collective or plural speech: a communism of writing" ("*Comité*: [The possible characteristics]"). Anonymity is achieved, then, by affirming plural speech. This is not a dialogue and not a complex conversation among several people but a contestation of unity. It is a theme of *The Infinite Conversation*, where

Blanchot keeps insisting that plural speech is "intermittent, discontinuous," and does not represent a point of view, or even several points of view, so much as establish a space of the "between" and open up "a relation of infinity."[65] This new relation ("the third relation": neither dialectic nor fusion) is the sheer otherness that marks a change of epoch, a revolution that will fundamentally change how human beings relate to one another.[66] If we are tempted to say that the affirmation of the third relation is less a political statement than a critique of metaphysics, being based on rejecting the One, then Blanchot would want us to say that it is a critique fraught with political consequences; and if we also say that it is less a political statement than an assault on the Abrahamic faiths, for God is One, then Blanchot would ask us to acknowledge that it is also a political critique of those faiths and their heritages. Communism too is brought under this contestation of unity, at least to the extent that it believes in dialectical meaning and insofar as its positions on the events of the day can be called into question. That was the case with the "Declaration," Blanchot thinks, and it will be the case time and again.

Plural speech is one way of approaching the fragmentary, which is at the heart of Blanchot's impossible politics. Consider what he says about the writings he wants for *Comité*: "Thus the texts will be fragmentary: precisely to make plurality possible (a nonunitary plurality), to open a place for it and at the same time never to arrest the process itself" ("*Comité*: [The possible characteristics]"). "Communism of writing" depends, therefore, on the fragmentary. This notion should not be confused with the fragment valued by Novalis and Friedrich Schlegel, still less with the aphorism, the epigram, and the maxim of writers such as La Rochefoucauld and Chamfort. These short literary forms contain their center within themselves and reveal it in a burst of insight or a sudden glitter of wit about politics, love, or literature. Fragmentary writing, by contrast, has no center within itself, and strictly no center at all: it abides in a shifting relation of texts that in principle can always be extended. (It is always a possibility, one that Blanchot darkly acknowledges, that fragmentary writing, if sufficiently supplemented, can freeze and become a countersystem.[67]) In short, Blanchot's idea of literary communism is of a writing that would enable a break with present times to declare and affirm itself. It would be what he calls a "disaster," a wandering away from a fixed star that has served as a guiding light. "Truth is nomad," he says in his presentation of the *Revue internationale* ("[The gravity of the project]").

Someone might object that all this talk of rupture and fragmentary writing seems very remote from political life as we live it in the United

States—voting in elections, lobbying our representatives in Congress, our Senators, and our President—and that affirming something entirely *other* might be entirely irresponsible. Blanchot would reply to this response with no understanding and perhaps not a little impatience as well. He would say, first, that this explosive affirmation of new, plural relations can at best be lived momentarily—in *les événements* of May 1968, for instance—and that it can only indicate a horizon to which we should move, a justice that is beyond any institutionalized justice (but one that is neither divine nor ideal).[68] Contestation may still have revolution as its aim; it is a communist revolution, though, not a nationalist one, and it affirms a communism that has not yet seen the light of day. ("There is no good nationalism," the leftist Blanchot states.[69]) And he would tell us, second, that we should continue to rally around causes of defiance, even at the risk of affirming unity or union. For all its commitment to difference and dispersion, Blanchot's politics is also pragmatic. It is worth remembering that, in November, 2002, his last political act was to express solidarity with the "Not in Our Name" appeal that was launched in New York against the war in Iraq.[70] In leftist politics we must always speak two languages at the same time, one dialectical and one neutral, which is his inflection of the French distinction between *la politique* and *le politique*.[71] For Blanchot, it is the language of *le politique*, the political, that guides how we should engage in *la politique*, politics, the contestation of settled positions, the decision not to accept complaisantly the advances in liberty that we have made over the decades and centuries. *La politique* is the "No" that opens the future in which there will be justice, but before one says that single decisive syllable, one must first hear the murmur of the Outside, which informs *le politique*. And if someone were to object to this language of the murmur of the Outside, Blanchot would probably respond by saying it is no more than a figure for the intellectual grasp of the third relation.

Equally, though, one could say, with Derrida (who learned a great deal from Blanchot about the political as well as the literary), that it is a structure of double affirmation ("Yes, yes") that opens the future. If the murmur of the Outside inclines one to say "No" to injustice whenever it confronts us, the whisper of *la différance* nudges one to say "Yes" to each and every prior affirmation of justice, no matter where it is found. It was in saying "Yes" to democracy that the ancient Greeks left us a heritage, which we can make our own only by joining our "Yes" to theirs. Democracy, which was once a male prerogative, is now something shared by male and female voters only because something deemed essential in democracy has been reaffirmed. In part this difference between Blanchot and Derrida is a matter of style, not substance, for they wish to say fundamentally the same thing. Blanchot avows the friendship of the No, and Derrida writes on the politics of friendship, which includes, as it happens, a critique of the unexamined fraternalism at the heart of Blanchot's political writings.[72] None of this is said to suggest that Blanchot and Derrida converged exactly in their senses of politics and the political. If Blanchot lived May 1968 with passion, regarding it as unique, as an "*explosive communication*" that affirmed itself "beyond the usual forms of affirmation," Derrida was more distant, more reserved, more nuanced in his response, for he simply did not believe in historical ruptures.[73] Yet he admired Blanchot and valued his political work. I well remember Derrida telling me, one evening in Melbourne, that once in 1968, when Blanchot was visiting him at the École normale supérieure, Blanchot leaned over toward him and said, "with a religious intensity in his voice, 'Would you ever write a *tract*?' " Derrida told me that he explained to Blanchot that he could never write in that genre. He preferred to analyze texts in a highly differentiated manner and not to make direct pronouncements or political interventions, to which Blanchot listened closely and silently before leaving. Derrida then said to me, "To think: he must then have been writing those tracts for the Students' and Writers' Action Committee. They are some of the finest political tracts ever written."

"It is undoubtedly the task of our time to move toward an affirmation that is entirely other." Blanchot wrote those words in 1953. If we take this remark in the frame of literature and philosophy, first in terms of post-Enlightenment horizons of thought (Marx, Nietzsche, and Freud), then by way of experiments with the forbidden (Sade, Hölderlin, Lautréamont, Bataille), then in modern literature (Mallarmé, Kafka, Char, Beckett), and finally in contemporary philosophy (Heidegger, Levinas, Derrida), we can see what he has in mind, even if the adverbs now seem extreme. The age is more modest, as Philippe Lacoue-Labarthe says, with the second half of the last century in mind.[74] Yet to the extent that Blanchot was thinking of a communist revolution, even one not countenanced by the Soviet Union, Cuba, or China, we must say that the age decided otherwise. The second half of the twentieth century marks a retreat from communism, first in Europe and Russia and then, in a more complex way, in China. True, at the same time we find a rethinking of community and friendship, but it is one that remains in the seminar room and does not take to the street.[75] It was the World Wide Web that was unforeseen and "other," that was able to join all manner of people in a way that is neither dialectical nor achieved by fusion, and that has had all manner of political consequences that are still in flux and that still require patient examination. "Our age" happened differently from how Blanchot thought it would. If he saw, rightly, that Christianity would come to live a greatly diminished life in Europe, he did not foresee the flourishing of Islam or conceive the affirmation of Allah as the One who is entirely other. Yet when May 1968 came, he recognized that something unique had taken place, something that was in deep accord with what he had had in mind in 1953.

While May 1968 saw Blanchot at an ecstatic height in his political life, that life was soon to end, at least in its main lines. Within a year of May 1968, Levinas received a letter from Blanchot in which the writer of tracts for *Comité* explains, in Levinas's words, why "He separated himself from his revolutionary friends when they opted against Israel." I quote from the end of the letter, which is all that Levinas gives us:

> No, I have always said that there was the limit beyond which I wouldn't go, but now I'd like to ask myself for a minute. . . . ask myself why these young people who are acting violently but also with generosity, felt they had to make such a choice, why they operated on thoughtlessness, on the usage of empty concepts (imperialism, colonization) and also on the feeling that it is the Palestinians who are the weakest, and one must be on the side of the weak (as if Israel were not extremely, dreadfully vulnerable). . . .
>
> But there is another reason, in my opinion. It is that in none of them is there any antisemitism, however latent, or even any idea of what antisemitism was.
>
> Thus it is not true that anti-Zionism is the antisemitism of today; that is why the meaning of Israel itself, in its most obvious aspect, absolutely escapes them; I find this serious; it is as though Israel were put in peril by ignorance—yes, an innocent ignorance perhaps, but from now on gravely responsible and deprived of innocence—put in danger by those who want to exterminate the Jew because he is a Jew and by those who are completely ignorant of what it is to be Jewish. Antisemitism will now have as allies those who are as if deprived of antisemitism.
>
> Isn't this a strange reversal, which proves that the absence of antisemitism is not enough?[76]

In 1984, in an essay brooding on the Dreyfus Affair and its lasting significance, Blanchot observed, "From the Dreyfus Affair to Hitler and Auschwitz, the proof is there that it was anti-Semitism (along with racism and xenophobia) which revealed the intellectual most powerfully to himself: in other words, it is in that form that concern for others obliged him (or not) to abandon his creative solitude."[77] The essay is testimony to what Blanchot himself had done: after 1968 he had revealed himself to himself and understood himself within his limits and the limits of his time, in terms of laws of responsibility that he would not transgress. In a letter to Bernard-Henri Lévy written in September 1989, a time of debate over the Church's decision to close down a Carmelite convent built near Auschwitz, Blanchot chose to end his letter by addressing the murdered Jews rather than Lévy: "You who are now dead, you who died for us and often because of us (because of our shortcomings), you must not be allowed to die a second time, and silence must not mean that you sink into oblivion."[78] The Blanchot who for many years had been revealed to himself, as it were, by death as dying, by the loss of the power to say "I," now sees himself in terms of responsibility to the Jewish dead.

Also in that essay of 1984, "Intellectuals under Scrutiny," Blanchot notes that when the intellectual, the writer, "makes up his mind and declares himself, he suffers perhaps irreparable damage. He absents himself from the only task that matters to him." What is that task? It is "to utter the unexpected [*la parole inattendue*]."[79] (217). Blanchot's letter to Levinas was the saying of an unexpected word, and all that he said after he posted it was a sequence of unexpected words. Intellectuals, he once wrote to Sartre, become aware of their peculiar power; it is a "power without power": not a power to vote on bills or sign presidential memos or anything of the sort. It is the power, rather, to contest power wherever it comes, but not to do so as a knee-jerk reaction. Thought is required, hard thought, thought that looks neither to the dialectic nor to fusion. The word that counts is the unexpected word, a word perhaps from left field, a word not always recognized or wanted by the political left but needed all the same. This book is full of them.

Introduction

"Affirming the Rupture"

ZAKIR PAUL

"Maurice Blanchot, novelist and critic. His life is entirely devoted to literature and to its own silence." These two laconic phrases replace the traditional biographical note in the majority of Blanchot's works published as French paperbacks. Given that they omit any mention of his political writings, and given the various self-perpetuating myths surrounding his work, the reader might justifiably wonder what brought a novelist and critic whose life was "entirely devoted to literature" to write texts of a political nature in the first place. We are given some clues in one of the last letters Blanchot sent to Georges Bataille, on January 24, 1962, in which he comments upon the proximity between René Char, Bataille, and himself. Implicitly placing himself between Char and Bataille, Blanchot ascribes their differences not to a varied temperament for "politics" but rather to divergent responses to pressures internal to the enterprise of writing. He goes on to describe dual forces that he has come to recognize in his own work:

> I do not at all think that an interest or disinterest in "politics" is at stake; this is merely a consequence and perhaps a superficial one. For my part, . . . I have seen better for some time now the double impulse [*mouvement*], necessary yet nonetheless irreconcilable, to which I must always respond. One (to express myself in an extremely vulgar and simplifying way) is the passion, the realization, and the speech of the whole [*tout*] in dialectical accomplishment; the other is essentially nondialectic, does not concern itself at all with unity and does not tend toward power (toward the possible).

These two vectors, which have opposite directions—one totalizing and dialectical, the other fragmentary and nondialectical—produce different discourses, as the letter goes on to explain:

> To this double impulse responds a double language, and for all language a double gravity: one is a speech of confrontation, opposition, and negation, meant to reduce any opposition so that the truth as a whole may be affirmed

> in its silent equality (a path the demand of thought must take). But the other is the speech that speaks before all, and outside of all, speech that is always first, without concord or confrontation, and ready to welcome the unknown, the stranger (where the poetic demand passes). One *names* the possible and wants the possible. The other *responds* to the impossible. Between these two impulses, which are both necessary and incompatible, there is a constant tension, often very difficult to bear, and truly, unbearable. But one can renounce neither one out of bias, nor the measureless search that imposes their necessity, and the necessity of uniting the incompatible, upon humans.[1]

This statement of Blanchot's conception of writing seems quite distant from the devotion to literature and its distinctive silence suggested by the two enigmatic phrases inscribed in his books. Here the whole is cleft in two, into "naming the possible" (the "demand of thought") and "responding to the impossible" (the "poetic demand"). It is between these two poles that Blanchot oscillates as a writer. They are related to the demand for a double language: a totalizing language of contestation and refusal, on the one hand, and a fragmentary language of hospitality and welcome, on the other. The texts collected in this volume are not exempt from the impulse to these two incommensurable languages, and often enough they comprise the very search that tries to bring them together. For Blanchot, "political writing" has little to do with lending one's signature to a cause as a writer; rather, it is an attempt to find the impossible language that would allow one to refuse and contest certain political events while watchfully preserving the possibility of others. The texts collected in this volume testify to the unbearable tension between the necessary and incompatible impulses that course through Blanchot's postwar political writings from 1953 to 1993.

These dates are largely arbitrary, given that Blanchot's political writings span from 1931 to 2002, if we consider the many manifestos to which he continued to lend his signature until his death.[2] To be sure, there are many reasons why this book should not exist in its current form. It could be argued that, since many of these texts were written anonymously and signed collectively, to assemble and publish them under Blanchot's name erroneously attributes them to a single authority. Moreover, the now familiar trajectory of Blanchot from a nationalism of the right to an internationalism of the left cannot be fully reconstructed until the interwar journalism is made available. This effort is already underway with the recent publication of all the uncollected literary articles Blanchot wrote for the *Journal des débats* between 1941 and 1944.[3] The majority of the political texts that Blanchot published earlier in the newspapers and journals of the extreme right—particularly *Combat* and *L'Insurgé*—have yet to be reprinted in French, although four exemplary texts were published and discussed in the final volume of a triple issue of *Gramma* by Michael Holland and Patrick Rousseau in 1976.[4]

What such attempts, along with Christophe Bident's monumental biographical essay *Maurice Blanchot: Partenaire invisible* (*Maurice Blanchot: Invisible Partner*) and Leslie Hill's *Blanchot, Extreme Contemporary*, have made clear is the complexity of the place where Blanchot began his political journalism. The milieu of Catholic nonconformism, notably around the young dissidents of the Action française led by Thierry Maulnier, was doubled by a close connection to Jewish nationalist groups around Paul Lévy and the weeklies *Le rempart* and *Aux écoutes*. Blanchot's position was one of contestation: anticapitalist, antiparliamentarian, anticommunist, anti-German and anti-Hitler. As early as 1933, he contributed articles denouncing the establishment of labor camps and the "barbarous persecution of the Jews."[5]

In addition to an underlying desire for a national spiritual revolution that would countervail what he then perceived to be the dual pitfalls of social democracy and communism, three major interdependent concerns have been identified in Blanchot's interwar journalism.[6] The first is the overwhelming necessity of opposing Hitler. The second is his growing distress at the undermining of national sovereignty by French foreign policy starting in 1924. In his view, French politicians were increasingly abandoning diplomatic traditions in favor of vacuous internationalism, as embodied by Aristide Briand's support for the League of Nations. Finally, he opposed the "abstract and juridical conception of politics" that allowed the leaders of the Third Republic to identify with the League of Nations in the first place, an identification that raised the threat of war by decreasing the defense of national interest. As he wrote in *Le rempart* in May 1933, "One of the main errors of democracy is to have defamed force. . . . It has done everything, to the greatest extent, to weaken the law [*le droit*]."[7] Blanchot conceives both the foundation and the defense of law as being inextricably bound up with the use of force. The government's weakening of force only intensifies the necessity of political action. And yet Blanchot's triad of concerns does not in the least amount to a political program. As Hill points out, there is no element of a future program beyond the will to depose an incompetent government. This is where "a call to just violence, to insurrection," is invoked and aporetically declared "the most sacred of rights and the most indispensable of duties."[8] Whatever future could follow such an act of "just violence" is apprehended "almost exclusively in terms of the self-presence of the nation, that is, beyond representation, the nation's self-identity and proximity to itself as political subject and origin."[9]

The difficulties of selecting "representative" texts from such a nonrepresentational context and presenting them as an appendix to the current volume would have been manifold, if not insurmountable. The very selection of texts as exemplary would be premised upon the notion that Blanchot had something resembling a political program before the war, and not a series of privileged issues to which he incessantly returned. Such metonymic logic would have been made problematic by the fact that, before the war, Blanchot was writing within and reacting to a distinct historical climate, which would have to be reconstructed along with these texts. Moreover, these texts appeared as columns and chronicles, which take on their full meaning only when read serially, echoing one another. However, as Blanchot argues in *Après-coup* (*After the Fact*), a critical text that revisits his first two pieces of short fiction, the process of historical restitution is never a guarantor of meaning, or vice versa: "History does not control meaning [*ne détient pas le sens*], any more than meaning, which is always ambiguous—plural—may be reduced to its historical realization, were this the most tragic and weightiest imaginable."[10]

Much difficult editorial work thus remains to be done, a task that is not facilitated by the inflammatory rhetorical tone of pieces bearing such titles as "Terrorism as a Method of Public Salvation" or "Dissidents Wanted." But even without delving into the issue further, two preliminary conclusions should be drawn. First, at no point can we afford simply to equate Blanchot's prewar writings with a "fascist" position, even if a particular strain of French nationalism is undeniable. This leads to the second, related point: Blanchot never refused to acknowledge or comment upon these articles when asked. In his correspondence and his writings he more or less explicitly characterized his journalistic activity of the time as profoundly misguided and, indeed, despicable for its nationalist tendencies, while taking the greatest distance from how his work would be analyzed in the future. In an open letter to Maurice Nadeau that appeared in *La quinzaine littéraire* in 1977, upon the publication of the volume of *Gramma* devoted to his interwar journalism, he wrote:

> I shall not defend the texts that I saw fit to publish at that time. There can be no doubt that I have changed. As far as I can tell, I changed under the influence of writing (at the time, I was writing *Thomas the Obscure* and *Aminadab*) and also through my knowledge of events. . . . I have always considered Nazism and anti-Semitism to be pure evil, against which we were ill defended. When the collapse came, I was present at the sitting of the *Assemblée Nationale* when, in a base and servile gesture, it handed its powers over to Pétain. . . . At that moment, I realized that Europe and perhaps the world were surrendering to the worst. My decision was immediate. Come what may, our duty was to keep alive centers of resistance in France, intellectual ones if nothing else. That is why I refused to leave for London, though I was invited to do so. That was how I met Georges Bataille, and also became involved in clandestine activity which I have never spoken about, and shall not speak about here. But the feeling of horror never left me.[11]

Blanchot's last distinctly political text of the prewar era was published in December 1937 and ended with an open call for dissidence. His parting words would turn out to be uncannily prescient of his future commitments: "The true communist dissident is the one who leaves communism, not to draw closer to capitalist values, but to define the true conditions of the struggle against capitalism."[12] This declaration was followed by almost two decades during which Blanchot refrained from publishing on political issues, continuing to establish himself as a prose writer and literary critic. He must have remained an acute observer of political changes, however, for he emerged from his literary reserve and reappropriated a political voice to expose the increasingly shaky foundations of the Fourth Republic, besieged with instability in Indochina and Algeria.[13] This contestation from the margins of literature signaled a growing refusal to accept the existing state of affairs, as well as a desire to find new forms of fragmentary and collective writing in order to express this refusal. A search for new kinds of political intervention is the absent center of the present collection. According to Blanchot's testimony to Nadeau, this change occurred through writing his novels and *récits*, while trying to theorize a separate sphere for "literary space." But such an attempt to account for a political turn in terms of a "turn to literature" remains insufficient to explain the underlying causes of the shift. In order to do so, one would have to understand what Blanchot means by literature, how writing invariably involves the loss of the power to say "I" and moves the writing self outside of the domains that structure, constitute, and institute the individual. During these years, the disaster of the Second World War and the Shoah revealed that humanity is capable of annihilating itself. As Sarah Kofman points out in her reflections on Auschwitz, *Paroles suffoquées* (*Suffocated Words*, 1987), Blanchot made a point of removing the word *récit* from 1947 onwards in all the texts he wrote and published after the war. This was not merely a question of genres and literary criticism but the sign that a fundamental disaster had transformed the grounds of speech itself. For Kofman, it indicates the struggle in Blanchot's writings to avoid being complicit with discourses of power and speculative knowledge. Even literature was no longer possible as it might once have been. As Blanchot wrote in 1983, "No matter when it may be written, every story will henceforth be before Auschwitz."[14] Placing literature in front of Auschwitz also means placing it at the cusp of the disaster, watching over a forever-imminent destruction that politics failed to avoid.

If one were obliged to find a continuity, despite this immeasurable gulf separating Blanchot's pre- and postwar politics, one might point to the persistent absence of a program, in favor of elevating refusal to the quintessential political gesture—if there were such a thing. However tempting, such a continuous view would be simplistic, since Blanchot in the thirties was close to volatile groups and individuals who did have distinct political agendas. After the war, he insisted that he was not a political writer, distancing himself from the dominant model of Sartrean engagement and emphasizing instead that it was in writing that he came to politics and the political. The stances he took were in turn complicated by the notion that political thought "remains forever to be discovered." Blanchot's earlier political writings remind us how deceptively facile it is to refuse established forms of authority. However, only after the war was he able to reformulate his task as one of learning not only how to refuse but how to sustain the power of refusal through "rigor of thought and modesty of expression."

In *L'Espace littéraire* (*The Space of Literature*, 1955), Blanchot writes: "Everything must become public. The secret must be violated. The dark must enter the day, it must dawn. What cannot be said must nevertheless be heard. *Quidquid latet apparebit.* Everything hidden: *that* is what must appear. And not in the anxiety of a guilty conscience, but with the insouciance of happy lips.—What, without risks, or perils?" He invokes the same phrase decades later in a letter to Dionys Mascolo, in relation to the possible publication of Antelme's correspondence: "Concerning the letters, you know my personal moral that applies only to me (not out of arrogance, but from a desire to escape biography), and still, I will correct it without illusion: *quidquid latet apparebit.* Nothing must, nothing will remain hidden." This phrase can perhaps judiciously orient our approach to Blanchot's political trajectory.[15]

To regard the years between 1938 and 1953, when this collection begins, as years of silence about politics would be misleading, not least because of the dichotomy between the literary and the political on which such a break would rely. The issues concerning sovereignty and violence in relation to the state and the law that thread their way through Blanchot's political journalism continued to provide the themes of his novels, especially *Aminadab* and *Le Très-Haut* (*The Most High*).[16] Just as the literary continued to provide a testing ground for the most ambitious part of his critical thinking—the part Paul de Man suggested Blanchot always reserved for literature and excised from his criticism—his criticism would increasingly come to focus upon the potentialities of literature, if only to insist that literature is "a kind of power not predicated on possibility."[17] In a text published in 1953, first in the *Nouvelle nouvelle revue française* (*NNRF*) and later collected in *Le livre à venir* (*The Book to Come*), he tried to come to grips with the question of where literature was headed. Beginning with a reflection on Hegel's dictum that art is a thing of the past, Blanchot describes the destination of literature as being reflexive, turning in toward itself, that is to say, toward its own disappearance. In a section titled "Literature, the Work of Art, Experiment," he argues that fragmentary tracts and anonymous documents should not be excluded from the domain of literature:

> we are irritated at seeing literary works replaced by an always greater mass of texts that, under the name of documents or reports, terms that are almost coarse, seem to ignore any literary intention. They seem to say: we have nothing to do with creating things of art; they also seem to say: accounts of a false realism. What do we know of them? What do we know of this approach, even failed, toward a region that escapes the grasp of ordinary culture? This anonymous, authorless language, which does not take the form of books, which soon disappears and wants to disappear, couldn't it be alerting us to something important, about which what we call literature also wants to speak?[18]

Blanchot's own experiments and experiences in writing move him from these reflections on the "book to come" to the pages concerning the "absence of the book" that close the 1969 *L'Entretien infini* (*The Infinite Conversation*). This movement toward a fragmentary, testamentary conception of writing, drawing on figures ranging from Hegel, Schlegel, and Nietzsche to Joubert, Mallarmé, and Artaud, was also informed by his participation in political experiments beginning in 1958. Once again, it was anticipated in the *NNRF* in a book review written in 1953 ("An Approach to Communism [Needs, Values]"), in which Blanchot considers the dialectic of needs and values in Dionys Mascolo's *Le communisme, révolution et communication ou la dialectique des valeurs et des besoins* (*Communism, Revolution, and Communication*). Teasing out the implications of Mascolo's definition of "communism" as the materialist search for communication, the review concentrates on whether it is possible for a writer to distinguish between private and collective relations. Having declared openness to the other to be an "essential mode of political decision and affirmation," Blanchot nonetheless expresses a critical desire to outstrip Mascolo's conclusions:

> Dionys Mascolo says that the writer must live both in the common world of need and in an intimate world of values and ends. But perhaps on this point one must go farther than he does, in the direction indicated by his statements. The poetic work, the artistic work, if it speaks to us of something, speaks to us of that which is removed from all value or repels all evaluation, articulates the demand of beginning (again), which is lost and muddled as soon as it is satisfied in value. Nietzsche wanted to transmute all values, but this transvaluation (at least in the most visible, all-too-well-known part of his writings) seemed to leave the notion of value intact. It is undoubtedly the task of our time to move toward an affirmation that is entirely other.

This "affirmation that is entirely other," which announced itself as a withdrawal from all preestablished value and a rejection of evaluation, drew Blanchot closer to Mascolo and the group that burgeoned around the rue Saint-Benoît—including Marguerite Duras, Robert Antelme, Edgar Morin, Maurice Nadeau, and Claude Roy amongst others—in 1958. Blanchot came into contact with this group after he had read the first issue of *Le 14 juillet*, a review that Mascolo and Jean Schuster started to contest the "coup d'état" of May 13, 1958, which brought de Gaulle back to power. His first letter to Mascolo declared: "I would like you to know that I agree with you. I refuse the past and I accept nothing of the present."[19] Mascolo, a reader at Gallimard, had already expressed his own growing dissatisfaction with institutionalized forms of political response to the present. Having resigned from the French Communist Party in 1949, he was at the origin of the 1955 Committee of Intellectuals Against the Pursuit of the War in North Africa, a venture in which he was joined by

Breton and the Surrealists, whose own relation to politics could be described as a series of refusals. Indeed, the first issue of *Le 14 juillet*, published in May 1958, was structured around the notion of refusal, a collective "No" addressed to the military's illegitimate elevation of de Gaulle into the role of head of state. The editors defended this decision to speak out against de Gaulle's accusations of idealist political chatter by invoking Pascal's phrase "We spoke only when we could no longer be silent without crime" and by placing a quotation from Spinoza about "usurped fear and hope" as epigraph to the review.[20] The review's approach was manifest from the title and epigraph on: "fidelity to the revolution, return to the resistance confiscated by Gaullists and Stalinists, [and the] unconditional refusal of providential power."[21]

It would be hard to overstate how difficult such refusal was in 1958. Despite signs of latent resistance to French colonialism, such protest had little place in the triumphalist public discourse of postwar France. Even the Communist Party was guarded about any question of Algerian independence. For Cornelius Castoriadis, against this background of official reticence, "through the struggle against the war, in demonstrations, draft resistance, secret organizing, aiding the Algerians, discussions about their revolution, a minority of students became conscious of what they opposed in *their own* society. . . . Algeria was the occasion, the catalyst for an opposition in search of itself, becoming more and more conscious of itself."[22] The total lack of institutionally sanctioned political discourse in favor of Algerian national independence distinguished the situation from earlier divisive instants in the history of modern French politics, such as the Dreyfus Affair or the Resistance. This lack of institutional backing, as well as the complexity of the situation, provided the occasion for Blanchot to enunciate his own conception of the political act, which must be based on a refusal of both compromise and opportunism—a refusal of the very idea that politics is adaptation to a difficult reality, or the art of pragmatism. Sartre had identified the ideology of political realism and pragmatism as the essence of collaboration. As Werner Hamacher has argued, drawing upon the implications of this identification, "putting this realism into question is an eminently political act, even if it is not articulated in explicitly political terms but rather in linguistic and philological ones."[23]

Armed with a heightened linguistic consciousness of the difficulty of formulating judgment in a case where what is perceived as "good" (in this case, national security and stability) and "evil" (a government propped up by the army) become intertwined, Blanchot would argue that it is precisely in such areas that an act of judgment becomes necessary. The writer becomes an intellectual momentarily, assuming this guise and responsibility in order to express a political judgment at a time when most are unable to exercise this faculty on their own, or are kept from being heard. As he wrote years later in a testamentary 1984 article "Intellectuals under Scrutiny":

> What is there to be said about intellectuals? Who are they? Who deserves to be one? . . . It would seem that you aren't one all the time any more than you can be one entirely. The intellectual is a portion of ourselves which not only distracts us momentarily from our task, but returns us to what is going on in the world, in order to judge and appreciate what is going on there. In other words, the intellectual is all the closer to action in general, and to power, for not getting involved in action and not exercising any political power. But he is not indifferent to them. In standing back from politics he does not withdraw from it, he has not retired from it, but rather attempts to sustain this space of retreat and this effort of withdrawal [*retirement*] so as to take advantage of this proximity at a distance and install himself there (in precarious installation), like a look-out who is there solely to keep watch, to remain watchful, to wait with an active attention, expressive less of a concern for himself than of a concern for others.[24]

This conception of power without power, captured in figures of retreat and withdrawal, would arrest Blanchot's attention in a particular theological trait when he began his critique of the "sacred" grounding of de Gaulle's power. In 1957, Blanchot was reading both the work of Gerschom Scholem, especially *Major Trends in Jewish Mysticism*, and Simone Weil, to whom he was also drawn by his interest in Jewish mysticism, which he owed to his longtime friend Emmanuel Levinas.[25] Especially impressed by the figure of Isaac Luria, the sixteenth-century Jewish mystic, Blanchot seized upon the kabbalistic notion of creation as the retreat of God: "For Isaac Luria, creation requires a double act: one is an act of retreat, the other an act of unfolding. The first consists in making emptiness and obscurity; the second in the making of the emptiness a clearing, sending a light into it—a double effort of withdrawal and bursting forth, of obscurity and revelation."[26] Like the double movement described in the letter to Bataille, this double understanding of creation as "withdrawal and bursting forth" should be considered in relation to Blanchot's ongoing attempt to reconfigure thinking as "retreat, abandonment, and the interruption of thinking."[27] The duplicity attributed to the task of thinking implies that the more a thought is fully expressed, the greater the degree of reserve. It would be in this space that a writer can inscribe his political judgment.

There is a crucial difference, then, between judgment and analysis. From a certain perspective, Blanchot does not offer an analysis of current political events. His remarks resist being circumscribed in such a narrow space. Nowhere is this more openly stated than in "The Essential Perversion," where we are asked what happens in political analysis: "What happens is precisely that it analyzes, it dissociates; it sees in what came about a plurality of facts of distinct origin and opposing meaning, correcting and neutralizing one another—de Gaulle compensating for the men of May 13. What was shadowy about them only intensified the bright light of the unique apparition."

By contrast, the aim of this text, which appeared in the second issue of *Le 14 juillet*, is to complicate and intensify the debate about de Gaulle's person at the moment he was brought back to power. And yet even this is only a pretext. At stake is a critique of representation, of the theatricality of sovereignty without power that Blanchot finds in de Gaulle. The particularity of this power conceals a contradiction—a perversion. Blanchot insists on the singularity of de Gaulle's character, which incarnates sovereignty in a manner that transcends the political. Instead, he instantiates the omnipotence of salvation; the text singles out the profoundly theological aspect of his power. The attribution of this theological power implies de Gaulle's lack of efficacy as an agent of government. Although Blanchot equates the dictator with the figure of the providential man in *The Book to Come*—also published in 1959—here he argues that de Gaulle is not a "simple and profane" dictator. He is guilty not of abusing power but rather of perverting the essential structure of authority. His name is confounded with a kind of enigma for political judgment, which must be exercised in order to identify the exact nature of the deformation at hand. The coup is saturated with "the feeling that something entirely different has happened, a serious mutation that partly escapes political judgment, for it throws into question decisions concerning a more fundamental agreement or disagreement" ("The Essential Perversion"). The singularity of the situation thus demands a hesitant judgment, which must refuse the appeasement offered by the figure of a providential man. Blanchot reduces the triangulation of singularity, judgment, and providence by declaring: "De Gaulle did not conquer power; he is not a man of action" (ibid.) This refusal might appear revisionist at first blush, but its unfamiliarity stems more from its concerted avoidance of cliché. Despite appearances, de Gaulle has very little to do with the cult of personality. Instead, he is marked by a sovereign affect that relies on

> the exaltation of a man. On the one hand, it glorifies a name whose glorious past it also uses; it says that this presence is irreplaceable, that it is unique (unique meaning that, from the point of view of political utility, de Gaulle has no rival, but that furthermore he has no peer, unique, then, because he represents the sacred and mystical value of the unique; this is why, psychologically, one puts the accent on his solitude, he is distinct, he is separate, he is the anointed one); finally, this person is providential. . . . The power with which a providential man is invested is no longer political power; it is the power of salvation [*puissance de salut*]. Its presence as such is salutary, effective in itself and not by what it will do. (ibid.)

Blanchot avoids analyzing the events that led to de Gaulle's reinstatement, choosing instead to translate the empty core of the problem. He translates the quotidian political reality in an attempt to unveil its onto-theological anchoring, which is supposed to remain absent or repressed. Doing so allows him to isolate the failure of an ongoing ideological transformation that relies on an associative chain leading from the nation to destiny, from destiny to government, symbolized by a man without a past or a future, the visible presence—the *parousia*—of a great, absent nation. The problem, again, is not that de Gaulle has too much authority but rather that the meaning of authority he invokes has been perverted to the point of ineffectiveness. It is too lofty and too great to exercise itself, as Blanchot sees it, quoting Malebranche's definition of providence as being incapable of any particular action, manifesting itself instead only in the most general ways. Blanchot's reading of de Gaulle builds upon a series of traditional theological questions: How is it possible that God can act in the world if he remains transcendent? How does the unity of the divine relate to the multiplicity of the phenomenal? By showing that sacred sovereignty is powerless, Blanchot underlines the paradox of the common public expectation that de Gaulle, once again, would save France. It might not be amiss to retrospectively overhear a Lacanian overtone of being turned toward the father (*Père-version*) in Blanchot's use of the word *perversion*. This perversion describes not only de Gaulle's transformation of military power into political power and the subsequent anointment of his figure but also the need for a father that the French nation expressed by instilling their hope in him.

For Blanchot, de Gaulle's name is indelibly linked with a colonialist movement, a nationalist drive, technocratic force, and the transformation of the army into a police force. The difficulty in naming the nature of the war in Algeria derives from the fact that the conflict overturns traditional political categories and representations. To name the conflict, in this context, is already to make a political judgment, to affirm whether or not there is a war or merely a national security issue, whether it is a war of liberation or secession, whether it is a matter for the army or for the police. As Blanchot put it in a meeting at the rue St. Benoît in 1958, the coup d'état created a void to which another void had to be opposed.[28] The judicial necessity of intervention was intensified by the activities and the impending trial of the Jeanson network, which helped the Algerian National Liberation Front (FLN) by carrying suitcases, transferring funds and identity papers out of metropolitan France to support the independence struggle. The central thrust of the "Manifesto of the 121" ("Declaration of the Right to Insubordination in the Algerian War") was precisely to declare the right to protest. Drafted in 1960, shortly before the Jeanson trial, by Jean Schuster, Dionys Mascolo, and Blanchot in cooperation with many others, this manifesto did not entail a call to insurrection. Instead, it declared that French soldiers serving in the army and those about to be drafted into the Algerian War had the right to desert in order to avoid practicing torture. Its 121 signatories did not conceive of the political act as a call to action—as opposed to a certain Marxist tradition, where the manifesto serves to incite collective insubordination. Here the Manifesto translates the current situation into another language, moving from the language of duty (*devoir*) to that of right and law (*droit*):

> What is civic virtue [*le civisme*] when, in certain circumstances, it becomes shameful submission? Aren't there cases where the refusal to serve is a sacred duty, where "treason" means courageous respect for the truth? And when, through the will of those who use it as an instrument of racist or ideological domination, the army places itself in a state of open or latent revolt against democratic institutions, doesn't revolt against the army take on a new meaning? ("Declaration of the Right to Insubordination in the Algerian War")

It is in this context that Blanchot and the other writers of the Manifesto posit the right to insubordination, denounce torture, and make striking comparisons between the French colonialists and the recently vanquished army of Hitler. It is illustrative to compare this declaration with Thoreau's essay on civil disobedience during the U.S. War with Mexico of 1846–48. Although speaking of a duty of disobedience, like Thoreau, does not necessarily exclude individual judgment, a right necessarily remains, in the words of the Manifesto, "a free power for which everyone is responsible, by himself, in relation to himself." This unprecedented right involves a judgment that is both ethical and cognitive. The text invokes truth, for judgment has to do with a truth claim and not a practical calculus. The

Manifesto seems strangely Platonic in its formulation, and its writers claim that truth, rather than pragmatic concerns, should dictate the course of political action: "a statement of this kind, a statement of judgment, owes all of its effectiveness precisely to the refusal to make it depend on calculations of practical and political effectiveness" ("Update"). This debt of judgment to language, rather than to praxis, is perhaps less surprising if we recall the importance Blanchot places on the role of vigilance in the task of the intellectual. Rather than getting involved—*s'engager*, in the Sartrean sense—his task is to watch over language and the transpositions of meaning that take place within it. One could certainly reproach this conception for having an untenable degree of abstraction, but, as Blanchot writes about the Berlin Wall, abstract divisions lead to concrete oppression, above all when division is abstractly concretized.

The recollections of those involved in writing the Manifesto indicate that each sentence was discussed at length, every expression weighed. The text would receive well over 121 signatures, including those of François Châtelet, Guy Debord, François Truffaut, Tristan Tzara, and Jean Wahl. At the same time, the group's open support for the FLN and the "suitcase carriers" alienated some of their close friends, who refrained from signing.[29] Responding to criticism of the unilateral character of the FLN, those who drafted the document argued that what would happen in the aftermath of Algerian independence was irrelevant when compared to the pressing need to support such a struggle.

In reaction to the Manifesto, the government banned those who had signed it from national French radio and television. *Le Figaro* refused to publish anything written by the 121. The Manifesto itself was discussed more than it was read, as it was not widely published in the French press. Offprints flowed in from Belgium, Italy, and elsewhere, showing international interest in the activity against the war in France. During the trial of the Jeanson network, Nadeau's lawyer went so far as to speak of a new Dreyfus Affair. As two short pieces on the judge's interrogation of Blanchot ("[Interrogation with the judge]" and "[Questioned by the judge]") reveal, the trial itself took on a fairly absurdist tone, insofar as all 121 signatories claimed to be the collective and anonymous writers of the text.[30] Indeed, the fact that Sartre, the most famous signatory of the Manifesto, was absent during its writing underlines this new conception of authority.[31]

Yet the notion of anonymous, collective authority did not curry favor for long with Sartre. The only known letter Blanchot addressed to Sartre (December 2, 1960), in which he insists on the importance of creating a new forum for the continued expression of refusal, went unanswered. Sartre's silence was not inexplicable, given that Blanchot was not merely asking him to support the nascent *Revue internationale* project but to do so while abandoning his own review, *Les temps modernes*. The idea of a new review had emerged from the meetings during which the Manifesto of the 121 was drafted. Once again Blanchot worked with the rue Saint-Benoît group (Mascolo, Duras, Antelme, and others), entering into contact with Italian, German, and English writers in order to lay the groundwork and imagine the form for a new multilingual, international journal. Commenting on Nadeau's intention to include more political pieces in *Lettres nouvelles* and Sartre's intention to create space for literature in *Les temps modernes*, Blanchot suggests that both editors signal the transition to a new era by discontinuing their respective journals. The necessity of a new journal, which would be neither "political" nor "cultural," was articulated in terms of a new direction, namely, total critique:

> I believe, rather, in a review of *total critique*, critique where literature would be understood in its own meaning . . ., where scientific discoveries, often poorly explained, would be put to the test of holistic critique, where all the structures of our world, all the forms of existence of this world, would enter into the same movement of examination, scrutiny, and contestation, a review where the word *critique* would once again find its meaning, which is to be global. ("[Maurice Blanchot to Jean-Paul Sartre]")

Although—or possibly because—the near-utopian scope of the review would awaken the interest of an impressive roster of European intellectuals, while failing to gather their unequivocal support, it was never published, except for the zero issue that appeared in the pages of the Italian journal *Il menabò* in 1964.[32] As Blanchot's letters to German and Italian colleagues testify, the multiple causes of this failure included the costs of translation, the difficulty of securing full editorial support from a publisher, the lack of a common language for discussion, and above all, a strong divergence concerning the formal value of fragmentation.[33] Initially conceived in accordance with a Hölderlinean ideal of solitude broken by the exchange of thoughts among friends, the review soon faced the reality of national and partisan borders. Uwe Johnson's resistance could largely be ascribed to his loyalty to Sartre, while, as Vittorini complained, much of the abstract French lexicon—especially the reliance upon "silence" and "absence"—sounded suspiciously mystical to the Italians. However, it was Blanchot and Mascolo's promotion of a fragmented rubric entitled "Course of Things" that came to be the main point of contention. As

Vittorini commented ironically, only writers from a country as centralized as France could ever dream of interrupting a fledgling relationship with friends from a country whose geographic separation and linguistic difference demanded the concentration of a common ground rather than dispersion into fragments.[34] This argument was even more applicable to the Germans, for whom the recent construction of the Berlin War had underscored the realities of the postwar period. Blanchot's own eagerness to transcend locality can be seen in "The Conquest of Space," his reflections on the voyage of Yuri Gagarin, the first man in space. He saw the experience of space as potentially breaking with the human *genii loci* in all their variations and with the sedentariness of civilization. Thinking the passage from one time and space to another, as well as its occlusion, was the explicitly stated task of the review, which hoped to create a "momentary utopia of some nonplace" ("The Conquest of Space") by allowing writers to criticize freely a shared unfolding political reality, while maintaining the powers of refusal that had been unleashed by the Manifesto of the 121: "Each person becomes responsible for assertions of which he is not the author, for a search that is not only his; he answers for a knowledge that he does not originally know himself. This is the meaning of the review as a collective possibility" ("[The gravity of the project]").

One of the formal innovations of the review was that events were to be analyzed only by writers coming from a different nation and a different language: thus the 1962 *Spiegel* affair, when the newspaper was accused of betraying West German state secrets, would be analyzed by the French or the Italians, while the Germans would comment upon de Gaulle's return to power and the war in Algeria. This linguistic and geographic "deterritorialization" was underwritten by a conception of the event as an interruption in the traditional course of values, which are inadequate for imagining ways of action when the event is truly that—namely, the arrival of the unprecedented. What the *Revue internationale* sought to provide, then, was a space where the event would not be subsumed under preexisting categories but rather exposed to the exercise of judgment, a judgment that ideally would refuse the form and authority of political analyses penned by famous intellectuals and instead operate through the anonymous authority of the fragment. In this sense, the review, as envisioned by Blanchot in the prefatory texts in this volume ("Letters from the *Revue internationale*," "[The gravity of the project]," "[A review can be the expression]," "[Review without division]," "Memorandum on the 'Course of Things,'" "Course of Things," and "Course of the World") was to rely on a distinct understanding of politics, one that opposed analysis in favor of judgment.

It would be ill advised to fault this venture, and Blanchot's oeuvre as a whole, for not producing an overarching theory of political action rather than a series of political judgments. On the contrary, one might even argue that Blanchot has no political "theory" to offer. Instead, his thinking takes the form of a series of strategic refusals, judgments, qualifications, specifications, and demands that straddle the divide between the normative and the descriptive. After reading "The "Essential Perversion," René Char wrote a note in 1964, which appeared later as a prose poem in his collection *Recherche de la base et du sommet* (*Search for the Base and the Summit*, 1971). For Char, something about the negative force of Blanchot's writing made it bound to unsettle the political certitudes of his readers:

> Politically, Maurice Blanchot can go only from one deception to another, that is to say, from courage to courage, for he does not have the forgetful mobility of most of the great contemporary writers. Blanchot is fixed at the depth that distress hinders, that revolt also electrifies but does not tap, the only depth that will count when everything will be ash or dust, having only the cold value, in a new present, of the past alone. Blanchot's work only begins, like a tree full of wind, on the other side of this "Sleep, you were not happy at all." It is here only to dig at clairvoyant minds and make them feel thirsty.[35]

Blanchot's aversion to traditional political commentary would remain intense. In a letter to Mascolo in 1962, he wrote: "There is nothing more illegitimate [*bâtard*] than political commentary, expressed by someone who believes he has something to say and the desire to say it."[36] The *Revue internationale* hoped to force writers to exceed the illegitimate boundaries of both their private convictions and the means of expression at their disposal. It hoped to "dig at clairvoyant minds and make them feel thirsty."

The failure of the project would, if anything, reinforce the importance of this experiment for Blanchot, his own work having taken a turn toward a postgeneric, fragmentary discourse, whose operative terms were those of *épuisement* ("exhaustion"), *l'entretien* (implying both "conversation" and "upkeep"), and *le neutre* ("the neuter" or "the neutral"). As Denis Hollier and Jeffrey Mehlman have suggested, the extent of Blanchot's ambitions for his writing and those for the review should not be underestimated: "It was as if, to play on the title of . . . the just published *Le livre à venir*, the journal was the book to come, both the book of the future and the future of the book, the site for the intervention of a plural authorship of a radically new type of writing agency that would relegate the single-author, traditional book to obsolescence."[37]

The dispersal of the book into fragments found its true expression during Blanchot's activity in 1968. The concern linking the refusal of de Gaulle's return to power, the contestation of the Algerian War, and the mass movements that would follow a few years later is, once more, to be situated in a dual impetus, here the two forms of responsibility distinct to the political and the literary: "There seems to result . . . an irreducible difference and even a discord between political responsibility that is both global and concrete, accepting Marxism as nature and the dialectic as the method of truth, and literary responsibility, a responsibility that is a response to a demand that cannot take form except in and through literature" ("[The gravity of the project]"). And yet the enigma persists that, despite this cleft, for Blanchot the problem of division is best expressed in literature. If the world allows itself to be grasped only indirectly, then those charged with the task of thinking the event must be prepared to follow the fragmentary, nondialectical paths unveiled by literature with no guarantee of arrival.

Although the events of May 1968 have been recalled and rewritten in truncated official versions as a counter-cultural revolution, a student movement, and even a sort of self-regulating collective purge of elements opposed to free-market capitalism and modernization, these bowdlerized histories only emphasize the need to look back at the documents the period produced. Blanchot's extensive contributions to the Student-Writer Action Committee in the form of tracts, posters, and bulletins bring us very far from what Kristin Ross has aptly described as a "police conception" of history.[38] In her rereading of May 68 and its afterlives, the media's intermittent commemorations, which focus on a few proper names picked from the ranks of ex-student leaders and the self-appointed "new philosophers," lead the spectator to believe that nothing happened.

As Ross notes, the French advertising industry's own term for such a blitz campaign—*matraquage*—conceals a long and uncanny history, which takes us back to the word's colonial origins. *Matraq* is the word for "club" in Algerian Arabic, and named the preferred weapon of the police against both the pro-Algerian demonstrators in 1961 and the activists of the mass movements of May 1968. The polysemic history of *matraque* serves as an admonition against reading 1968 as a spontaneous upheaval orchestrated by the youth of an insurrectional generation.

Granted that 1968 was a singularly "arrogant" instance of demands made in the name of the "here and now," as Jean-Claude Milner has argued, such forces of rupture can take on meaning only when placed in the context from which they seek to break away.[39] The fault-lines of this break are above all linguistic. They are to be found everywhere, addressed to the passerby, whose fleeting glance is seized by the bold typography of tracts, posters, and bulletins written in the "Hegelian-Marxist" dialect that was the privileged idiom of the moment:

> In May, there is no book on May—not due to a lack of time or due to the necessity "to act," but because of a more decisive obstacle: it is written elsewhere, in a world devoid of publication, it is distributed with the police and in a certain way with their help, violence against violence. This arrest of the book [*arrêt du livre*] is also an arrest of history that, far from leading us back before culture, designates a point well beyond culture, and this is what most provokes authority, power, and the law. May this bulletin prolong this arrest, while preventing it from being arrested, suspended, ended. No more books, never again a book, so long as we maintain our relation with the upheaval of the rupture. ("[Tracts, posters, bulletins]")

The ironies of reciting these words, meant to incite passers-by to action, within the inherently conservative space of academic commentary are too corrosive to be lingered upon. Like many others written anonymously for the pages of the Student-Writer Committee's eponymous review, *Comité*, these words were later attributed to Blanchot by Mascolo. These furtive pages, written and distributed in haste, attest to a radicalization of Blanchot's breach with political orthodoxies. The mass movements of May—which claimed to conjoin the demands of workers and those of students, those of citizens and those of immigrants, the cities' and the provinces', the colonizer's and the colonized's—are said to be the sole power capable of laying open a future untouched by "political death."

Blanchot insists that de Gaulle's France is a massive political dead zone, where no communication is possible due to heightened police surveillance, which guarantees the stasis of ordinary citizens as well as their unquestioning adherence to the political body. After the occupation of the Sorbonne and the workers' strikes of May 1968, de Gaulle hastened to dissolve various political organizations by presidential decree, modifying laws from 1870 and 1936 concerning "combat groups and private militias." For Blanchot, this decree amounted to a political death sentence, and refusal became the primitive manifestation of life, insofar as the politics it imagined were an articulation of refusal expressed before it was possible even to name what was being refused. The conceptualization of "political death" is doubled by the notion of "political crime," which, for Blanchot, is the regime's desire to suffocate any voices or gestures of refusal emanating from the body politic.

Hence the urgency of exploiting any remaining modalities of rupture, which are necessarily anonymous, plural, fragmentary, collective, and proffered without commentary, to be put at the service of those who cannot speak for themselves. The correlation between literary and political liberation is acute. In anonymous writing, the individual writer is not only liberated from his authority, he can also accede to a new form of writing in "communism," presented here as the ultimate stage of writing. Blanchot's startling notion of literary communism takes root in the work of Georges Bataille, Jacques Derrida, and Jean-Luc Nancy, to name a few who paradoxically share and contest a legacy of communism without heirs. In its most economical definition: "Communism is what excludes (and excludes itself from) any already constituted community" ("[Communism without heirs]").

Significantly, the text titled "[Communism without heirs]," published in *Comité*, is the first in which Blanchot speaks of the exit from religion, family, state, and history in terms of "a call to the outside" and of the world of communist demand and liberal capitalism as being merely held together by the trait, the hiatus of a disaster. The end of alienation heralded by the call to the outside is not a topic that can be treated thetically or thematically, and it inaugurates a quest for new modes: a writing of the disaster. The refusal to write "on" a political situation becomes a refusal of analytic discourse, of discourse tout court, in favor of more ephemeral forms, whose incisiveness owes much to their transitory, para-textual existence. A political truth expressed in this manner has more to do with an interpellation or a call than an enunciation, as it is intended to provoke disorder rather than resolve the issue at hand.

Blanchot's resistance to pragmatic expediency, to solutions as such, in favor of the search for new forms of exposition continues in his approach to Marx. In "Marx's Three Voices," a text later collected in *Friendship*, he lingers on the philosopher's style. Marx's discursive heterogeneity allows him to consider the same object differently, and by intertwining these different orders of discourse, he alters our understanding of science. For Blanchot, to interpret Marx's political philosophy one must begin with his language. While this may seem to be a heedlessly aesthetic take on one of the most programmatic thinkers in the history of political philosophy, in his reading of Marx Blanchot reveals how the possibility of literature holds new vectors for politics and the world. The attention to Marx's language should be read as part of a general strategy of transformation and redundancy. As Denis Hollier writes, for both Bataille and Blanchot "literature does not expect to be made possible by a transformation of the world; rather, in a transformed world literature will be able to realize its own essence by ceasing to be possible."[40] Although Blanchot may accept the premises of Marxism, this acceptance does not lead to being doctrinaire, since he takes Marx as above all a reminder that incessant contestation always takes place in multiple languages, bound to remain untranslatable and strictly nonhomologous.

That such multiple speech was the true site of the events of May distinguished it from other revolutions for Blanchot. As he wrote fifteen years later in *The Unavowable Community*, this insurrection was "without project [*sans projet*]," and, unlike more traditional revolutions, did not revolve around the siege and occupation of a symbolic center. Instead, what mattered was allowing the possibility of "being together" to emerge, a possibility that "gave back to all the right to equality in fraternity through a *freedom of speech* that elated everyone."[41] What was said mattered less than the right to say it, or to question the unspoken premises of those who had monopolized the right to speech until then.[42] To use Blanchot's most Levinasian formulation of the underlying ethical tenor of the moment, "Saying was more important than what was said [*Le dire primait le dit*]."[43] The priority of the saying over the said is another reminder that for Blanchot "politics is embodied in speech, in the power to say no, in refusal, the only power "irreducible to any power," and that "language watches over," if language is indeed the possibility of hospitality, a space open to the disposition of the entirely other."[44]

Yet it is clear that for Blanchot, even in 1968, the space of hospitality was so consistently threatened that he was willing to align the year's events with the Second World War by claiming that France under de Gaulle was still an occupied country, a state at war with itself. What may surprise readers, beyond the discernable insistence on a "permanent revolution" that would make insurrection a quotidian reality, are the parallels Blanchot draws between this struggle and the civil rights movements in the United States and South Africa. Here liberation is construed in the broadest sense possible, as an escape from privative claims made in the name of universal liberal humanism on the behalf of Western, capitalist colonialism.

Indeed, if one accepts Mascolo's description, Blanchot's overarching strategy also involves a liberation from the exclusionary powers of concepts themselves. Mascolo saw Blanchot's thought as "a revolt against the concept, . . . which must be stripped at all costs of its unbearable power of exclusion." Herbert Marcuse recognized such a promise of nonexclusionary thinking in Blanchot. In *One Dimensional Man* (1964), his famous critique of the repressive tendencies of Western industrial societies, the critical theorist of the "Great Refusal" turned to Blanchot in the final section, "The Chance of the Alternatives." For Marcuse, pure domination amounts to a total administration of life, which finds its defense in the guise of progress: "in the overdeveloped areas of mass consumption, the administered life becomes the good life of the whole, in the defense of which the opposites are united."[45] Any refusal of such a "good life of the whole" necessarily appears to be purely negative, incapable or unwilling to contribute to society, demanding only the end of its domination. While "the established system" incorporates topical instances of resistance by putting them to work, it can merely point to the unreasonableness of absolute refusal, which is bound to appear ever more so, as increased productivity "alleviates the burden of life." Faced with the seeming impossibility of alternatives to the status quo, Marcuse quotes a passage in French from Blanchot's "Refusal" on the value of what is being refused and the necessity of its refusal. He introduces the passage by insisting that "if the abstract character of the refusal is the result of total reification, then the concrete ground for refusal must still exist, for reification is an illusion. By the same token, the unification of opposites in the medium of technological rationality must be, *in all its reality*, an illusory unification, which eliminates neither the contradiction between the growing productivity and its repressive use, nor the vital need for solving the contradiction."[46] Refusal becomes necessary when what is being refused is not without value or importance. The seeming unreasonableness of absolute refusal is merely a sign that the contradictory conditions that give rise to it need to be transformed.

The remainder of the texts collected in this volume attest to a growing, almost unique attention to the preservation of a space in which to welcome the other. While affirming the rupture that had been produced and rejecting the lure of reconciliation, Blanchot's thinking constantly turned back to the most singular instance of exclusion in memory. The texts in the third section of this book often take the form of a reflection on Judaism and the Shoah, as if the slogan popularized in May 1967 upon the exile of Daniel Cohn-Bendit, the Franco-German student leader—"We are all German Jews"—never stopped resounding for Blanchot, especially since, as Milner points out, the very success of this slogan, which qualified the name "Jew" with the "German" nationality, left the question of solidarity with French Jews or Jews without nation in abeyance.[47] Starting in 1971, Blanchot began to address the Shoah and Israel explicitly in his writing, entering into dialogue with Levinas and especially with Antelme, who had written about his internment in the camps at Buchenwald, Gandersheim, and Dachau in *L'Espèce humaine* (1947; *The Human Race*). Their dialogue would remain a touchstone for later thinkers such as Sarah Kofman and Philippe Lacoue-Labarthe.

Although in the seventies and thereafter his publications became increasingly sparse, he did break his silence to express his support for Israel even while criticizing Begin's expansionist policies ("What Is Closest To Me"), to defend threatened writers, and to sign manifestos against impending conflicts. Above all, he commented upon the work of his friends. In addition to Antelme and Lacoue-Labarthe, he wrote on Marguerite Duras, Dionys Mascolo, Louis-René des Forêts, Jacques Derrida, Jean-Luc Nancy, Michel Foucault, Henri Michaux, Paul Celan, Samuel Beckett, Edmond Jabès, Leslie Kaplan, and Vadim Kozovoï. Blanchot returned repeatedly to Heidegger, whose writings had so deeply influenced many of these writers, and to Levinas, the first conduit of Heidegger's thought into France. The charged question of Heidegger's political affiliations with National Socialism from 1933 to 1934, while he was rector of the University of Freiburg, drew Blanchot's attention. The importance of elucidating the extent and nature of this affiliation was bound up with the significance of the philosopher's work. Heidegger's greatest fault, for Blanchot, was to have used his inimitable philosophical idiom "to call for votes in Hitler's favor, to justify Nazi Germany's secession from the League of Nations," or to praise party ideologues such as Schlageter ("Thinking the Apocalypse"). This perversion of language was like a "wound to thought," in Blanchot's words, a wound that he would repeatedly examine during this time.

The debate concerning Heidegger's politics took on a more polemical tone in 1987, when Victor Farias's book *Heidegger et le nazisme* revisited then-familiar accusations, mixing anecdotes with a few unpublished facts while failing to lend any serious consideration to Heidegger as a philosopher. As Ethan Kleinberg argues, the French reception of Heidegger's thought had already gone through three major phases from 1927 to 1962. First introduced to a French readership by Levinas and by Alexander Kojève's Heideggerian interpretation of Hegel, the thinker gained a wider audience through Sartre and Jean Beaufret's divergent interpretations and then through Levinas's ongoing opposition of a primordial "ethics" to Heidegger's ontology, questioning the anteriority it accorded to Being over beings.[48] Yet none of these investigations raised the curiosity of the mass media as much as Farias's book did. Even Philippe Lacoue-Labarthe's dissertation, published the same year and dedicated to Blanchot, failed to register in the sensationalistic discussions of the press.[49] It was in response to Catherine David in *Le nouvel observateur* that Blanchot wrote "Thinking the Apocalypse," a letter that contains his most direct statements concerning Heidegger's silence about the Shoah and his wartime political affiliations.

Blanchot's writings about Heidegger's politics were always in dialogue with, if not explicitly addressed to, Levinas, who had introduced him to the philosopher's work during their student days in Strasbourg in the 1920s. Blanchot wrote on his friend's lifelong reflections on ethics and Judaism on various occasions ("Our Clandestine Companion," "Encounters," "Peace, Peace Far and Near"). In a striking parallel to Blanchot's discussions of Levinas, Levinas read Blanchot's work as providing an extensive critique of Heidegger's conception of the work of art: "Does Blanchot not attribute to art the function of uprooting the Heideggerian universe?"[50] The mutual homage in these writings could be read as part of a larger reflection on absent friends that Blanchot began in 1971 with the book *L'Amitié* (*Friendship*), a volume that collects a series of studies devoted to his friends. This became the central focus of his writings from 1986 onwards, in such works as *Michel Foucault tel que je l'imagine* (*Michel Foucault as I Imagine Him*, 1986), *Une voix venue d'ailleurs* (*A Voice from Elsewhere*, 1992) and the offprint *Pour l'amitié* (*For Friendship*, 1996), included in this volume. While these essays are inflected by the laudatory register that Eleanor Kaufman has dubbed "delirium of praise"—reserved for commentary on and among friends—they also move beyond the pale of friendship and *philia*.[51] At the end of this book, we are left with an enigmatic invitation addressed to Salman Rushdie and the Ayatollah Khomeini, convoking them to join Blanchot in the presence of the Koran in order to settle their differences. This unbounded sense of openness to the radically other remains a call extended to his readers.

No amount of contextualization can avoid the translator's question of whether it is possible to translate texts that resist the spirit of anthology not only for a host of syntactic and lexical reasons but in their very form. How can one translate mural writing? Here we are dealing above all with a mode that is "neither inscription nor elocution," that does "not need to be read" but is posed "like a challenge to every law, words of disorder, the speech outside of discourse that marks our steps, political cries—and bulletins by the dozen . . . everything that disturbs, calls, threatens, and finally questions without expecting an answer, without resting in certainty, never will we enclose it in a book, which, even when open, tends toward closure, a refined form of oppression" ("[Tracts, posters, bulletins").

Is there an impertinence in publishing these texts under Blanchot's name, an act made doubly treacherous by translation? "Languages are never contemporaneous," we are reminded in these pages, "How is one to maintain this difference of historical level in a translation?" ("Course of Things").

Two infidelities then: the book and its translation. The problems in translating the political writings necessarily lead to a questioning of translation in the largest sense—of historical context, of translation from "one" language to "another," of theory toward praxis. Blanchot's French prose, above all when he writes these texts, remains a foreign language even to those who speak French. It disturbs the security of having privileged access to a "mother tongue." While it respects classical grammar and syntax, his prose undoes every accent of familiarity, depriving the reader of immediate understanding. It is written in its own idiom. The reflexivity of this idiom, as in such impersonal reflexives as *se traduire*, *se contester*, and *s'affirmer*, seems far more pervasive than is allowed by common usage. In a letter to Ilija Bojovic, a representative of the Yugoslav media, concerning May 68, we read: "The great Law was shattered; the great Theory collapsed [*s'est effondré*]; the Transgression was accomplished, and by whom? By a plurality of forces escaping all the frames of contestation, coming literally from nowhere, unlocalized and unlocalizable. This is what I believe is decisive" "[Letter to a representative of Yugoslav radio-television]"). Without the believing "I" that ends the letter, there is no subject, and the passive structure of the prior sentence is left grasping at the sources of an unnamed agency. Barring the possibility of clearly attributed actions, one falls into the passive voice, which writers of English are taught is to be avoided at all costs, at the peril of losing the reader's attention. The attention that such reflexivity demands of the reader, in French and in English, is closely correlated with the concentration demanded by the problems of political judgment. Can one claim to extrapolate a politics from these collected instances of judgment? If so, is it best understood as a gesture or as a theory?

There are strong reasons to claim that Blanchot lacks a fully articulated political theory. This absence should be conceived not as a lack but as an alternative to theory. Yet even the most cursory readings retain refusal as Blanchot's characteristic political gesture: a refusal that is above all a refusal of stories rich with political lessons. "The past does not enlighten us very much; there is something different here, the promise of a new oppression. . . . all roads are closed off to us for now, it depends on us to find an exit, precisely from here, by refusing to yield at every moment and in every way" ("Refusal," note). For Blanchot, 1940, 1958, and 1968 matter not merely as dates on which something took place, but because of what was refused then. In 1940, refusal did not have to be exercised "against the invading force (not accepting it was self-evident)" ("Refusal"). In 1958, refusal was not "in relation to the events of May 13 (which are refused by themselves), but in the face of this power that claimed to reconcile us with them honorably, by the mere authority of a name" (ibid.). The parallelism is noteworthy: what one believes occurred is presented as self-evident and reflexive, whereas the true site of contestation is the refusal of this self-evident account, as well as any unexpectedly happy solutions it has to offer.

This decision of refusal, which belongs above all to those who cannot speak, can be followed like Ariadne's thread through the labyrinth of the postwar period. As Nancy wrote shortly after Blanchot's death, one is often left with the impression that his work is less thinking than a stance or a gesture. Trying to trace its movement, Nancy writes:

> In truth, less a thinking than a stance or a gesture—a gesture of a certain trust. Above all else, Blanchot trusts in the possibility of *entretien* ["conversation" or "maintenance"]. What is maintained in the conversation (with another, with oneself, with the proper pursuit of the conversation) is the perpetually renewed relation between speech and the *infinity* of sense that constitutes its truth. *Writing* (literature) names this relation. It does not transcribe a testimony, it does not invent a fiction, it does not deliver a message: it traces the infinite journey of sense in so far as it absents itself. This self-absenting of sense is not negative; it is sense's chance and what is at stake in it as such. To "write" means relentlessly to approach the limit of speech, that limit which speech alone touches and in touching it unlimits us (us speaking beings).[52]

The interest of these writings, then, is not just the particular set of positions Blanchot adopts with respect to specific political problems—from colonialism to a capitalist mode of production and its cultural effects—but even more the way in which such analyses are mirrored by a constant reflection on the gesture of writing as a highly distinctive and mediate form of political intervention. Whether or not it is possible to translate Blanchot's double sense of the political into another language and a recognizable, repeatable gesture remains to be seen. The present attempt hopes to partake in the infinite conversation about the possibility both of translation and of politics.

Chronology

This chronology is a translation of Christophe Bident's "Repères Chronologiques," featured in *L'Énigme Blanchot, Magazine littéraire*, no. 424 (October 2003), p. 27–28. I would like to thank him for graciously allowing me to reproduce it here.

1907 Maurice Blanchot is born in Quain, a small town in Devrouze (Saône-et-Loire), on September 22, in a house inherited from the maternal side of his family, who were affluent Catholic landowners. He has two brothers and one sister. His family will move frequently: his father is a teacher and a private tutor who offers his services from Paris to Elbeuf, from Sarthe to Chalon.

1923 Blanchot graduates from secondary school. A duodenum surgery, which he will later deem useless, delays his departure for university by a year. All his life he will enjoy an "irrésistible petite santé," ("irresistible delicate health"), to use Deleuze's phrase about many artists and writers.

1925 A student of philosophy and German, Blanchot meets Emmanuel Levinas at the University of Strasbourg. Together they read German phenomenology, Proust, and Valéry. Derrida will later write that "the *friendship* between Maurice Blanchot and Emmanuel Levinas was a grace, a gift; it remains a benediction of our time" (Jacques Derrida, "Adieu," in *Adieu to Emmanuel Levinas*, trans. Pasquale-Anne Brault and Michael Naas [Stanford: Stanford University Press, 1999], 8).

1930 Blanchot submits a graduate thesis, a Diplôme d'Etudes Supérieures, on the Skeptics at the Sorbonne.

1931 He begins medical studies at St. Anne Hospital. But journalism attracts him more than the university. He publishes his first article, on François Mauriac. He contributes to newspapers and journals of the far right, notably around young dissidents of the Action française, led by Thierry Maulnier. He begins a novel, whose various drafts he most probably destroys.

1933 Anticapitalism, antiparliamentarianism, and anticommunism are his constant watchwords, at the service of a spiritual revolution, likewise anti-Germanism and anti-Hitlerism. Blanchot is also close to nationalist Jewish groups swift to denounce the Nazi demands. In *Le rempart*, a daily newspaper led by his friend Paul Lévy, he protests the first deportations of Jews to labor camps.

1936 Blanchot's father dies. A year of radicalization ensues. He participates in the monthly journal *Combat*, edited by Jean de Fabrègues and Thierry Maulnier.

1937 He writes a polemical political column, as well as his first literary column, in *L'Insurgé*. He will put an end to this double contribution during the course of the year and will sign no further political texts for the far right. Claude Séverac, a close colleague from *Aux écoutes*, the newspaper directed by Paul Lévy, dies. This is probably also the year when he meets Jean Paulhan.

1940 Blanchot covers the government in the dissolution of the Third Republic and the formation of a puppet government under the Nazis at Bordeaux, then at Vichy, for the *Journal des débats*. He then renounces his editorial activity. At Jeune France, a state-sponsored cultural institution, he directs the research unit on literature; with some others, he plans to use "Vichy against Vichy." In December, he meets Georges Bataille, who would later describe their immediate rapport of "admiration and agreement" in an autobiographical fragment.

1941 He begins a series of 171 literary columns for the *Journal des débats*. His first book, *Thomas the Obscure*, a novel, is published that autumn. He hosts and finds shelter for the wife and daughter of Levinas.

1943 At Dionys Mascolo's request, *Faux Pas* is published, collecting fifty four of the literary columns from the *Journal des débats*.

1944 Stood up by German soldiers against the wall of the house where he was born, Blanchot is saved in extremis when the Germans turn out to be Russians, from the Vlassov army, who allow him to escape at a moment when their Nazi lieutenant's attention is diverted by Resistance fighters. The miracle of his escape leaves him with feelings ("the instant of my death henceforth always in abeyance") of which he will write fifty years later in *The Instant of My Death*.

1946 Blanchot publishes in *L'Arche*, *Critique*, and *Les temps modernes*, participates in various literary juries, and begins to be recognized as the most important postwar critic in France. His relationship with Denise Rollin begins. He leaves Paris to settle down alone on the Mediterranean, in Èze village, even though he continues to make frequent visits to the capital.

1946–58 Blanchot's articles change form: longer and denser, they testify to a new authority and concerted research. In 1953, he begins contributing monthly to the *Nouvelle nouvelle revue française*. He creates his own literary space: the interminable, the incessant, the neutral, the outside, essential solitude. *The Space of Literature* appears in 1955. These are also the years of the *récits* written in Èze, in the "small room" evoked later, at the beginning of a text devoted to Louis-René des Forêts, "Anacrouse." He writes a second, more concise version of *Thomas the Obscure*. He publishes *Death Sentence*, *When the Time Comes*, *The One Who Was Standing Apart from Me*, and *The Last Man*. His mother dies in 1957.

1958 Blanchot returns to Paris. He writes to Dionys Mascolo, who has just established the review *Le 14 juillet* against de Gaulle's "coup d'état": "I would like to express my agreement with you. I accept neither the past nor the present." He publishes "Refusal" in the second issue of the review. He becomes close to Robert and Monique Antelme, Marguerite Duras, Louis-René des Forêts, Maurice Nadeau, and Elio and Ginetta Vittorini.

1960 "Declaration of the Right to Insubordination in the Algerian War," called the Manifesto of the 121, appears. With Dionys Mascolo and Jean Schuster, Blanchot is the primary writer. The project for the *Revue internationale* is born. With Mascolo and Vittorini, Blanchot is its main initiator. Robert Antelme, Michel Butor, Louis-René des Forêts, Marguerite Duras, Michel Leiris, Maurice Nadeau, Italo Calvino, Pier Paolo Pasolini, Ingeborg Bachmann, Hans-Magnus Enzensberger, Günter Grass, Uwe Johnson, Martin Walser, and others participate in the meetings. Others, like René Char and Jean Genet, propose texts. The project fails at the end of four years of effort and leaves Blanchot without hope.

1962 *Awaiting Oblivion*, Blanchot's first fragmentary book, is published. Death of Georges Bataille; Blanchot writes a text in homage to his absent friend: "Friendship."

1964	Blanchot writes his first letter to Jacques Derrida, beginning a sustained correspondence.
1966	The review *Critique* devotes a special issue to Blanchot, with texts by René Char, Françoise Collin, Paul de Man, Michel Foucault, Roger Laporte, Emmanuel Levinas, Jean Pfeiffer, Georges Poulet, and Jean Starobinski. Foucault's article, "The Thought from Outside," sets the standard. Elio Vittorini dies.
1968	Blanchot joins the demonstrations, writes tracts, and presides over meetings of the Student-Writer Action Committee. He anonymously writes more than half of the first and unique issue of the review *Comité*.
1970	Blanchot suffers many serious health problems.
1972	He writes a text in homage to Paul Celan (*The Last to Speak*), included in *A Voice From Elsewhere.*
1973	*The Step Not Beyond*, his second book of fragments, is published.
1978	In January, his brother and Denise Rollin pass away in close succession.
1980	*The Writing of the Disaster*, a third book of fragments, is published.
1983	With *The Unavowable Community*, Blanchot responds to "The Inoperative Community," an essay by Jean-Luc Nancy that would later be put together with others in a book of that name. His writing is increasingly limited to offprints, re-editions, prefaces, homages, responses to questionnaires or surveys, public letters, and political interventions.
1990	Robert Antelme dies.
1996–97	Emmanuel Levinas and Marguerite Duras die in 1996, followed by the death in 1997 of Dionys Mascolo and Anna Wolf, the widow of Blanchot's brother René, with whom he had lived since René's death.
2003	Maurice Blanchot dies on February 20. Four days later, during the memorial service, Derrida delivers a speech in homage to the "perennial witness [*le témoin de toujours*]."

Political Writings, 1953–1993

Part I

Le 14 juillet and the *Revue internationale* Project, 1953–1962

An Approach to Communism (Needs, Values)

In a book on communism, Dionys Mascolo has tried to show that what is essential in the revolutionary movement is in part the movement of satisfying needs. Nothing else is certain: nihilism is irrefutable, but irrefutable nihilism does not suspend the play of needs for human beings as a whole. Human beings, deprived of truth, values, and ends, continue to live and, living, continue to try to satisfy their needs, thereby continuing to sustain the movement of searching in relation to this necessary satisfaction.*

Dionys Mascolo also says that communism is the process of the materialist search for communication. This can be put simply—too simply: the movement of satisfaction of needs clashes and discovers that it clashes against an obstacle, which is the existence of an economic nature. This nature, which long went unperceived, gives men a market value for one another, makes them things that are exchanged as such. Thus certain men are hired out, bought, employed by others; they become instruments and tools. This instrumentalization, this relation of utility between men, gives men the value of things; this is clear for the slave and even for any man who hires out his work—trades his time to another—but it is also clear for the master. The one who, even without his knowing it and perhaps especially then, treats another person as a thing through the unperceived detour of economic relations, this person treats himself as a thing, accepts belonging to a world where men are things, gives himself the reality and the figure of a thing, not only breaks off communication with the one who is similar or dissimilar to him, but breaks off communication with himself.

Nonetheless, in our world these relations of things are partly masked, partly scrambled by the interference of values and relations between values. Men employ other men, that is to say, in fact they treat them as things, but they respect them (ideally). From this there ensues the confusion, hypocrisy, and absence of rigor that make up our civilizations. The essential task of Marxism would be, in terms of collective relations, to liberate man from things by taking the side of things, by somehow giving power to

*Dionys Mascolo, *Le communisme, révolution et communication ou la dialectique des valeurs et des besoins* (Paris: Gallimard, 1953). Let me recall that this book was published in 1953—which dates the commentary, too. The third note below is more recent.

things, that is to say, to that which reduces man to being nothing but useful, active, productive, that is, by excluding any moral alibi, any phantom of value. The essential task of Marxism (at least understood as such and restrictively) is to give man mastery over nature, over that which is nature in him, by means of the thing.* All other means of liberation by recourse to ideal hopes would only prolong his subjugation and, moreover, trick him and let him remain in a false state, where he soon loses his footing and becomes oblivious to what is. From this perspective, the liberator would thus be the man who is, from now on, most purely a thing, the man-tool who is already reduced, without disguise, to his material condition, who is "nothing" but useful, the man of necessity, the needy one, the man of need—it is to him that power must be relegated: the working man, the producing man, that is to say, the man who is not immediately man (for he is "nothing," he is only lack, negation, need), but is work itself, anonymous and impersonal, and the things produced by work, works in their making, in which man, undergoing violence and responding with violence, would come to himself, to his real freedom. But it is self-evident that any man, if he wants to "see" through the unreality of values what he is (that is to say, nothing) is also this man of need.

The immensity of the effort to be carried out, the necessity of questioning all the values to which we are attached, of returning to a new barbarity in order to break with the polite and camouflaged barbarity that serves as our civilization, the unknown toward which we are heading—for we absolutely do not know what man might be—the terrible violence provoked by inequality in the satisfaction of needs, the subjugation to things, government by things, as well as technology's own dialectic, finally inertia and fatigue—all this would contribute to deferring the actualization of such a movement to a dreamt of (or bloody) deadline, if the pressure of needs did not represent a force, a very large reserve of time. We can say that the movement's rapid progress is astonishing, but in any case it takes time. What matters is not to arrive but to depart; the beginning of man would be the event par excellence, and we cannot say that we are at such a preliminary point—perhaps we can make it out, maybe one has to begin again and again, that is to say, never rely on the word *beginning*. In any case, no one doubts that Marx's phrase—"The reign of liberty begins with the end of the reign of needs and external ends"—promises nothing other

*But perhaps it would be more correct (very rough, nonetheless) to say that it is only when man has reached his end (has been superseded) as a power that the relation to man will cease to be a power and will become a possible relation, "communication."

to contemporaries than the quest for a just direction and the determination of a possible future.

It follows that men today and no doubt also those who will come later, if they do not want to run the risk of living in relations of illusion, have apparently no other solution than to limit themselves to the form of the simplest needs: they must convert all values into needs. This means that, in collective relations, we should have no other existence than the one that makes possible the movement by which the man of need is brought to power. It might also mean that we could not have any other existence than this collective impersonality and that all forms of private, secret life would have to be banned and considered guilty, as happened in France during the Terror. But Dionys Mascolo refutes this last consequence in the most inventive part of his work. We have two lives that we must try to live together, even though they are irreconcilable. One consists of so-called private relations.* Here, we do not need to wait, nor can we wait. Here, it seems that through desire, passion, the exaltation of extreme states, by speech, too, man can become the impossible friend of man, being precisely related to the impossible. Plenitude is broken, communication is no longer that of separate beings who promise each other recognition in the infinitely distant future of a world without separation, it does not content itself with bringing particular individuals closer, in the intimacy of desire, it affirms itself alone, it does not affirm itself as a movement that affirms what it unites, but negates, a movement itself without fixity, without certainty.

Can we live these two lives? Whether we can or not, we must: one is linked to the future of "communication," when the relations between men will no longer, insidiously or violently, make them into things, but for this it engages us, profoundly, dangerously, in the world of things, of "useful" relations, "efficacious" works, where we always come close to losing ourselves. The other welcomes communication, outside of the world and immediately, but on the condition that communication be the upheaval of "the immediate," the opening, the shattering violence, the fire that burns

*But here a question arises: Can we distinguish so easily between private and collective relations? In both cases, are we not dealing with relations that could not be subject-object relations, nor even subject-subject relations, but are such that the relation of one to the other could be affirmed as infinite or discontinuous? Hence the exigency, the urgency of the relation through desire and speech, a relation perpetually in displacement, where *the other*—the impossible—would be welcomed, constitutes, in the strongest sense, an essential mode of political decision and affirmation. I think that Dionys Mascolo would admit this. What finally remains is that the concept of need is not simple and that need, too, can be distorted, just as, in a certain state of oppression, men can fall below their needs.

without waiting, for that is also, that is first of all, what communist generosity is, this inclemency, this impatience, the refusal of all detours, of all ruses, and of all delays: infinitely hazardous freedom. Certainly, alone, the first relates to a possible "truth," it goes alone—but with what vicissitudes and what pains—toward a world. We can see clearly, however, that it does not take the latter much into account: intimate "life"—because it does not belong to the day—is without justification, it cannot be recognized and could only be recognized by dressing itself up as value. Who is not aware that tragic and possibly intolerable divisions result from this? If there is a tragic dimension specific to our times, it would be found here.

We thus have two lives, and the second is without right, but not without decision. "Communication," as it is unveiled in private human relations and withdrawn into works that we still call works of art, may not indicate the horizon of a world rid of false relations, but it helps us refuse the authority that founds these relations, forcing us to find a position from which it would be possible to have no part in "values." Dionys Mascolo says that the writer must live both in the common world of need and in an intimate world of values and ends. But perhaps on this point one must go farther than he does, in the direction indicated by his statements. The poetic work, the artistic work, if it speaks to us of something, speaks to us of that which is removed from all value or repels all evaluation, articulates the demand of beginning (again), which is lost and muddled as soon as it is satisfied in value. Nietzsche wanted to transmute all values, but this transvaluation (at least in the most visible, all-too-well-known part of his writings) seemed to leave the notion of value intact. It is undoubtedly the task of our time to move toward an affirmation that is entirely other. A difficult and essentially risky task. It is to this task that communism recalls us with a rigor that it itself often shirks, and it is also to this task that "artistic experience," in the realm that would be proper to it, recalls us. A remarkable coincidence.

Refusal

At a certain moment, when faced with public events, we know that we must refuse. Refusal is absolute, categorical. It does not discuss or voice its reasons. This is how it remains silent and solitary, even when it affirms itself, as it should, in broad daylight. Those who refuse and who are bound by the force of refusal know that they are not yet together. The time of common affirmation is precisely what has been taken away from them. What they are left with is the irreducible refusal, the friendship of this sure, unshakable, rigorous No that unites them and determines their solidarity.

The movement of refusal is rare and difficult, though equal and the same in each one of us, as soon as we have taken it up. Why difficult? Because we must refuse not only the worst but also a reasonable semblance, a solution that will be deemed happy and even unhoped for. In 1940 refusal had to be asserted not against the invading force (not accepting it was self-evident) but against the chance that Marshal Pétain claimed, no doubt in good faith, to represent and against all the justifications he was able to invoke. Today, the exigency of refusal has not arisen in relation to the events of May 13 (which are refused by themselves), but in the face of this power that claimed to reconcile us with them honorably, by the mere authority of a name.

What we refuse is not without value or importance. This is precisely why refusal is necessary. There is a kind of reason that we will no longer accept, there is an appearance of wisdom that horrifies us, there is an offer of agreement and compromise that we will not hear. A rupture has occurred. We have been brought back to this frankness that does not tolerate complicity any longer.

When we refuse, we refuse with a movement free from contempt and exaltation, one that is as far as possible anonymous, for the power of refusal is accomplished neither by us nor in our name, but from a very poor beginning that belongs first of all to those who cannot speak. Today, one might say that it is easy to refuse, that the exercise of this power carries little risk. This is no doubt true for most of us. I think, however, that refusal is never easy, that we must learn how to refuse and to maintain intact this power of refusal, by the rigor of thinking and modesty of expression that each one of our affirmations must evidence from now on.

The Essential Perversion

When one reflects calmly, as one must, on the events of May 1958, one quickly realizes the following: if these events are considered only in their political aspect, and if this aspect is thought to be sufficient to define them, then any judgment that one passes on them, even an unfavorable one, will be implicitly favorable. This is why the refusal of politicians often appeared without force and more obstinate than firm. What happens in the case of political analysis? What happens is precisely that it analyses, it dissociates; it sees in what came about a plurality of facts of distinct origin and opposing meaning, correcting and neutralizing one another—de Gaulle compensating for the men of May 13. What was shadowy about them only intensified the bright light of the unique apparition. Similarly, although the military revolt may have seemed regrettable, de Gaulle the military man, but a special kind of military man, was precisely well chosen to defuse the political ambitions of the army. Finally, there was the mediocre former regime, its incapacity to reform itself or to resolve serious problems. Here again, we have obtained an interesting solution, in sufficiently legal conditions, even if it is subject to criticism: Who would fight against this Constitution, and in favor of the other one or for any other one? Hence the conclusion: de Gaulle is really better, after all, and when you think of what we might have had, more than we can hope for.

This commonsense judgment is so natural that it must be present in each of us. This is politics conceived of as opportune behavior; opportunism is thus political truth. Considered as an opportune decision, the solution that bears de Gaulle's name can seem dubious or satisfying (one always finds facts for or against him)—the discussion is endless and almost useless.

Nonetheless, even with those who use the arguments of opportunism to justify their approval or disapproval, as is the case for the largest number, who remain silent because they cannot sort out the difficult mix of good and evil, there is the feeling that something entirely different has happened, a serious mutation that partly escapes political judgment, for it throws into question decisions concerning a more fundamental agreement or disagreement. Here too we can continue weakly to approve or disapprove; we can also maintain a neutral attitude; but we feel, in our unease and discomfort, how much damage (in an almost physical sense) is inflicted on thought by this way of shirking events that question thought. A deeper understanding or misunderstanding is hidden behind each one of our choices. And the refusal to see clearly already makes up a part of the "yes" that secretly commands our assent and constrains us.

The power that issues from the events of May has a singular appearance. This character of singularity contributes to the difficulty of judgment, and to the appeasement it settles on. It is a power that bears a name, that of de Gaulle; this name qualifies it and covers it over, but does not suffice to determine it. Is it a dictatorship? No. Dictatorship is the power invested in an individual who has struggled for power and concentrates it around his highly individual person. It is certainly nothing good, but it is not anything disturbing for thought, either. Dictatorship is a human power, the dictator is a marked man [*un homme manifeste*], his regime is the exercise of force without constraint. Naturally, dictatorships change quickly. Dictators use up the magic of their person; they make themselves emperors, they dominate. But it is always as individuals that they rise. They are men. The combat against them is a simple and wordless combat. None of these features directly suits de Gaulle or the regime that he represents. De Gaulle did not conquer power; he is not a man of action. He politicized himself briefly some time ago with embarrassment and awkwardness, drawn into this role by his own bizarre passivity, but he was quickly convinced of his error; this is why attacking him by reminding him that he used to be a party man does not mean anything. He is not a man of action. Action does not interest him. His extreme care not to take power, but to let power come to him, to offer itself to him, thanks to people of impure action with whom, however, he didn't want to seem to be connected, is remarkable. Was it the desire to save legal appearances? No, since he first refused to take those little steps necessary to his enthronement. Is it because of a too proud and slightly vain idea of himself? I don't think so. It is not due to a respect for his person, but from respect for the impersonal power that he represents, from the feeling of sovereignty that is his to affirm and that is only compatible with a minimum of action.

This sovereignty that he incarnates is apparently the exaltation of a man. On the one hand, it glorifies a name whose glorious past it also uses; it says that this presence is irreplaceable, that it is unique (unique meaning that, from the point of view of political utility, de Gaulle has no rival, but that furthermore he has no peer, unique, then, because he represents the sacred and mystical value of the unique; this is why, psychologically, one puts the accent on his solitude, he is distinct, he is separate, he is the anointed one); finally, this person is providential. This title, which was immediately attached to him, is already explicit. Providential means designated by providence and affirming itself as providence. The power with which a providential man is invested is no longer political power; it is the power of salvation. Its presence as such is salutary, effective in itself and not by what it will do.

From here, the perspective changes. The omnipotence that fell to this man alone from the beginning was quite extraordinary; everyone wondered: What won't he do with it? But one had to notice with surprise (and cowardly relief) that he wasn't doing anything with it. He couldn't do anything with it. That's because the meaning of the authority that belongs to him is that it is too high and too great to be exercised. Hence the following situation gradually became clear: de Gaulle can do anything but, in particular, he can do nothing. He is omnipotent, but the respect that he has for this omnipotence (the feeling of being the whole of France, the sense not only of representing her, but of making her legible and distantly present in her timeless reality) forbids him from using it for any determinate political decision. Thus even if he had political ideas, he could not apply them. He is not a man of policy, of a certain politics, but rather he is comprehensive sovereignty itself ("*Je vous ai compris*"[1]), which comprehends everything and, through this comprehension, satisfies everything. This sovereignty is distant, unshared, and always in the background in relation to the demonstrations that are expected of it. We are far from a simple and profane dictatorship. A dictator does not stop parading; he does not speak, he screams; his speech always has the violence of the scream, of *dictare*, of repetition. De Gaulle manifests himself, but only out of duty. Even when he appears, it is as if he were foreign to his appearance. He is withdrawn into himself. He speaks, but secretly or under the veil of majestic commonplaces, and the people of the faithful live by the exegesis of these uncertain words. Truly, he is the providential man, if Providence, according to Malebranche, is incapable of any particular action and can only manifest itself in the most general ways.

I admit that this view might be a little simplified, but even as such it does not alter the main feature, which remains the transformation of political power [*pouvoir politique*] into a power of salvation [*une puissance de salut*]. Destiny is now in power; not a historically remarkable man, but some power that is above his person, the force of the highest values, the sovereignty, not of a sovereign person, but of sovereignty itself insofar as it identifies with the possibilities of destiny thus brought together. What destiny? Here, the answer is easy: it is the august affirmation, superior to all historical accidents, of a nation as destiny. De Gaulle's past clarifies this response, which is necessarily linked to what he thinks of himself. In another time, he was called the Symbol. In dire moments, he had to represent national permanence and certitude over and above a disastrous void. He was the visible presence of a great absent nation. He personified it. It is always dangerous to identify the reality of a country with a person, and even more so to ideally elevate his story above history; but then de Gaulle himself was nothing, a man without a past, without a future, and the value of his gesture came from the firmness of a refusal that was not connected to any power. A surprising experience—in a way, he does not stop being passive; he does nothing, he can do nothing, at most he preserves, he safeguards through his presence, and he haughtily maintains nullified rights, an authority without content and the immense active forces—in which he has only a nominal share—work little by little at translating the affirmations of an Idea into reality.

From this experience arose the consciousness of a sovereignty of exception that coincided, during the dramatic hours of the void, with the essential presence of the national destiny. What is characteristic here is the manifestation of this void: in 1940, nothing was more pathetic and more obvious; where France had been, there was nothing more than the void, and beyond this void of history, the almost visible, almost perceptible affirmation, in an unknown and faceless man, of France as persistent Destiny, as the very prophecy of her salvation. De Gaulle has held onto the horror [*hantise*] of this void, but also its intimate knowledge and the feeling of its necessity. He inscribed it into the Constitution. He made it legal in a way. For France to raise herself into a Destiny and for the power that represents her to become a sovereignty of salvation, she must become conscious of this void, which, owing to its institutions and its divisions, does not cease to threaten her. In 1946, de Gaulle abruptly withdrew so that the country, discovering its void, would come to decisions that would guarantee its integrity. But the country saw nothing and the operation failed. In 1958, the operation is a masterful success. Faced with the problems of an unreasonable war, and in the despair—transformed into agitation—that was provoked by the problems of this war, doubt organized itself (and was organized). The void makes itself felt, even as the essence of national Sovereignty, which alone can fill it, approaches in the guise of the providential man. But it is striking to see that de Gaulle is no sooner in power than in fact there is (apparently) no longer anything but him and the void. Political forces crumble. Social forces withdraw. Everything becomes silent. It is like a mysterious conditioned reflex. Even those who are capable of opposition for strong internal reasons remained silent, as if they were absent. The void must not be disturbed. The Yes of the referendum is nothing but the inordinate word of this void. And the void does its work, which is to *consecrate* the authority of one man alone as the power of salvation. What would happen if we lacked such a man? The response is now clear: there would be nothing but the void.

But this is a misleading answer. History does not repeat itself. From 1940 to 1944, the great active forces of the Allies left de Gaulle behind, but at the same time he was free from his ideal authority. Today's allies, whose actions have brought him almost passively to power, have not at all faded, especially since one consequence of the inactive sovereignty of sacred power is that these powers have the greatest possible latitude for action, thus giving a political content to a power majestically without content. These forces are known, albeit still insufficiently, and only according to their anecdotal aspect, which does more to hide them than to define them. Above all, because of this insistence on anecdote and analysis, they have been presented as isolated forces and not as having a meaningful relation to the power that issues from them; or else, on the contrary, some have tried to establish anecdotal relations between de Gaulle and the conspirators. This amounts to seeing things solely from the point of view of the spectacle. What is important is that what happened on May 13 and what happened afterward constitute a whole, which has reality and meaning only as a whole. What is important is that in their intertwining relations, of different origin, form, and character, these movements—which one can designate roughly as a movement of colonial affirmation, a nationalist upsurge, the pressure of technocratic demands, the transformation of the army into a political force, the transformation of political power into a power of salvation—constitute a single phenomenon, unstable in its meaning but unique and, as such, very grave.

One of the consequences is that this regime is not what it appears to be, constantly occupied as it is by different forces that are using it to work toward their own realization and from which it cannot differentiate itself without losing face. At the forefront, we have the sovereign Presence, affirming a power not only political but essentially religious and putting into play the crudely perverted values of the sacred (the privileged destiny of one man, his predestined appearance: he saved us once, he will save us every time, he is the savior; he is the eternal fatherland [*patrie*]; every time the country is in danger, she incarnates herself in this man, the depositary of providential decisions).

To the extent that the colonial reaction is a movement of despair (just as the nationalist upsurge is a form of distress)—that is, a collective despair brought together in a collective unrest giving rise to movements of agitation that one could at times call racist, at others fascist—we see how the Destiny of Salvation symbolized by de Gaulle constituted an appropriate response. But agitation requires slogans, fetish-words (if only one would pronounce the word *integration*, peace will be made, the beautiful past will return); it wants violent satisfaction, spectacular undertakings, executions, warlike operations or, failing that, clandestine conspiracies (secrets and spectacles are equally necessary for such movements), and this form of disordered affirmation does not suit the lofty Sovereignty that is aloof from this vulgarity, does not intend to identify with it, but cannot condemn it either, for it is here to comprehend it (in every sense), to recognize it and to protect what is essential in these intentions, yet without realizing them directly, which in any case would be impossible.

Through a series of emanations that are fading imperceptibly, the supreme authority of the One must therefore be communicated, unaltered, to zones of power that are increasingly realistic, authoritarian in form, and dictatorial in their aims, designed to meet the ends in the name of which May 13 was decided upon (French Algeria; war pursued to the point of outrage, dominating everything with its logic; the army continuing to exercise its authority, which will be necessarily political, in the name of this logic). Thus, behind this sovereignty with its religious (and anachronistic) form, much more modern manifestations of political activism are announced or affirmed, ranging from the permanent intrigues of diverse factions to the threat of the praetorians (if de Gaulle goes away, you will get the paratroopers), by way of the already dense network of police control, all the way down to political gangsterism pure and simple. Similarly, we see the forces of neo-capitalism use the mystique of sovereign unity, turning it from its ideal meaning to make it meet the demands of economic domination, which needs a centralized power at the service of planning and in view of technocratic efficiency. Here, the Sovereign is not the Savior that the despair of instinctive crowds is calling for; he is not the commander that the army wants, capable of taking power both in the name of war and in the name of the army; he is the Director, a being of impersonal character who directs, monitors, and decides according to the necessities of modern capitalist organization.

I understand that these forces are divided, that they secretly fight each other, and that the violent contradictions, far from calming down behind the noble facade of unity, have moved into power, each one trying to translate the hymn to Sovereignty in their own way via the mediation of simple and narrow Debré-style nationalism.[2] This struggle has only just begun. We are at the beginning of a process in which war, a senseless war, lacking meaning as it lacks an exit, remains the determining factor. What will come of it? I am not here to prophesy. I will only observe that rarely has a regime been more false, not by the falseness of men but by the essential alteration of political power: an authoritarian regime, yet without authority; in the guise of unity, yet the most divided unity; with the appearance of an active power, incapable of determining itself and of choosing; laying claim to a personal responsibility and a personal appointment, only to cover with the name of a single person a multiplicity of irresponsible actions, as well as the supremacy of impersonal economic forces. A strange regime, a grave story, and not just grave, but insufferable, in which everything is perverted in an unfortunate confusion, where one sees de Gaulle's opponents place all their hope in him, his zealots profane him (blasphemy is part of religion), and his closest friends, those whom he placed in the government himself, have no other concern than to ruin what he would like to represent. This is why, at times, one might be tempted to conclude with the unreal strangeness of this whole situation, an unreality whose light, unfortunately, is often seen when a story is about to end. As for those who say (openly, silently), yes, we are for de Gaulle, we defer to him and are happy about this vocation of sovereignty that religiously elevates him above all protests because, were he to disappear, we would have the worst, we would have dictatorship, one must respond to them: you have saved nothing by betraying the essential, for, behind the Sovereignty that is everything and can do nothing, you already have in latent form what you will have exploding tomorrow: this dictatorship that necessarily follows as soon as political power is corrupted into a power of salvation.

Declaration of the Right to Insubordination in the Algerian War

[Manifesto of the 121]

Early last July, the following declaration was submitted for the consideration of writers, artists, and academics, at the initiative of some of the signatories, and up to now it has received the approval of 121 among them.

A very important movement is developing in France, and it is necessary that French and international opinion be better informed about it, at a time when the new turning point of the Algerian War must make us see, rather than forget, the depth of the crisis that erupted six years ago.

In ever-increasing numbers, French nationals are being prosecuted, imprisoned, and condemned for refusing to participate in this war or for helping Algerian fighters. Misrepresented by their adversaries, but also downplayed by the very people who would have the obligation to defend them, their reasons generally remain misunderstood. However, it is not enough to say that this resistance to public powers is respectable. As a protest by men attacked in their honor and in the right idea that they hold of truth, this resistance has a meaning that exceeds the circumstances in which it was asserted and that it is important to recapture, no matter how things turn out.

For the Algerians the struggle, whether pursued by military means or by diplomatic ones, contains no ambiguity. This is a war of national independence. But what is it for the French? It is not a foreign war. French territory has never been threatened. Moreover, it is being waged against people whom the State ostensibly considers French, but who are fighting precisely to stop being considered so. It would not even suffice to say that we are dealing with a war of conquest, an imperialist war, coupled with an outgrowth of racism. There is some of that in every war, and the ambiguity persists.

In fact, in a decision that constituted a basic violation, the State first mobilized entire classes of citizens with the sole aim of carrying out what it itself termed a police action against an oppressed population, one that had revolted only out of an elemental concern for dignity, as it demanded finally to be recognized as an independent community.

Neither a war of conquest nor a war of "national defense," the Algerian War has almost completely become an action specific to the army and a social caste that refuses to yield before an uprising whose meaning even the civil power, realizing the general collapse of colonial empires, seems ready to recognize.

Today, it is mainly the will of the army that maintains this criminal and absurd combat, and this army, by the political role that many of its high ranking representatives make it play, sometimes acts openly and violently outside of any legality, betrays the ends that the entire country entrusts to it, and compromises and risks perverting the nation itself by forcing citizens under its orders to make themselves accomplices in a factious and degrading action. Is it necessary to recall that fifteen years after the destruction of the Hitlerian order, French militarism, as a result of the exigencies of this war, has managed to reinstate torture and to make it an institution in Europe once again?

It is in these conditions that many French people have come to question the meaning of traditional values and obligations. What is civic virtue when, in certain circumstances, it becomes shameful submission? Aren't there cases where the refusal to serve is a sacred duty, where "treason" means courageous respect for the truth? And when, through the will of those who use it as an instrument of racist or ideological domination, the army places itself in a state of open or latent revolt against democratic institutions, doesn't revolt against the army take on a new meaning?

This moral dilemma was posed from the beginning of the war. As the war dragged on, it was to be expected that this moral dilemma would be concretely resolved through increasing numbers of acts of insubordination and desertion, as well as protection and help for the Algerian fighters. Freedom movements have developed in the margins of all the official parties, without their help and, in the end, despite their disavowal. Once again, outside of the preestablished official framework and slogans, a *resistance* was born, through spontaneous awareness, seeking and inventing forms of actions and means of struggle in relation to a new situation, whose true meanings or demands political organizations and newspaper editorials have agreed not to recognize, either out of inertia or doctrinal timidity, or by national or moral prejudice.

The undersigned—considering that everyone must come to an opinion about acts that it is henceforth impossible to present as trivial episodes of an individual adventure, and considering that they themselves, in their place, and according to their means, have the duty to intervene, not to give advice to men who have to decide personally when faced with such grave problems, but to ask those who judge them not to be taken in by the equivocal aspect of words and values—declare:

—We respect the refusal to take arms against the Algerian people, and we judge this to be justified.

—We respect the conduct of the French citizens who consider it their duty to bring help and protection to the oppressed Algerians in the name of the French people, and we judge this to be justified.

—The cause of the Algerian people, which contributes to ruining the colonial system in a decisive way, is the cause of all free men.

(Signatures)
Arthur Adamov, Robert Antelme, Georges Auclair, Jean Baby, Hélène Balfet, Marc Barbut, Robert Barrat, Simone de Beauvoir, Jean-Louis Bédouin, Marc Begbeider, Robert Benayoun, Maurice Blanchot, Roger Blin, Geneviève Bonnefoi, Arsène Bonnafous-Murat, Raymond Borde, Jean-Louis Bory, Jacques-Laurent Bost, Pierre Boulez, Vincent Bounoure, André Breton, Guy Cabanel, Georges Condominas, Alain Cuny, Jean Czarnecki, Dr. Jean Dalsace, Hubert Damisch, Adrien Dax, Bernard Dort, Jean Douassot, Simone Dreyfus, Marguerite Duras, Yves Elléouet, Dominique Éluard, Charles Estienne, Louis-René des Forêts, Dr. Théodore Fraenkel, André Frénaud, Jacques Gernet, Louis Gernet, Édouard Glissant, Anne Guérin, Daniel Guérin, Jacques Howlett, Édouard Jaguer, Pierre Jaouen, Gérard Jarlot, Robert Jaulin, Alain Joubert, Henri Kréa, Robert Lagarde, Monique Lange, Claude Lanzmann, Robert Lapoujade, Henri Lefebvre, Gérard Legrand, Michel Leiris, Paul Lévy, Jérôme Lindon, Éric Losfeld, Robert Louzon, Olivier de Magny, Florence Malraux, André Mandouze, Maud Mannoni, Jean Martin, Renée Marcel-Martinet, Jean-Daniel Martinet, Andrée Marty-Capgras, Dionys Mascolo, François Maspero, André Masson, Pierre de Massot, Jean-Jacques Mayoux, Jehan Mayoux, Théodore Monod, Marie Moscovici, Georges Mounin, Maurice Nadeau, Georges Navel, Hélène Parmelin, Marcel Péju, José Pierre, André Pieyre de Mandiargues, Édouard Pignon, Bernard Pingaud, Maurice Pons, Jean-Baptiste Pontalis, Jean Pouillon, Denise René, Alain Resnais, Jean-François Revel, Alain Robbe-Grillet, Christiane Rochefort, Jacques-François Rolland, Alfred Rosmer, Gilbert Rouget, Claude Roy, Marc Saint-Saens, Nathalie Sarraute, Jean-Paul Sartre, Renée Saurel, Claude Sautet, Jean Schuster, Robert Scipion, Louis Seguin, Geneviève Serreau, Simone Signoret, Jean-Claude Silbermann, Claude Simon, René de Solier, D. de la Souchère, Jean Thiercelin, Dr. René Tzanck, Vercors, Jean-Pierre Vernant, Pierre Vidal-Naquet, J.-P. Vielfaure, Claude Viseux, Ylipe, René Zazzo.

Update

Michel Cournot's reflections on the Declaration of the 121 call for a few remarks.[1]

Cournot criticizes the form of the Declaration. He calls it bourgeois; to him it seems too subtle to be understood by the "proletarians." Let us leave aside the kind of contempt for proletarian intelligence that such a judgment betrays. And let us not get involved in the critique that the recourse to this old vocabulary would require: bourgeois style, proletarian style, the latter being the only one appropriate when one wants to speak to the people. Let us simply remark that the text of the Declaration was composed collectively by intellectuals of every origin and every background. They expressed themselves according to their means, in a language that Cournot judges too subtle, that others judged too trenchant, and that strives first to analyze a situation appropriately, then to judge and to decide. Each sentence was discussed, thought over and meditated upon. It was never a question of stylistic research, but on the contrary of speaking as if anonymously in order to attain the simplicity of a just conclusion.

"This is not language that one addresses to proletarians," says Cournot, thus suggesting that the Declaration is directly intended for young workers and young farmers. An irritatingly thoughtless statement. (Analyzing a banned text that no one can read and whose interpretations cannot be controlled by anyone, Cournot had, it seems, the duty to respect its intentions more scrupulously.) In fact, the Declaration explicitly specifies to whom it is addressed: not to the young men who, faced with the Algerian War, have to take the decision to refuse or to participate in it, but to all those who judge these men, who judge and condemn them lightly, by invoking traditional values that, in the present circumstances, no longer hold sway. And we know these institutions: it is not only the judiciary bodies, it is, more decisively, organizations, press agencies, and everything that contributes to form or deform the judgment of a people in a country governed by opinion.

As for the criticisms of some Communist Party leaders against the Declaration, criticisms whose meaning Cournot poorly grasps, we will limit ourselves to the following remarks. First, it is a fact that this Declaration was signed by many Communist intellectuals. It is another fact that it was welcomed favorably during the first few weeks, even in *L'Humanité*.[2] And it took time for Maurice Thorez to express his disagreement more clearly.[3] But since, at the same time, Communist leaders were distancing themselves from the projects of the UNEF,[4] projects that nonetheless totally excluded any demonstration in favor of insubordination, one must conclude that it is not the content of the Declaration nor its form that prompted Thorez's unfavorable judgment but a more general reservation that translates, in such a decisive moment, into a practical immobilization of a large part of the working class.

Cournot, finally, following many others, including some Communists, accuses the *Declaration* of being ineffectual—a strange accusation. It is important to recall what the Declaration is: an act of judgment, doubtless a very serious act, but an intellectual one, firmly deciding, in the situation defined both by the war in Algeria and the transformation of military power into political power, what is just and what is not. To look for orders and practical advice in this Declaration would be not only to alter but to *weaken* its impact. And why did it have such a force of upheaval, not only in France, but in the whole world, as numerous responses have confirmed for us? For a reason that is clear: in a simple act of speech, and with the distinct authority of speech, at a moment when these words needed to be spoken, it was recalled by men of culture and reflection (many of whom are not politically active) that when the State engenders or allows to be born, within or alongside itself, an oppressive force that threatens essential freedoms, it is then the right of each citizen to refuse and denounce it. Nothing more. Is this ineffectual? It may be, although all the political developments out of this simple act of speech are already casting that into doubt. We will nonetheless say that a statement of this kind, a statement of judgment, owes all of its effectiveness precisely to the refusal to make it depend on calculations of practical and political effectiveness; at a certain moment, it must be said, whatever the consequences may be, whatever it may cost, that is its truth, that is its force; it is a just statement.

Naturally, the subsisting order can always strike and attack those who speak. But speech itself will remain outside their grasp. It was said and will remain said. Here, in the *Declaration*, what was said is one word alone, the serious word of extreme refusal. At all the decisive moments of humanity, some men, and sometimes a large number, have always known how to preserve the right to refuse. "*We cannot*"; "*Here I stand, I cannot do otherwise.*" This is the fundamental recourse. We must all be vigilant about such a right, be vigilant so that it is not used without rigor, be vigilant so that, reaffirmed and maintained, it remains what it is: the ultimate recourse as the power to say no.

[The Declaration of the Right to Insubordination that we have signed]

The Declaration of the Right to Insubordination in the Algerian War that we signed collectively is an act that is sufficient in itself and that any particular commentary would risk weakening or attenuating. I draw attention only to the fact that it is not a simple protest manifesto but an essential affirmation by which we state that in a situation defined both by the Algerian War and the transformation of military power into political power capable of changing governments, of overthrowing regimes and imposing decisions of its choice, there is a vacancy of the State and a void as it were [where] traditional civic duties have ceased having the value of obligation.

I specify that the Declaration is in no way a declaration of anarchy. It is, on the contrary, the destitution of the State that we denounce, its anarchic erasure before the factious power of the army. Today, behind the façade of an archaic kind of sovereignty and with the alibi of an authoritarian government without authority, anarchy is in power, this power that has declared, through the mouth of the head of what we mistakenly call the State, that the Algerian War was absurd, thereby reducing the exercise of military duty to the absurd.

A situation of extreme seriousness to which this serious declaration responds—a declaration that we have made, and for which we will assume until the end, personally and collectively, all responsibility.

Concerning my relations with the law, I would say only this: our personal cases have very little importance. I'll add this, however: yesterday, M. Debré himself made an effort to destroy the juridical pretext of the procedures initiated against us. By specifying that only those signatories will be judged by the courts who "distinguished themselves through a particular disturbance," M. Debré frankly warned us that he plans to mobilize the judges against any political action, against any political opposition. Here is a statement that we will not forget. It testifies to a strange contempt for judicial power. It shows that we have entered into a violent situation where it seems entirely natural for the powers that be to reinstate the crime of political opposition. Finally, and this is perhaps the most characteristic feature, the astonishing expression, *those amongst them who distinguished themselves through a particular disturbance*, reveals that the government reserves the right to choose at will amongst the signatories of the Declaration, without any rule other than fear, hatred, or political caprice. This is pure arbitrariness.

[The Declaration . . . is not a protest manifesto]

The Declaration of the Right to Insubordination in the Algerian War is not a protest manifesto. It constitutes an act of judgment and decides, in serious speech, faced with the absence of an authority in power, what is right and what is not.

1. The Declaration both denounces and demands. It denounces the moral violence inflicted upon French youth when the government, by obliging them to participate in a war of oppression, one that it itself defines as absurd, reduces to absurdity the military duty to which it obliges them.

The Declaration denounces this absurdity and refuses to allow civic obligation to be contaminated by oppression and by absurdity.

2. The Declaration denounces the political violence that is done to French youth when young people see themselves obliged, by military service, to belong to an army that is not only a military power at the service of the nation but a political power and a kind of political party at the service of a colonial caste and its factious activists.

The Declaration denounces this violence by which a young Frenchman, by helping to wage the war, not only participates in a criminal and absurd action but favors willy-nilly the antidemocratic schemes of the heads of the army and thus himself contributes to the infringement of his own political freedom.

3. The Declaration states that in this specific situation, defined both by the Algerian War and by the transformation of military power into predominant political power, there is a destitution of the State, an anarchic slippage of the State before the factious power of the army.

The Declaration is not a declaration of anarchy. It does not deny the authority of the State in every circumstance. On the contrary, it denounces the current government as being anarchic and not founded on veritable authority. Behind the anachronistic appearance of a sacred kind of sovereignty and with the apparatus of a violently and arbitrarily authoritarian government, it is anarchy that is in power, and where the authority of the State should be, there is nothing but a disordered and violent semblance of power, a void where traditional civic values have ceased to have the value of obligation.

The word *insubordination*, which the Declaration pronounces, unites, in a unique refusal, the right to be opposed to these three forms of violence.

The word *insubordination* says: the Algerian War must be refused because one must refuse the absurdity and oppression that this war represents.

The word *insubordination* says: the false authority of the State and the confusion of civic power in a quasi-religious force must be denounced, because this confusion threatens our sovereignty.

The entire force of the Declaration is in the simplicity of this word: *insubordination*. Insubordination is extreme refusal. The right to insubordination designates the right that founds or maintains itself in this refusal and from this refusal: the right to not be oppressed and not to be an oppressor.

[For us, the first fact]

For us, the first fact, the essential fact, is insubordination. And it is as such that the Declaration is a serious act. It affirms that, in the situation that we are in, characterized both by the Algerian War and the political reign of the army, there is a vacancy of the State before factious military power. And we are saying that it is a right for a young Frenchman to refuse to participate in this war defined as absurd by the authorities themselves, that it is a necessary exigency not to allow civic obligation to be contaminated by this absurdity.

This is what is essential. Once this has been said, everything has been said. And helping the Algerians? Help to the Algerians only comes afterwards, as a consequence, but, as a consequence, we recognize it as being justified. How, exactly?

First, the young Frenchman violently and illegally obliged to participate in this war realizes that in carrying arms against the Algerian people he carries arms against himself, for he plays the army's game, which is to lay claim to political power and expect to destroy democracy (and the army needs this war to reach this end). He thus realizes that, in helping with this war, he destroys himself, he destroys what matters to him most, and he helps introduce military dictatorship into his own country. A situation of outrageous absurdity.

Henceforth, it is natural and dramatically justified that this situation be turned upside down: when the young Frenchman realizes that in fighting the Algerians he is fighting himself, he comes upon the idea that he and the Algerians have something in common, that the violence he suffers under civil and military authority is the same violence that is exercised against the Algerians; it destroys freedom as the aspiration to national independence. From this point of view, there is an understanding between the Algerians and the young Frenchman to the extent that both have experienced violent constraint being carried out against them. This understanding takes shape and expresses itself in help and support for the Algerians.

But this is not all; this is not even the beginning of reflection. Indeed, the young Frenchman is obliged to recognize that, if he himself runs the risk of being colonized by the army and having his political freedoms colonized by the colonial caste and the military dictatorship, for one hundred and fifty years the Algerian people have suffered this oppression that he himself suffers for twenty-seven months and that threatens to become his future. This violent oppression, which has lasted for so long, is organized in the name of the French people. He thus feels responsible for this oppression, and this responsibility creates a duty for him not only not to add to the misfortune and oppression suffered by the Algerians but to help and protect them.

It seems to me that this is where the meaning of the Declaration lies. The Algerian War has revealed—in a way that is tragic but also, in a sense, liberating—a community of destiny that unites in freedom all those who fight for it.

But if we want to be more precise, we must still add the following: the feeling of a community of destiny can be developed either by yielding to moral demands (we are responsible for the long colonial oppression, we must help the Algerians who are subjugated by it) or by laying open political possibilities. Here, one must question the revolutionary value of the Algerian struggle. For my part, and for the time being, the conceptions of the FLN seem ideologically insufficient and uncertain to me. I refrain from commenting on them or fighting for them. I do see, however, that once one abstracts from ideology, the sole fact of the Algerian struggle has a meaning that we could call revolutionary. I do see that, if the war continues, it will develop, attracting the revolutionary power of China into our own space, precipitating imbalance, quickening the upheaval. Am I ready to welcome this consequence? I withhold my judgment. But I will say that, as the co-author responsible for the Declaration, [not only do I not accept it, but that] this does not implicate it. The Declaration is destined, in pronouncing the serious word *insubordination*, to render the absurd and impossible character of the war apparent, so that it is brought to an end by Algerian independence. If, above all, we desired the development of the revolutionary process that is perhaps the future of the Algerian War, then we would refrain from making this more difficult by speaking about insubordination and refusal now: we would speak instead about French Algeria and we would sign the manifesto of the *Académiciens*.[1]

[It is as a writer]

It is as a writer that I signed this text, not even as a political writer, nor as a citizen engaged in political struggles, for I do not participate in them, but as a nonpolitical writer led to comment seriously and firmly on essential problems that matter to him and concern him as such.

How do these problems present themselves? We know that young Frenchmen are prosecuted, imprisoned, and condemned for having refused to carry arms against the Algerian people, others for having helped Algerian fighters. These facts exist. They exist in front of us, they are known by all, everyone discusses them, and everyone judges them, the newspapers, the parties, and the judges. It seems to us, to us writers and intellectuals, that, faced with such serious facts, before this debate laid open before French and international opinion, we have the duty not to remain silent but to comment openly and calmly. This decision to speak is contained in the final declarations of this text.

Why these declarations? What do they intend to explain? That in all intellectual rigor and honesty, you judges, ministers, and you bodies of political opinion can no longer apply to these acts that you incriminate or to these men that you indict the habitual use of words and values: that, when you speak about treason and insubordination, you make an illicit and guilty use of terms and legalities that no longer apply here.

Why? For two essential reasons. Indeed, for five years on the one hand and for the past two years on the other, we have entered into a situation where the usual civic criteria are no longer valid, a situation defined by the war in Algeria, an oppressor's war, which is moreover unspeakable, and by the transformation of military power into the predominant political power.

The first reason is that the Algerian war is an illegitimate, indefinable, unspeakable war, scandalous to the point that no one has the right to name it (but simply the duty to do so). Truly unnamable, yet a war directed against ourselves, a violent and often awful action radically dividing the French, waged for the benefit of a small cast against a community of men who are legitimately demanding their independence; this right to independence whose full legitimacy was acknowledged by the head of state himself.

The Algerian War, which has no national justification, which is directed against the French no less than against the Algerians, is such that civil power has no right to draw the entirety of its conscripted soldiers into it. On the contrary, by mobilizing French youth for something that was touted as a mere police operation, the civil power has committed a fundamental violation that it is the duty of each one of us to denounce. If the government has the right to mobilize conscripts in this war, if this is a war where the fate of the nation is at stake, then it should also have the right, even the duty, to declare a general mobilization. A mass levy would have to be declared, yet the absurdity, the fundamentally illicit, criminal, and mad character of this mobilization, would immediately be apparent. But if the mobilization of all French citizens in the Algerian War would be a crime, then it is also a crime, almost a more serious crime, to mobilize all French youth in such a war. And to the government, to the military power, we are saying: you no longer have the right to enlist French youth in this war, the most unjust and the basest of wars, exposing them to mortal risk and to a true inner destruction. And to the judges, we say: you no longer have the right to condemn those who refuse to undergo the violence that is inflicted upon them by mobilizing them illegally for this war.

But there is yet another reason, a reason that gives the first one its seriousness. For two years now, since May 1958, we have known in all certainty that the army has become a political power that, as a political power, intends to decide national destiny as a whole. We know that the army, in the enormous material power that it represents and in the importance that the Algerian War gives to it, has the power to overthrow governments, to change regimes, to impose decisions of its own choosing. This transformation of military power into political power is a fundamental fact of unprecedented gravity. You judges and you military men, I imagine that you are aware of this gravity, whether to approve of it or to regret it. But this is a fact, an essential fact for our country.

Apparently, the army is the nation itself, because it is made up of conscripted soldiers: but this is where the trap lies. The army as an institution, the meaning of the army as an institution, is what its executives, its leaders, its active elements have made of it. It is a kind of political party, with enormous material power at its disposal, laying claim to conscripts bound to strict obedience, in order to make believe that this political party is the nation itself.

Now, what we will be saying from here on, following this radical transformation of the army as an institution, is that the refusal to submit to military duty takes on an entirely different meaning. In claiming for itself the right to have a political attitude and to play the political role that it does, the army gives each person the duty to judge whether or not he accepts being enrolled in the political party that the army has become. Some accept it; there is nothing more to be said. Others refuse: this refusal is a fundamental right. To the extent that the army is an instrument of ideological and racist domination, the young people who are enlisted in it not only take part in an unjust war but, due to this very fact, already carry arms against the remaining democratic institutions and prepare, despite themselves, for an explicit dictatorship tomorrow.

I would also add this: Why does the Algerian War continue? Why does this criminal, unjust, absurd war continue, while the civil power affirms that it is ready to render the right of independence to the Algerians, a right that is justifiably theirs and that was violently taken from them one hundred and fifty years ago? Why? It seems to me that a great number of French people agree with this fact: the war doesn't end because the army does not want it to end. And the army does not want it to end because it is linked to this war professionally, morally, and politically, this kind of conflict being the only one capable of satisfying its ambitions. Through this war, it assumes a determining role in national destiny as a whole and has at its disposal a power that it will never renounce.

But if this is the case, we can see the terrible spiral in which we are caught: the army will never give up the Algerian War, because it is from the Algerian War that it draws its power and its political determination. Without the Algerian War, it would not be able to achieve its schemes of political domination.. But as long as the war continues, and the more intensely it is waged, the more violently the army will have power over all the citizens of this country, this army that is a political power. Today we see clearly—and only on the emotional level—what is happening. French people, profoundly and confusedly, are almost all convinced that this war is unjust. We could thus believe that they will revolt against the fact that their sons participate in it. But the reasoning must be reversed: because their sons are participating in it—automatically, by the mad automatism of military service—they can no longer recognize that this war is unjust, and they make themselves accomplices. The army thus has a hold on everyone: the sons, physically, and because it perverts them little by little; the parents, because they can only be supportive of their sons. This is the trap. The army at war in Algeria is this trap. This must be said. This is what we are saying.

[Interrogation with the judge]

S.I.:[1] *Do you admit to being the main author of this text? (Or else) What do you mean when you admit to being its coauthor?*

[M.B.]: I would first like to make a preliminary declaration. As an intellectual, I declare that I recognize myself as entirely responsible for this text, from the moment that I signed it. The fact of the signature is essential. It means not only that I agree with this text, but that I am merged with it, that I am this text. Each one of the signatories identifies with the text, just as you have it before your eyes, just as it was made public.

The approach that consists in dividing responsibilities, in an effort to establish a pseudo-hierarchy of responsibility, is a fundamentally erroneous one; it fails to recognize the truth of all collective texts, signed collectively: that is, that "each one has his share and all have it entirely." Everything you are trying to make me say that would go against this affirmation, which is the meaning of every collective text, will be false, and I revoke it in advance.

I will add that, if I recognize myself to be fully responsible for the text, each one of the signatories needs to be considered *equally* its unique author; I assume this responsibility globally, in its entirety; I will not go into details. I admit it on whatever level you may want to consider, but I do so on the basis of the intellectual and theoretical responsibility that is defined by my signature. Translate this theoretical responsibility into terms of material responsibility, if you wish: I accept this concrete translation as the consequence of my global and theoretical responsibility. But you are the one doing this translation, for you seem mistakenly to recognize only material responsibility: I am not participating in this translation.

S.I.: *When did the idea of producing such a text first come about?*

[M.B.]: In May [19]58. Since May 58, we have known clearly that the army has become a political power that has the power to overthrow governments, to change regimes, and to impose decisions of its own choosing. The transformation of military power into political power is the essential fact, a fact of unprecedented gravity, that sanctions our text.

S.I.: *Do you admit to being one of the initiators of this text?*

[M.B.]: I declare that it is fundamentally erroneous to distinguish between one person and another in an effort to identify who could have been the initiator. That said, I am ready to recognize myself as its "initiator," along with hundreds of other people, based on a theoretical and intellectual responsibility that I fully assume as such. The initiator of this text is the event, it is May 58, it is the Algerian War, it is the army, and it is de Gaulle.

S.I.: *But the introductory text specifies that the initiative was taken by some people in particular?*

[M.B.]: That is a text that does not belong to the declaration, about which I have nothing to say, except that it is ineptly formulated and that in my opinion it signifies only that the Declaration was not made in a day, that it was in gestation for a long time, that it was submitted to reflection—an essentially active faculty—by writers, artists, and academics, that the agreement that they gave to it is a considered, active, and unqualified collective agreement.

S.I.: *Did you collect signatures?*

[M.B.]: This expression is entirely inaccurate. When one is dealing with such a grave text, one does not present it to writers and tell them: sign here. The signature is effective participation in the text. No one collected signatures in the way that you said, but each person was able and obliged to invoke, with other intellectuals, the problems set down in this text.

S.I.: *Do you admit to having distributed copies of this text?*

[M.B.]: What do you mean by "distribution"? It is obvious that as soon as a writer signs a text of this kind, in the unqualified collective sense I invoked, it is not so that he may then keep it within his heart. Now the text exists. Signing it means authorizing it, wrapping it in one's authority, making it come and go, already by the simple fact that the one who authorizes it comes and goes. If I speak about it to friends, I am already distributing it. I distribute it if I write to acquaintances: "There is an important text that says such and such." If, in a private letter, I copy passages or if I send it sealed like a private letter, I do nothing more or less than distribute it. Today there are thousands of distributors, for the Declaration is the object of conversations among intellectuals all over this country and abroad.

S.I.: *Do you admit to being guilty of the crime of inciting insubordination, etc.?*

[M.B.]: Not only do I not admit to being guilty, I am saying that it is you judges, you the government, who make yourselves guilty of an abusive and illicit use of the words *treason* and *insubordination* when you apply them in the current situation, characterized both by the scandalous Algerian War and by the transformation, through the fact of this war, of the army into a political power—situations where traditional civic obligations are no longer valid (etc.).

[Questioned by the judge]

Questioned by the judge . . . concerning the new charge against us of provoking soldiers to disobedience, I told him, among other things, the following: the French courts, in particular the military court of Bordeaux in January 1953, in condemning German soldiers because they had not disobeyed the inhuman orders that were given to them by their superiors, morally and legally founded the right to military disobedience.

When we claim the right to insubordination, we claim the right of the French soldier not to behave culpably, in a way that would expose him in the future to the rigors of international law, and we ask French judges to remain consistent with the law they applied in the recent past: the law that it is a duty for all, even against supposedly national demands, not to be inhuman and not to be oppressors.

Maurice Blanchot

[First I would like to say]

Why did you sign this Declaration?

First of all, I would like to say that this Declaration is a serious act that is self-sufficient; any given commentary might weaken it, appease it, or even take away its collective character, which is one of its most important features. Given these reservations, I will answer that it is as a writer that I signed this text, not as a political writer or as a citizen involved in political struggles, but as a nonpolitical writer led to comment on problems that essentially involve him. How do these problems present themselves? We know that young Frenchmen are being tried for refusing to carry arms against the Algerian people, others for helping Algerian fighters. These facts exist. They have not been created by us, they are known to everyone, everyone talks about them, and everyone judges them: the newspapers, the parties, the judges. It seemed to us that, faced with such serious facts, in these debates set before French and international opinion, we had the duty not to remain silent but to express our judgment firmly. This decision to speak is present in the final declarations of the text. One of the important meanings of the Declaration is to make apparent the specific responsibility of intellectuals: when the democratic order alters or undoes itself, it falls to them, apart from any purely political alliances, to say, in simple words, what seems just to them.

And so are you saying that insubordination has become a right?

Indeed. I think that the force of the Declaration, all its force of upheaval, comes from the authority with which it pronounced this word alone, the word *insubordination*, a solemn word, an extreme refusal: the Right to insubordination. I say Right and not Duty, as some thoughtlessly wanted to hear in the Declaration, undoubtedly because they believe that the formulation of a duty goes farther than that of a right. But this is not so: an obligation refers to an interior moral that enfolds, guarantees, and justifies it. Where there is a duty, we merely have to close our eyes and blindly accomplish it; then, everything is simple. A right, on the contrary, refers only to itself, to the exercise of the freedom of which it is the expression; a right is a free power for which everyone is responsible, by himself, in relation to himself, and which completely and freely engages him: nothing is stronger, nothing is more serious. This is why one must say: the right to insubordination. Each person must make a sovereign decision. But it must be added: the right to insubordination in the Algerian War. In fact—and it is important to point it out—the Declaration is not a claim to anarchy, denying or contesting State authority in all circumstances. Here too, those who would have wanted the Declaration to affirm more, affirm the right to refuse any military obligation in general, were really only looking for an alibi, the refusal always offered to good conscience by a theoretical expression of an absolute right, disconnected from reality. What is important, what is decisive, is to affirm that, in the situation precisely defined both by the Algerian War and by the transformation of military power into political power, traditional civic duties have stopped counting as obligations. This is what the Declaration essentially reminds us.

Aren't you afraid that speaking of insubordination will lead the country to anarchy?

But anarchy lies in the fact of letting the army become a political power as well as in the fact that the current regime owes its rise to a military coup d'état that thereby sealed from the beginning the illegality of the imperious order that in its august manner it claims to represent and to impose upon us. Since May 1958, we have been in a situation of anarchy; this is the truth that everyone has vaguely grasped. For since May 58, everyone has known that the army has become a political power with the intention of determining national destiny in its entirety. We know that the army, with its enormous material force, and because of the importance that the Algerian War has given it, has the power to overthrow governments, to change regimes, and to impose decisions of its own choosing. This transformation of military power is a capital fact of unprecedented gravity. Well, we are saying that henceforth the refusal to assume military duty takes on an entirely different meaning. For, in claiming the right to have a political attitude, the army must recognize, in turn, in each young Frenchman the right to judge whether yes or no he accepts being enrolled in the kind of political party into which its high-ranking representatives have sought to transform it. Some accept that there is nothing to be said about it. Others refuse: this refusal is henceforth a fundamental right.

Insubordination is a very serious act. Aren't you afraid of pushing young people, whose entire lives will be changed by it, to this serious act?

As soon as we can accept saying that the Algerian War is unjust and criminal, we say everything necessary to justify the refusal to take part in it. When, on three occasions after Melun, General de Gaulle solemnly declared that the war and battles in Algeria were absurd, he himself warned young Frenchmen (or else the words he uttered are meaningless) that from then on to participate in these battles was to participate in nonsense. We have said and we are now saying nothing more. However, I would like to add a remark: deep down, and in a confused way, the great majority of French people are convinced that this war is unjust, indeed absurd. We might thus believe that they would revolt against the fact that their sons are participating in it. But the thought must be reversed: because theirs sons are participating in it—albeit automatically, by the automatism of military service—they can no longer recognize that this war is unjust, and they make themselves its accomplices. The army thus has a hold on everyone: it has a hold on the sons both physically and because it slowly changes them; it has a hold on the parents, who feel support for and complicity with their sons. That is the trap. The army is the trap. We can neither see nor say this too much.

Do you think that the fact of signing such a Declaration can have a political impact?

You mean to say: won't it be politically ineffective? I think one must reply: it does not pretend to any immediate political effectiveness, or more precisely: it must be effective to the very extent that it has not taken into account calculations of practical and political effectiveness, for example, in seeking to rally the greatest number with a text that is a compromise. It is an act of judgment, such is its meaning and such is its force. This is not a simple protest manifesto. It is a Declaration, a declaration that makes a decision, in the absence of legitimate authority, concerning what it is appropriate to refuse and to demand. Mere speech? Indeed, but having all the authority of serious speech, which makes all those who pronounce it feel responsible from now on, ready to support it calmly, firmly, as much as necessary, whatever the consequences may be.

[Maurice Blanchot to Jean-Paul Sartre]

Paris, December 2, 1960

My dear Sartre,

I would like to share with you my reflections on the project of transforming the review. I consider it very important that you have conceived it in relation to the event that was the Declaration. The intellectual future could depend on the way in which it will be realized.

What has taken place—you recognized it right away—is a movement of great meaning. Intellectuals, I mean many of them, writers, artists, scientists, who until now seemed to have no concerns other than their own activities, recognized the demanding character of this activity and recognized that this demand must, today, lead them to political affirmations of a radical character. They perceived (at times in a moral *contre-jour*, but it doesn't matter) that their word had a power of decision to which they themselves had to respond, in a movement intended to go well beyond the mere feeling of responsibility. They have also experienced—and this is not the least meaningful feature—a way of being together, and I am not thinking of the collective character of the Declaration, but of its impersonal force, the fact that all those who signed it certainly lent it their name, but without invoking their particular truth or their nominal fame. For them, the Declaration represented a certain anonymous community of names, by a remarkable relation that judicial authority precisely endeavors, instinctively, to break.

The intellectuals thus became aware of the novelty of the power that they represent and, although in a confused manner, of the originality of this power (a power without power). At the same time, representative political institutions, be they official or part of the opposition, have also become aware of this power, with astonishment or irritation, and have momentarily taken part in affirming it, some by taking note of it, others by rejecting and criminalizing it. Hence the disorderly reaction of the government, its awkward violence, its decision first to strike us, then, today, its will to tranquilize and silence the event, to appease this history, to render it insignificant.

You reminded me of what I must have said at times and what I have always thought privately: that the Declaration would find its true meaning only if it were the beginning of something. I add that many of those who have thought about what happened share this feeling and try, according to their means, to express this kind of initial truth. I have learned, for example, since I saw you, that Maurice Nadeau had a project similar to yours: just as you wish to make more room for literature in *Les temps modernes*, in order to make the new relations of political and literary responsibility more perceptible, as the Declaration showed they are, so, in a contrary way but within the same perspective, Nadeau might have the intention to dedicate an important part of his review to political and social critique.

All of this seems remarkable and meaningful to me.

But I must admit that in neither of these two cases do these changes seem sufficient to me, neither of them is up to the measure of the transformation that they should signify. What will we end up with? Finally, seen from the outside, a more literary *T[emps] M[odernes]*, a more political *L[ettres] N[ouvelles]*: this is a lot and a little, especially since in each case old habits are likely to hold sway. Experience shows that, not without risks, one can renew a review, but one cannot make an old review a new one, charged with new power; in any case, it is very difficult, it requires an even greater will to rupture, since this will has only partially renewed material means for its realization.

I want to state my own feeling: I believe that if we want to represent the change that we are all sensing, as we should unequivocally, if we want to make it more real and to deepen it, in its moving presence, in its new truth, we can do so only by means of a new instrument. In that sense, if one sees Sartre, and others among the 121 with him, decide to express themselves in this form deliberately chosen as new, everyone—and I am thinking not only of writers and the general public but also of intellectual youth as a whole—will understand that we are entering into a new phase and that something decisive is taking place and trying to affirm itself. I'll add that, if I am thinking of a new instrument, it is also for another reason: I do not really believe it is of the greatest interest to have a review in which one finds beautiful literary stories, beautiful poems, political commentaries, social or ethnological investigations etc.; this mixture always risks being ambiguous, without truth or necessity. I believe, rather, in a review of *total critique*, critique where literature would be understood in its own meaning (with the help of texts as well), where scientific discoveries, often poorly explained, would be put to the test of holistic critique, where all the structures of our world, all the forms of existence of this world, would enter into the same movement of examination, scrutiny, and contestation, a review where the word *critique* would once again find its meaning, which is to be global. Such a review, today, precisely today, would have a very great importance and force of action. A naturally debatable project whose difficulties I see, but one that could serve as a point of departure, about which we could at least question ourselves.

In any case, knowing the strong aversion that I have both to participating in the kind of literary reality that a review is and, when I do participate nonetheless, to taking on a role that suits my means only quite poorly, I would feel capable of overcoming this repulsion only if the project were strong enough to maintain and develop all the reasons that made me participate in the Declaration. We all know that we are headed for a crisis that will only make our critical situation more manifest (a crisis in which a military coup would merely be another mediocre aspect). From this perspective, as well as from a more distant one, I would be happy to work with you, as we have so usefully begun to do with the Declaration, upon the condition, of course, that this agreement be not only between us but also with all intellectuals who are fully aware of what is at stake today. It is this agreement that a new review would have to represent.

Maurice Blanchot

Letters from the *Revue internationale*

Maurice Blanchot to Gaston Gallimard

July 18, 1962, Paris

Dear Gaston Gallimard,

I am taking the liberty of writing to you about the review. Louis-René des Forêts, who is away at the moment, showed me the letter you recently wrote to him and left me in charge of responding to you. We were interested in the way you spoke about our project and we noted with satisfaction that you do not fail to recognize its importance. For my part, and after all these conversations we continue to have with French and foreign writers, not only do I not doubt that it will be realized, as it meets a demand one might call historic, but I am tempted to believe that the intellectual future may depend on the way in which it will be realized. That is how the efforts that each one of us is ready to devote to it, both here and abroad, can be explained: it is thus that our persistence is to be understood; nothing, to my mind, will make us renounce it.

Certainly, there remain difficulties of a practical kind. They do not seem insurmountable. I think that I can conclude from your letter that you stand by the propositions formulated in the letter of May 16. These propositions are as follows (I remind you of them in order to dispel all imprecision): (1) you will finance the production; (2) you will put a space at our disposal; (3) you will handle distribution. This agreement, you said, will be valid for two years. And you add that, for our part, we would have to take on the editorial work. It seems, then, that you wish to leave responsibility for the latter problem to us, which is to say, all questions concerning not only the organization of the editorial committee, of course, but also the financing of inevitable expenses for that part of the work. Such a prospect, as you know, is not without difficulties. To overcome them, many projects are under scrutiny, and diverse contacts have already been made, abroad as well as in France. And it is precisely in order to carry out these discussions with greater clarity that we would need to learn from you whether the propositions that you make are valid in any case. In other words, it would be necessary to know how you evaluate this problem yourself, insofar as another or many other silent partners could be brought to cooperate, albeit in an entirely indirect way, with no other intermediary than ourselves—a cooperation that the existence of a nonprofit corporation, which will soon be established, would facilitate legally. In any case, it would be useful to have new discussions with you in order to enter into more details concerning questions that still need to be settled, but I think that, given the absence of many of our friends and the imminence of the holiday season, it is preferable to postpone them a little.

I would nonetheless like to add a more personal remark. About a year ago, you suggested that the review should not be published by anyone other than Gallimard; if some of us insisted that these proposals be accepted, it was not only for opportune reasons or even for reasons having to do with a friendly preference, for we could not invoke the latter for a project of this sort. What seemed essential to us was that a publishing house as powerful as yours, which has played such a large part in the history of French literature, should remain capable of doing so in its future as well, by knowing how to face with resolution, lucidity, and imagination the new problems that this future poses. We all know that we are heading toward great upheaval, on every level; it is in relation to these changes that the project of the "review" was conceived and must try to be achieved. It is thus important, even in our eyes, to know whether Gallimard is ready to welcome these changes or whether it prefers, on the contrary, to avoid them by contenting itself with the brilliant ease of current success. Pardon me for expressing myself with such frank simplicity. I believe I had to so that there would be no ambiguity about the meaning of what is at stake—for us and perhaps also for you—in this enterprise and in the choice of the publishing house that will be associated with it in France.

Please accept, dear Gaston Gallimard, all my very best wishes,

Maurice Blanchot

Maurice Blanchot to Dionys Mascolo

Wednesday, November [?] 1962

Dear Dionys,

Here is a very hastily transcribed translation of this astonishing letter. It is clear that we are facing the greatest misunderstanding. According to the conception that Johnson seems to have of the review, each group works in isolation, nationally and autonomously, without lifting its gaze toward other horizons, the only function of the international conference being to allow for technical adjustments.

It is necessary to write to him as soon as possible, in the most frank way and with the greatest care, that our conception is entirely different, that what matters to us in the review is *collective work, the effort of reflection in common* at the international level itself, *work and reflection* for which the review will only be the *means of concrete affirmation.*

You will see, moreover, that Johnson seems ready to abandon "the Intellectual Course" for futile and false reasons based on current events, as he is far from sharing our view that it is the backbone of the publication. He must thus be reminded once again that according to us this section must be the center of the review, and that elaborated in close exchange between the three editorial committees, it is intended to reflect, to say the world as it affirms, questions, and denounces itself though the *collective conscience of writers*, that finally this section made up of *numerous texts of varied and rather brief forms* will lay claim to any event of whatever kind (philosophical, poetic, scientific, or sociological). It lays claim to the political process and the general movement of the world, but considering it from the writer's perspective, that is to say, by engaging in a dialogue, perhaps elaborating a new questioning.

He must be reminded that Enzensberger not only always expressed his agreement, but also his group's agreement to this section, as well as to the conception of the review.[1]

It seems to me that it will be equally essential that Vittorini write to him on his own about this, in a way he deems right and with his characteristic authority.

Fundamentally, it seems that the current work should consist in preparing the international meeting (in elaborating themes: selecting questions, etc.), but the real work on the issue can only begin after this meeting, whose date should perhaps be advanced . . .

Please forgive me, dear Dionys, for these all too hasty thoughts. . . . Generally, it is Suhrkamp's influence that I perceive in this way of seeing things.[2] Suhrkamp always wanted a specifically German review. Unable to have it, he is satisfied with a specifically German third . . .

Maurice Blanchot

Maurice Blanchot to Dionys Mascolo

Thursday, November [?] 1962

Dear Dionys,

It seems to me that fate has definitively overwhelmed us now. However, so that we do not respond thoughtlessly, I consider it necessary, faced with the varied demands, to search one last time for all the possible answers, in order to see whether there is one among them that could be right (which I doubt).

Paradoxically, I am mainly worried by the German demands, because they may well ruin the very reasons for our enterprise (which goes far beyond the horizon of our review).[3] I can see many possible solutions, all more or less bad. They are as follows. (1) We collect the 70 pages that are expected of us for December 15. In consequence, it is almost certain that the first issue, in its very configuration, will not satisfy our intentions at all. Hence the second solution: (2) the issue (with or without our quota) will be sold only in Germany; for us, it would be issue zero, and the true first issue would be the second, which would come out around September-October. (3) We are trying to argue that the five-month delay for technical preparation that he is demanding is excessive. But here, I am sure in advance that we will fail, for he has already replied that it is impossible, and he will continue to invoke the supposed technical necessities with typically obstinate determination. (4) We reject the ultimatum.

Finally, it seems essential to me to make a decision only in agreement with the Italians. This is why I attach a lot of importance to the solution that they seem to have found and are proposing to us. If their letter does not arrive by Friday morning, could you call Elio, so we may present their proposals in the afternoon session?

A demand or rather a deficiency—I do not see any solutions. But I wonder whether, just as you suggested to your interviewer, we should not purely and simply delegate the task of finding one to Gallimard. Let's tell them, then, in a very short letter (without bitterness): you are responsible for the cost of publication and distribution; you put a space at our disposal—very well. The editorial part remains to be financed, which, reduced to a minimum, will include fees for the contributors, for the translators, for a secretary, and for running a secretarial office, as well as travel expenses. Since you reasonably dismiss the solution of a double partnership, we ask what solution you are suggesting to us to resolve the last problem, which your son Claude, as you told us on many different occasions, has been dealing with for a long time already. If you both share this opinion, would Louis-René [des Forêts] agree to prepare some model letters that we could discuss tomorrow? (Naturally, we can also reply by saying that we have had enough of this behavior, which has more to do with a mental institute than with reasonable negotiation and express our final break—we will come to this one day, it is almost destiny).

Forgive me for this new written intervention. But I fear that if we do not prepare for tomorrow's session, it will result only in confusion and not allow us to decide clearly and seriously, as we should.

Your friend,
Maurice Blanchot

Maurice Blanchot to Uwe Johnson

February 1, 1963

Dear Uwe Johnson,

Louis-René des Forêts and the other members of the French group present in Zurich have authorized me to write you to try to clarify the situation, as well as to specify the tasks that we need to accomplish by February 15.

First of all, we are all delighted about the positive results of this meeting: the agreement on the editors' guarantees—the agreement on the review's publication date and on the work schedule—the agreement on the date and locations of our next meetings—the agreement on certain particular points, notably this: in the event of disagreement with other groups, it is as a last resort that the national group will judge which literary texts to give to the review. And on this point as well: we agree that texts published by the review should, as far as possible, be written precisely for the review or, in any event, not be excerpted from more general works, especially novels. (Concerning Günter Grass's text, after the explanations that you have provided, we agree entirely that it should be part of the first issue.) The title of the review could be *Gulliver*, unless it is impossible for legal reasons for us to use it or unless we were to find a better title in the meantime. We do not agree about the format yet, but we are in agreement that each one of our editors, in relation to their respective editorial boards, will work on a model and make proposals; a decision will be made later. The review will appear every three months and should include 210 pages (naturally, this figure is not definitive, for the final format will have to be taken into account). Each editorial committee will be responsible for about a third of the issue, including the contributions of writers from other countries that it provided. All this is settled. We are glad about that.

We are also glad about the contact that we have had with each other. I, for my part, was very happy to have been able to speak with you personally and I would very much like to continue such conversations. Unfortunately, we had very little time, and we were sorry that you had to leave so early. We have only met three times in working sessions; this is extraordinarily little for everything that we had to say and to decide. A fourth encounter, at least, would doubtless have been necessary after the Sunday morning session when so many serious topics were brought up.

This is why, in order to fill this gap, we thought it indispensable to communicate to you a few concerns that might help us to prevent greater misunderstandings from arising.

1. On hearing presentations by Boehlich, as well as by Leonetti and Vittorini, it is clear that we do not conceive of our role as critics, and consequently as review directors, in the same way the Germans and Italians do.[4] As a matter of fact, the Italians and the Germans have criticized our texts—and as for the Italians, have criticized yours—in the style of "*Kulturkritiker*" and ideologues. This attitude seems dangerous to us, for it amounts to judging the literary act by making it depend upon implicit aesthetic and ideological criteria, to which, in our view, it is impossible to submit a writer's texts. For me, the literary act or experience is indivisible; this act or experience has to be accepted or rejected in its entirety. Let's take your text, if you don't mind. Elio Vittorini has accused you of "repeating" yourself or, to be more accurate, has expressed regret that your essay does not add anything new to what you published in English in the *Evergreen Review* and in French in *Les temps modernes*. As I have already said publicly, I find this regret strange, for this supposed repetition is (at least in part) the very meaning and truth of what you wrote and it seems to us, on the contrary, necessary that not only you but also other German or non-German writers return *many times again* to this Berlin situation and to division in general: all important issues are inexhaustible and must be spoken of inexhaustibly. (This is also, among other reasons, the justification for the "Course of Events [Cours des choses]" and the "short form," given that both represent the possibility of a reflection that is infinite, obsessive, and harassing—as the world is today). Likewise, it is difficult to agree with the critical method applied, perhaps in an entirely accidental way, to Jean Genet's text, a method that consists in extracting a few sentences, isolating them, then finding an ideologically suspect meaning in them, as if a text did not have only a global meaning. Likewise

again, and without any other justification, a ban seems to have been placed upon René Char. If this is the case, it would be inadmissible. What would the Italians have said if we had declared: we do not want Gadda, or we don't want Moravia, without giving any reasons? I would prefer that such attitudes be abandoned (supposing that I am not misinterpreting our interlocutors' thinking). It is the opposite of what literary research represents to us. We think that it is often when a writer is "mistaken," when he is wrong or seems to us to be wrong, that he happens to speak to us the most profoundly, if we listen well.

I'll add that reading a writer's text is a very important and very difficult act, all the more so when it is a text written in a language that is not our own. We must learn to read each other slowly and even humbly, in a spirit of mutual attention.

2. Another opposition came to light, this time of a philosophical order. We were denounced as being philosophically guilty, guilty of abstraction, guilty of ignoring the "concrete," of satisfying ourselves with "sublime intellectual heroism" and of turning away from the flesh. I began to respond to this complaint in Zurich. I would like to add some brief remarks. I must say that this refusal of abstraction and defense of the concrete seemed essentially abstract to us and of a more dangerous abstraction than the kind that we were reproached with, because it is idealizing and, in the end, ethical in nature. (To say: "One must stop being abstract, one must be concrete" without worrying whether such a slogan has the least meaning in the state of exploitation of our societies is what I call pure idealism.) In truth, I was struck by the fact that the reproach addressed to us is exactly the reproach that the right wing addresses to leftist intellectuals in France, that is, that they are people enthralled to principles, busy splitting hairs and capable only of lengthy, impoverished investigations, uncertain of attaining truth. In France, people from the right unanimously denounce philosophy because they are afraid of *contestation* and of the *questioning* that is essentially "philosophy" for us and because, under the pretext of praising the concrete, of praising empiricism without principles, they aim to hold onto the social *status quo* and sociological comfort.

That said, we have no intention of imposing on you our own intellectual demands, in the form in which they imposed themselves on us. (Moreover, as it should be, in the French group each one of us has distinct "philosophical" concerns.) Quite the contrary—and this is where I come to the essential point. We are saying that we accept you as writers and as thinking men, absolutely, just as you are, in your difference, and it is precisely this difference that matters to us; but reciprocally, we ask you to accept us as we are in our difference, even if this difference disturbs or even disappoints you at first (disappointment is enriching at times), and we ask you not to "judge" hastily in the name of cultural references that, in our opinion, do not apply here.

3. The third order of difficulties concerns the conception of the review. But here, taking for granted that the preceding principles will be admitted and respected by all, we must also recognize that it will be a very long task that only common experience will allow us to carry out better. The French group has presented a certain form, since what we call "The Course of Events" stands for both a particular section and the principle of a more general structure connecting all the other texts in a flexible way. Naturally, we are attached to this form, first because we have worked on it a lot and also because it represents something new, I believe, in comparison with both foreign reviews and French ones. And finally because—here is the essential reason—for us it seems to correspond to the decisive task that we ought to pursue: attaining a *plurality* of objects and possibilities of the world, through a *plurality* of *different* reflections, ordered in an *arrangement* that alone truly determines their meaning. But the thought of brutally and externally imposing this conception on you is far from us. We only hope that you will consider it and perhaps, gradually, through experience come to admit its significance and importance. We must work in common without exclusions and constraints while deeply respecting the demands that are specific to each of us: this is the humble starting point of our enterprise; little by little, it will deepen and perhaps be unified in its diversity.

When it comes to our respective tasks between now and February 15, I think that we can say this: you recall Elio Vittorini's last proposals, which, it seems to me, were accepted. Vittorini asked the three groups to *supplement* their contributions in order to bring them closer to each other. He committed himself, in the name of the Italian delegation, to giving several short texts that could fit alongside ours and yours. On our side, we will strive to supplement our collection (a) with other texts, (b) with a longer essay (if possible), (c) with a literary text. What are your intentions in this regard? Do you think, as we hope, that you could supplement the contribution of the German group with several texts that could find their place in "The Course of Events"? It would equally be necessary that we all gather "information" in the sense that was evoked on Sunday morning, either short or longer and even unpublished pieces of information, as Günter Grass fortuitously suggested.

Forgive me for writing to you at such length, but truly, and I am sure you felt it, the remarks that I present to you are essential, and your agreement on these general remarks is also essential for us, as is the agreement of our Italian friends, to whom we are writing by sharing this letter with them.

I would like to express once more, along with the expression of my sincerest regards, the hope that our relations will be able to flourish in the future.

Maurice Blanchot

P.S.: During breakfast on Sunday, Günter Grass told Robert Antelme that the Ford Foundation offers grants to foreign intellectuals who want to stay in Berlin for a one to three month period. Günter Grass expressed the desire that several of us take advantage of this opportunity. I would like to say that I am now seriously considering such a stay in Berlin this summer if circumstances allow me to do so.

Maurice Blanchot to Uwe Johnson

[Undated letter, between February 1 and March 5, 1963]

Dear Uwe Johnson,

I am worried that I have not yet received a reply to the letter I wrote to you on February 1. To explain your silence, I have begun to wonder whether it reached you. I was told that you have been traveling for the last few weeks. It is very important to us here to know your judgment of the serious questions raised in that letter. Since we have to run such a review together, it would be unreasonable for us not to question each other further about what it should be, as well as its structure and the goals that we are pursuing in preparing it. I would particularly insist once again on the necessity of elaborating a form for this review, that is, establishing its architectonic. We are convinced that if, out of laziness, fatigue, or theoretical suspicion, we are satisfied with a publication without structure or form (where arbitrarily collected texts will be assembled without any coherence other than a vague, instinctive harmony), we will very rapidly end up with the most sterile failure. To elucidate this question further, I have attached to my letter the memorandum on the "Course of Events" considered as a structural principle, but this time translated into German. (When we sent this text to you in French, I think it had not been translated by Suhrkamp due to a lack of time and thus could not have been brought to your attention.)

Dear Uwe Johnson, we are deeply convinced that our task is as important as it is difficult. But if we want to carry it through or at least try to do so, we must learn to speak to each other. Speaking is our peril and our necessity.

With all my best wishes,
Maurice Blanchot

P.S. We very much regret that the title "The Other Review" is not acceptable to you. For us, and for the first time, this was the true title capable of designating, very simply, this *traurig namenlose Zeitschrift* [sad, nameless journal]. Would it not be possible to find a similar title that would not risk being confused with "Die andere Zeitung [The Other Newspaper]"?

Maurice Blanchot to Elio Vittorini

February 8, 1963

Dear Elio,

Dionys first read me your letter, after translating it with his distinctive rigor. However, he asked me to wait for the translation that he had requested from a professional translator, according to your wishes. I now have the text before me, as we all do. Surely, in writing to us, you have yielded not only to the proposition of friendship (and allow me to tell you that from now on it seems to me that this friendship is a place where I have always lived) but to the exigency of our difficult enterprise. We must speak to each other. This simple speech, it is true, is itself difficult. It risks spreading misunderstandings and destroying the happy certainty of the possibility of immediate understanding that we might have held. This does not matter. Speaking is our peril and our necessity.

The same thought that led you to write to us brought me to write to Uwe Johnson. You read the letter. It too continues the Zurich conversations. At the same time, it seeks to draw Johnson out of the formal reserve in which he has been entrenched from the beginning, while everything has me persuaded that he is not only an important writer but a sensitive and impassioned one (in his rigid coolness). I will tell you what our fears are in relation to this attitude on the part of the Germans and regarding the future of the project. All of us, almost all of us, attach the greatest importance to this project. Many of us are momentarily sacrificing personal activity for the project, and it seems to us that you too, our Italian friends, are not devoting less attention to the review from your perspective. But when it comes to our German associates, everything is more obscure. The ease with which they were close to breaking things off on at least two occasions is unsettling. The fact that most of the preliminary texts that we have sent them (particularly on the "Course of Events") were simply "thrown out" (as Miss Kirchner said) shows their lack of attention and curiosity. (What's more, it may be Boehlich's fault; this is why we are writing to Johnson directly in German from now on.) This is worrying; indeed, it does not suffice to have a theoretical interest in such an undertaking. One must work at it. A considerable, almost terrible, amount of work. When I see that we meet every week, that writers are close to each other, easy to reach, and easy to stimulate, yes, when I see how difficult it is to overcome the profound laziness endemic to every writer (an idleness [*désoeuvrement*] without which, indeed, he would not write), it frightens me to think about Johnson isolated in Berlin and the other German writers spread out, each entrenched in private activity and perhaps half-heartedly interested in our common task. I am ready to prosaically attribute their disgust for cooperating with "The Course of Events" to this inveterate laziness. We must try, if not to cure them, at least to convince them gradually of the importance for themselves of a project different from all others.

This brings me to express another fear. We have tried to develop a certain structure, and in a large sense a certain "form," for this review. I have explained this once again in a letter to Johnson. We can discuss it. But we are convinced that if, out of laziness, fatigue, and theoretical suspicion, we satisfy ourselves with a review lacking structure and form (in which arbitrarily collected texts would be assembled without any other coherence than a vague, instinctive harmony), we will very quickly end up with the most sterile failure. I don't know how it is in Italy and Germany. In France, it is clear. All the reviews are dying; the genre "review" is dead. Why? There are many reasons, but one of them is simple and striking: writers no longer feel concerned about this mode of publication. Why else? Because there is nothing in such an exhausted genre that would incite one to write for it. Even if they feel that their activity as writers could also be carried out elsewhere than in the space of their work [*oeuvre*], they are absolutely reluctant to participate in current political and literary publications, because these do not at all meet a demand to which they would like to respond. These reviews do not bring them anything, do not provide them with the new possibility they might expect to find as writers or with the issues that escape them, even as they live through them.

Now, it is this possibility that the "Course of Events" should bring to them, while giving them the ability to enter into a *form* where the meaning of the common task presents, prepares, and affirms itself at the same time. What we are calling a "short form" or, more precisely, a "fragment" is essentially linked: (1) to the idea that each written piece does not contain all its meaning in itself and is nothing but a fragmentary unit whose meaning depends on its relation with all the others; (2) thus, to the idea that meaning is not here once and for all, in the text where it emerges, but varies according to the way a collection of texts is arranged, that is to say, according to the operative rule that decides the organization and the combination of diverse fragments (or plural units). (This is why Boehlich's error, and at times your error, has been to read each one of our texts as if it were alone in the world, rich or poor with a unique, determined meaning, whereas in reality the meaning of these texts is still to come, depending both on your texts and on those of the Germans, and above all on the structure of the whole.) (3) The "fragment" is linked to the necessity of giving expression to a plurality of different reflections, that is to say, to connecting the plural multiplicity of objects and possibilities of the world through this diverse plurality, without threatening the review with formlessness, which would happen if the diversity of these multiple texts could not be composed and articulated in an overall project.

I will stop here. I would only add that we have been deeply struck by how much the "form" and the "structure" that we propose, as well as the general scheme of the "Course of Events" interested and attracted writers who were apparently the least close to us. This is what I found necessary to tell you today. Concerning your letter, after having thought about it a lot, I think it more judicious to wait so that one day we can try to reduce misunderstandings through the free movement of the spoken word. Basically, dear Elio, you wrote us a philosopher's letter, and this is where the error lies. We cannot recognize ourselves in the philosophical vocabulary that you use—I mean, to comprehend its scope and value in relation to ourselves. Ideas [such as] the refusal of epistemology and ontology: I can assure you that nothing in the reasons that make us express ourselves, whether within the review or outside of the review, finds expression even remotely in these words. And when it comes to me, what could I say? My entire life seems to have disappeared in a movement of seeking that is perhaps the experience of writing, the responsibility for which I try to bear, poorly but absolutely.

In truth, I am more worried about the possible misunderstandings concerning the "short form," because they threaten the project directly. But as Roland Barthes will be in Milan around February 15, when I hope he will see you, and as I know that he can express what we understand by "fragmentary speech" better than I can, thanks to his distinctive language, I will leave it to him to continue this letter.

The difficulties are immense, to be sure. Every night, when lucidity is greater, I see them so clearly that I wonder whether they will not win out. But each day I think that even if the nights are not wrong, still nothing should discourage us. There is thus a nocturnal madness and there is diurnal madness—put together, they must constitute a kind of firm reason to which one can remain faithful.

Maurice Blanchot

Maurice Blanchot to Elio Vittorini

Paris, March 11, 1963

Dear Elio,

I am responding hastily to your letter, and almost without thinking, not to tell you anything new but to maintain the movement of words between us and also in gratitude for the force of friendship that it expresses even when you get slightly angry, for reasons that are no doubt justified.

I think we were wrong not to answer you more explicitly about some propositions in your letter to Louis-René des Forêts. We had the impression we had already answered in advance. Indeed, in my letter to Johnson, I indicated to him that we have all accepted the compromises you proposed: that is, that the Italians and Germans should strive to contribute to the "Course of Things" with shorter texts, whereas the French, on their side, would bring longer texts, which would be either literary or, if possible, in the form of essays. When it comes to the news section, it is true that we value the search for meaningful information that has not yet been commented upon, simply given form (as the word *in-formation* indicates); but (1) this does not exclude the information that you call "developed," even though we hardly distinguish it from the other texts in the "Course of Events"; (2) we must admit that we ourselves have not developed this section as would be required, due to a lack of time and organization. For my part, I think it is nonetheless important, because it is through it that we can connect directly with world events and particularly political events.

There is a convergence of good will on all these points, even though the Germans have strictly limited themselves to the long form until now (but mainly because they remain disorganized and held up by other preoccupations: this situation may, of course, be only temporary; Suhrkamp has, it seems, the intention of setting up an office for the review in Berlin, and, from that point on, they could begin to concentrate).

This, then, is not what poses a problem. And yet we sense that such an agreement is somehow a formal agreement—undeniably necessary, but one that does not suffice to dissipate the critical difficulties that we all became aware of in Zurich: by "we" I mean, above all, the Italians and the French, for as was recently confirmed, the Germans were satisfied. They came to Zurich with great suspicion and skepticism, and they all, except Boehlich, left with the conviction that the review would surely come into being and that the conference had been a success. (I share these details with you not for the pleasure of the anecdote but because they hold a certain interest for the future of the enterprise).

So where does the "uneasiness" come from? This is very difficult to determine. In an attempt to specify it negatively, I was recently saying to Robert and Dionys that, if our goal were simply to create a review of international politics, well then, we would not be encountering any of the difficulties that have surfaced and are now looming over us. Our agreement, on this level, is certain. But it remains true that political agreement doesn't suffice to allow us to master this other understanding, whose slow development our enterprise presupposes. And we must conclude from this that it carries an additional, even more serious, and in any case more difficult demand—a demand where the very truth of our life, our most intimate raison d'être, is at stake. Hence the dramatic aspect of our contestations, the violent and almost desperate movements that we are going through, without our friendship being able to protect us from them, and yet also without this friendship ever being harmed.

What kind of difficulty is this? In your letter to L.-R. des Forêts, you sought to define it in philosophical terms. And in this regard, I would like to clear up the misunderstanding that my letter seems to have brought about. We have never claimed to revoke your concern for philosophical elucidation, even less to evade such contestation. What seemed necessary to me was to avoid getting lost in terminological discussions, and so to defer such discussions, which are easier to have orally, to an upcoming meeting. (For example, when you speak of phenomenology, which kind are you referring to? There have been at least ten since Husserl, without going back to Hegel, and when you speak of logical positivism, I am afraid that for us this designation represents something that does not have any life here in France.) If we hold onto this plan of cultural diversity, we merely risk increasing the opportunities for error. We also risk forgetting what has been the point of departure for all reflection since Hegel and Marx: namely, that we belong to "the end of philosophy." A necessarily ambiguous end, about which we have to decide whether it takes the glorious form of its fulfillment in the world or the more melancholic form of its pure and simple liquidation, as overcoming or as renunciation, and which, as an ending, does not end but can last for long historical eras, and yet which, as such, entrusts us with radically different tasks, to which the old labels no longer correspond.

Basically, and to say it in a spirit of simplification for which I apologize, I think that the most visible concern at the origin of our project was a unitary one: working for political, social, cultural, and philosophic unity, working in the perspective of the whole and for the development and realization of the whole. This concern is surely also deeply yours. And we certainly also have this worry, but we do not have it only because (how can I avoid expressing myself with clichés?) we too already feel mainly responsible for the demand that will persist once unity is achieved: the postunitary and postcultural demand that is perhaps the "artistic" demand par excellence. In other words, we know—Robert [Antelme] often says with an entirely convincing force—that as writers we are already within "communism" and that, insofar as we are there, the *response* has been given: this is the response of communist unity; but from here on, when speech is asked to be something other than a response, then the demand specific to all literary language begins to be affirmed: being essentially a question or a radical interrogation, which it remains uncertain that man can bear, just as it is uncertain that he is capable of literature. Perhaps one of the misunderstandings that trouble us comes from here: our texts could seem "reactionary" to those who persist in reading them in a preunitary perspective, while for us they represent an approach to the question laid open from now on insofar as we belong to the "end of philosophy." Thus everything takes place as if the world always had to be thought of—spoken—twice, first from the perspective of unity and in relation to the coming of the whole, and a second time in the affirmation of difference and the demand for discontinuity.

Forgive me for these words, which are written so rapidly and which I ask you to read as rough approximations. What I would like to say is simply that today, at the point where we are, after Marx and Lenin, it is not responding that is difficult, but rather questioning and speaking while questioning. This is the possibility that we are striving to maintain above all. This is why we may seem to be less men of culture than our partners, because we have an almost exaggerated consciousness of the gap that exists between cultural affirmation and artistic or literary affirmation, and that this gap is precisely what escapes any process of unification. But I will add immediately: we still do not deny a contribution that would be different from ours. On the contrary and from the perspective that I mentioned, it seems so essential that we will seek to take it on so far as is in our power, just as, surely, you will come to cooperate with our effort and, moreover, to carry it to a degree of maturity and of truth of which, without you and your criticism, we would be incapable.

Now I will end by dealing with one last question: you say that we came to Zurich with a project very different from the one that we had developed together, especially concerning how the international editorship would function. This is not correct. We arrived extremely open-minded (we still are), as well as very tense (we still are slightly so), but above all anxious to persuade our partners of the meaning and the importance that we attach to the "Course of Events," both as a section and even more as a general structure (and on this point "The Memorandum on the Course of Events" had clarified our intentions to you several weeks ago). It is true that it was Maurice Nadeau who raised the question of international authority in relation to the literary texts, in the Saturday afternoon session, but he did so at his own initiative (I mean, spontaneously) and, frankly, what he proposed had already been asked by Enzensberger as early as 1961, during the Paris meeting. Nonetheless, in the critical state of our debates (which remain difficult to analyze), the question immediately took on a new character of seriousness. This is why I did not take a position at the time; it seems to me that you didn't do so either. All the Germans were in favor of it precisely because it was becoming clear that they suspected us, the French (quite mistakenly, quite mistakenly), of imperialism and even of intellectual terrorism and that they desired first of all to secure the possibility of liberty (liberty that Boehlich, moreover, took away from us with his abrupt criticisms on the very next day). This was very clearly the point of view shared by Grass and Johnson. Finally, and gradually, everyone became aware that, in the current state of things, the exercise of international intellectual authority, as we had too abstractly conceived of it, implied a positive agreement that was at the time merely presupposed (and as a point of arrival, not as a point of departure) and was liable to bring about a disastrous rupture from the beginning. Moreover, we had to realize that, as our aim was not merely to start a review, it was no longer possible to run our enterprise as reviews are habitually directed in every country: in a unitary and authoritarian way. Does this mean that every possibility of international editorship has disappeared? Not at all, in our opinion. As Dionys must have told you and as Roland Barthes was supposed to tell you but did not get a chance to do so, if international editorship cannot be exercised in an authoritarian way directly over the content of the texts (this would only be possible if the "review" claimed to embody an ideology), it can and must be exercised over the structure, form, coherence, and collective movement of each issue, a structure that will finally hold the ultimate meaning of our enterprise and its future possibilities.

Maurice Blanchot

[The gravity of the project]

I

1. The gravity of the project: we are aware that we are approaching an extreme movement in time, what I would call a change of times. This alludes not only to particular possibilities of upheaval (in France, a regime incessantly threatened with being overwhelmed by forces that it has itself called forth; in the world, the question of Berlin and many others); but, much more seriously, gravely, it means that all problems are international and that the smallest international problems become intractable because they serve only to carry and translate such a state of tension, so that return to the traditional idea of peace is henceforth radically excluded and so that even war—a good old, classical war—might seem a relief from this state of tension (hence, the tension of war).

At such an extreme moment in time, the idea of starting a new review, one that would merely be more interesting or better than the others, seems derisory. It is therefore necessary that such a project be ceaselessly focused on its own gravity, which is the attempt to respond to the grave enigma that is the passage from one time to another.

2. This reference to the essential must be affirmed in reference to a certain number of principles:

—The project is essentially collective, for it is international in scope. This does not mean that we are looking for a thought common to all, to all the participants, but that by pooling our efforts, questions, and resources, and above all by internally going beyond our own thoughts, we can give rise to new ones.

Thus the editorship must be collegial without restraint, so that everyone can fully participate in it, not only by expressing agreement but by working effectively, by giving their ideas and time, and by orienting their thinking toward the achievement of the project. If we have not fully decided on this collective effort, it is better not to undertake anything at all. At the same time, it is possible that a collegial editorship may not be practically attainable; that may be; in that case, we will renounce it, but we have to verify it through experience and, if it is a utopia, accept failing utopically.

—This review will not be a review, that is to say, a panorama of cultural, literary, and political activities of our time. There are very few things that should interest us in this review, or in other words, we should not give the impression that we are interested in and curious about everything. Or again, we should be interested only in the whole, where the whole is at stake, and always regain this interest and this passion for the whole; then we must ask ourselves if the essential interest does not also lead to that which is outside of the whole.

—Thus the review will not be a cultural review: the interest, for example, that we have in literature is not a cultural interest; when we write, we do not write to enrich general culture. What matters to us is the search for truth, or a certain just demand, perhaps a demand for justice, for which the literary affirmation, by its interest in the center and its unique relation to language, is essential.

—Practically, this must translate into the importance given to the central chronicle, around which the rest of the review should be organized—into the importance given to the tone of the review, to its language, to its form—and into the exclusion of everything that is secondary (reading notes, etc.)

II

1. A review can be the expression of an already-constituted doctrine or of a preexisting group (Surrealism). It can help to shape still vague but latent tendencies. Finally, it may be a collective, creative work of going beyond, a work of oriented demands that, by the very fact that the review exists, leads participants farther along its own path and also perhaps on a slightly different path from the one they would have followed on their own. Each person becomes responsible for assertions of which he is not the author, for a search that is not only his; he answers for a knowledge that he does not originally know himself. This is the meaning of the review as a collective possibility. It is an intermediary status between author and reader. Hence the necessity of a great work of elaboration in common, and since unanimity is neither possible nor desirable, discussion and dialogue within the review itself become a necessary pursuit.

2. For this review project, such a necessity is even more imposing; it must essentially be an international review, not only multinational or universal in the sense of an abstract universality, maintaining only a vague

and void identity based on the problems addressed; but it must be the putting in common [*mise en commun*] of literary, philosophical, political, and social problems, as they are posed according to the determination of each language and within each national context. This supposes that each person renounce the exclusive rights of both ownership of and intervention in his own problems, recognize that his problems also belong to everyone else, and thus agree to conceive of them in a common perspective.

Thus, it will be not only a review of exchange but also a space for questioning, discussion, and dialogue.

3. There should still be some initial principles admitted by everyone involved:

Concerning the *political horizon*: on the one hand, this means putting everything into question to the extent that we agree to carry out a fundamental interrogation of our time, seeking to give the word *question* all its force and dignity, even questioning the value of the question itself.

On the other hand, there is no point in putting everything into question in a simply skeptical and superficial manner or else under the pretext that history has not brought us sure evidence and definitive facts. For example: whatever our personal choices concerning Marxism may be, it is still the case that we are leaning [*adossés*] on Marxism, pressed up against it, albeit in order to contest it. The necessity of thinking about all problems as if they were uniquely political problems *at a certain moment*, then *at the same time* thinking of all problems not as purely political but as putting into question a global demand that we cannot only call political, this necessity comes from Marxism, and it leads us to affirm Marxism as dialectical, yet without being condemned to repeat the Marxist dialectic.

4. The demand of literature and the arts: literature and the arts can perfectly well be subjected to a critique of a Marxist kind (for example): this is perfectly acceptable; it is even necessary, on the condition that this critique says something new and does not rehash hackneyed commonplaces. But we must also grant that literature, still today at least, constitutes not only its own experience but a fundamental experience, questioning everything, including itself, including the dialectic, for if it is true that the dialectic can and must take hold of literature and make it serve its movement, it is also true that the literary mode of affirmation escapes the dialectic and does not belong to it. Literature represents a power of a particular sort that perhaps does not have to do with possibility (whereas only possibility has something to do with the dialectic): art is infinite contestation, contestation of itself and contestation of other forms

of power—and this not only in simple anarchy, but in the free quest for original power that art and literature represent (*power without power*).

To put it very briefly and schematically, we can thus imagine literature as:

—the affirmation of works (*oeuvres*): the movement toward the work is essentially enigmatic;

—as the search for itself, experience that must not be subjected to any restriction, any dogmatic surveillance, to the extent that it is a creative kind of contestation, contesting itself by the sole force of creation;

—as the search for the search [*recherche de la recherche*] itself in which perhaps something other than literature alone speaks. (Literature, even so-called pure literature, is *more* than literature; why? What is this "more"? Why is literature not completed by the necessary illusion of being more than itself, as the affirmation of an extra-literary truth?)

5. There seems to result from this an irreducible difference and even a discord between a political responsibility that is both global and concrete, accepting Marxism as nature and the dialectic as the method of truth, and literary responsibility, a responsibility that is a response to a demand that cannot take form except in and through literature.

This discord need not be resolved from the outset. It is a given; it exists as a problem, not a frivolous problem, but one to be borne with difficulty, all the more difficult given that each one of its discordant terms engages us absolutely, as does their dissonance, in a way.

6. Elements of a solution do exist, though: one of the tasks of the review should be to explore them in more detail.

III

A review without any division between the critical and the anthological section—because critical knowledge must appear to be as essential as the beautiful texts or readings in it, and because the latter can implicitly play a critical role (but never an illustrative one), and vice versa.

THE INTELLECTUAL COURSE OF EVENTS

I believe in the importance of a column or section established collectively by each editorial board with the help of elements provided by foreign editorial boards, giving a certain idea of the intellectual course of events. This column, implicit or explicit, will respond very freely, I mean in a varied form, to all kinds of aims: first, to represent a specific type of literary critical information by presenting a global review of books published, with a predominance of Italian, German, and English books in France, the French part being more limited or included with the rest for comparative purposes (since the weeklies or other reviews have already made them known); this column must also, and perhaps primarily, focus on a specific intellectual event, be it philosophical, poetic, or sociological (publishing trends, review articles, etc.)

Naturally, the other arts also belong to this column. However, I think that when it comes to music, painting, etc., it is more important to have a more intensive study on any given issue, from time to time, whether it is related to current events or not.

Moreover, there should be critical notes on the French and foreign books that it seems necessary to consider separately, and to draw them away from the course of events. The works in the "column" will be part of a movement and a process. In this other part, they will be nothing but themselves.

THE COURSE OF THE WORLD

In a similar column, with a form that is of course different, but also varied, there will appear *short* texts of critical interest, engaging in a dialogue, such as some "remarks" on the political process or the general evolution of the world. For example, today, reflections *by writers* on Gagarin's adventure, what it means, Khrushchev's use of the word *fatherland* ["*patrie*"], the first cosmic word, etc.

IV. Memorandum on the "Course of Things"

It is necessary for us to summarize very precisely the propositions concerning the meaning and the structure of the "Course of Events" that we agree on, in order to submit them to our foreign friends. Two points must be emphasized once again:

1. The purpose of the review is to try to prepare a new possibility, which would allow the writer to *say* the "world" and everything that takes place in the world, but as a writer and from his own perspective, with the responsibility that comes to him from his writer's truth alone: thus a form of responsibility entirely different from (yet no less essential than) that which brutally marked the relations of literature and public life from 1945 on, known under the simplistic label of "Sartrian commitment." One important result of this is that the review will not be able to address political

reality as such directly, but always indirectly. This search for the "indirect" is one of the great tasks of the review, given, of course, that an "indirect" critique, that is, by detour, does not mean only an allusive or elliptical critique but the most radical critique, going to the hidden meaning of the "root" (for example: the *Spiegel* affair[1] does not interest us for the governmental crisis that it provoked, nor even for the political authority's interventions into the judiciary, but for its underlying implications: the myth of military secrets; the necessity and exigency of saying everything without taking any question of timeliness into account; the affirmation of the authority and responsibility of writers).

2. The purpose of the heading "The Course of Events" must be revealed and clarified by its *structure* and its *form*: (a) This section must run throughout the issue, which will begin and end with it. As this section will be interrupted each time that texts with different forms appear, it must be identifiable with a special mark. We propose that each text of this section be numbered, the series of numbers thereby affirming the discontinuous continuity of the section considered as a "series." (b) In this section, a *short form* (in the sense that this term has in music today) will be attempted. By which we mean that not only will each one of the texts be short (from half a page to three to four pages), but also that it will make up something like a *fragment*, which does not necessarily have all its meaning in itself but rather opens onto a more general meaning still to come or even accepts the demand of an essential *discontinuity*. Let it be repeated that in this "short form" each one of us will deal with everything that concerns him, a very difficult task, in everything that happens (and also does not happen): poetic, philosophical, and political questions prompted by the intellectual, scientific, and general state of affairs, proposed in a still invisible or, by contrast, in a spectacular manner, coming from books or from everyday life. (c) The structure of this section must be such that, in addition to commentaries ("fragments"), it can admit other texts printed in a different font and constituting a kind of relay: (i) citations, for example, "Aby Warburg": "der Liebe Gott steht in Detail";[2] or else: "By thousands of routes and never gaining a step, to always return to the same point" (*Theaetetus*); (ii) kinds of aphorisms (aphorisms of thought, rather than of style); (iii) above all, very plainly written "information," information valuable not as information but as meaning: a sort of ephemeris constituted by a few rare events, which would punctuate [*scander*] the "Course of Events" and which we would take the responsibility of choosing, this choice being necessarily partial, that is to say, meaningful. (For example: the *Spiegel* affair is an event, but the recent French elections are not an event. The

censorship of certain books belongs here, but not, of course, literary prizes.) Each one of our editorial committees should thus prepare a "news in brief" series, which we could discuss and agree on at our meetings. The importance of this lies in the attempt, at our risk and peril, to bring to the fore elements of a true and more secret history, confronting them with official and apparent history, and also insofar as it will use the event in its brutality and its nudity as commentary itself, brutality that will reinforce the (somewhat tendentious) stiffness of the form that we will give it. Our correspondents from the Eastern, Anglophone, and Hispanic countries have agreed to cooperate attentively.

V. Course of Things

ON TRANSLATION

1. The translator will, in a certain sense, be the true writer of the review. Hence the problem of translation must be raised starting with the very first issues. The translator may well be an overtly facile vector of unification. Languages are never contemporaneous: How is one to maintain this difference of historical level in a translation? Similarly, dialects pose a problem: literary German and in particular poetic language is often dialectal language, and it seems the problem of the translation of dialects has never been solved appropriately. (Just as, I think, Italian is not as unified as French.) Leyris, Bonnefoy.[3] For the latter, bad French translations of Shakespeare in the past are related to an implicit metaphysical opposition.

2. Translation as the original form of literary activity. The translator is the secret master of the difference between languages, not to abolish this difference but to use it, in order to awaken, in his own language, by the changes he brings to it, the presence of the differences that are in the original work. The translator, a nostalgic man, feels as a lack in his own language everything that the original text promises to him in the way of possible assertions: privatively possessing French, for example, and yet rich with this deprivation.

3. The example of Hölderlin: a man fascinated by the power of translating. The translations of *Antigone* and *Oedipus*, works on the verge of madness, were carried out with the intention not of transposing the Greek text into German or of bringing the German to its Greek sources but of unifying the two powers (Orient, Occident) in the simplicity of a total and pure language. To translate, in the end, is madness. (Perhaps Laplanche . . .)[4]

The review will be made up of fragments, not articles (the essay in search of a form). To simplify, we could say that there are four kinds of fragments: (1) The fragment that is only the dialectical moment in a greater ensemble. (2) The obscurely violent aphoristic form, which is already complete as a fragment. Etymologically, the aphorism is the horizon, a horizon that limits and does not open. (3) The fragment linked to the mobility of seeking, of the traveling thought that fulfills itself in separate affirmations and demands this separation (Nietzsche). (4) Finally, a literature of the fragment that places itself outside of the whole, either because it supposes that the whole is already realized (all literature is the literature of the end of time) or because next to forms of language in which the whole builds and expresses itself—the speech of knowledge, work, and salvation—it senses an entirely other speech that frees thought from being only thought oriented toward unity, in other words, that demands an essential discontinuity. In this sense, all literature is a fragment, whether brief or infinite, on the condition that it designate a space of language where each moment takes on its meaning and its function by making all others indeterminate or else (this is the other side) where some affirmation that is not reducible to any unifying process is at work.

(Naturally, this question of the "fragment" can be approached in an entirely different way, but I think that it is an essential question, particularly for this project. It is always the question concerning the review as form, as the search for its own form.)

This is a reflection on our projects: we always speak about themes and questions, but are we sure that the "world" is thematizable? There is perhaps a profound athematism, which we discern, for example, when we refuse to speak about someone who is close to us, to transform him into a theme, into an object of reflection, accepting only speaking to him. Hence the strong aversion that one feels in becoming a hunter of questions, a swarm of questions, and even more, in obliging other writers to see nothing in the world but questions for a review. There is surely some violence here, maybe a demand that we could tolerate for ourselves but that cannot be made into a felicitous and constraining method.

Some other thoughts: the "questions" that are of interest to the review will differ: (a) in subject or theme, (b) in the development of these themes, (c) in the way in which the texts will be ordered into a whole, (d) but also in the form or the essence of the questions. What should this difference in form or essence imply? There are, for example, questions that have their origin in an insignificant, barely noticed fact, from which an important meaning can be drawn (the passage from the implicit to the explicit) and by this very act could well crush the fact. Thus it seems to me that the essential feature of the *everyday* is not to let itself be captured, to escape; it is insignificant, it is uneventful, without subject; this is its profundity. The everyday, in this sense too, perhaps refuses thematization. What will we do about other kinds of questions that have already been developed and are considered important (de-Stalinization)? Will we refuse to show an interest in them as such? Will we try to deal with them only indirectly, approach them tangentially, from the side, or even break them apart? A bias in favor of reduction. Finally, there are borderline questions, which are not posed, are always held in reserve, and are betrayed as soon as they become the object of a special problematic. Here a new questioning is secretly elaborated, as if there were a questioning where, in questioning, one would question more than one can question, more than the power to question can tolerate, more than there are questions. An excess of questioning over the power to question. Maybe, through literature as a work, only solitary reflection can receive and maintain such a questioning demand in itself, one that is completed precisely when there are no more questions.

—The conquest of space: reflections on the "place." What was momentarily felt as decisive when man became spaceman is the rupture with place: a man existed, in principle, outside of all horizons and in the absolute of an almost homogeneous space. This liberty acquired in relation to place (albeit in a still illusory way), this kind of lightening of human substance obtained by the detachment from place, prolonged and provisionally completed the work of technics, uprooting sedentary civilizations, destroying human particularisms, leading man out of the utopia of childhood (if he seeks a return to place).

But hardly had Gagarin left place behind than Khrushchev saluted him in the name of the earth, his "fatherland." Thus, the statesman sees in the cosmonaut not the one who calls place into question, but rather the one who consecrates its prestige.

1. The relation to the Outside was not radically modified, it was phenomenologically modified. Speech as the only relation with the former place: the cosmonaut must speak and must do so constantly. Certainly technics is dangerous, but less dangerous than "the genius of place." There is perhaps something to be said against the paganism in which anti-Christianity seeks to shelter itself—Heideggerian paganism, the poetic paganism of rootedness. Truth is nomad.

—Boulez and Mallarmé. *Pli selon Pli.* Boulez's lecture at Donaueschingen in which he shows the incompatibilities of music-poetry. It is from these incompatibilities that a meeting is possible. And Boulez finds this meeting point in verbal, rhythmic, architectonic structures and their musical equivalents. All the difficulty lies in linguistic equivalence. This evokes Wittgenstein's problem: each language has a structure about which one can say nothing in this language itself, but which one can address in another language that in turn has a structure which we can only deal with in another language . . .

2. The new treatment of text in contemporary music.

3. There is also the very difficult question concerning the relations between "modern" literature and the "modern" arts. Is it possible to find relations between them that are less superficial than the ones culture uses to situate Einstein, Picasso, Joyce, and Schönberg within a single perspective?

—The myth of the savant. When Teilhard de Chardin elaborates his random syntheses, he does not forget to say, albeit naively rather than presumptuously: I am not leaving the territory of scientific observation; I speak as a scientist. Charon, who confirms Chardin's conception, according to which there are no corpuscles without psyche,[5] presents this hypothesis of universal psychism (already endorsed by Nietzsche) as a *scientific discovery*. When does a scientist stop being a scientist? For instance, how can we call the models of the universe or unified theories scientific?

—Questions that could be drawn from books: Claude Levi-Strauss's *The Savage Mind*, Pernoud's book on the bourgeoisie, Ellul's book on propaganda, Leroi-Gourhan's book on the anthropological structures of the imagination, Fanon's book on violence.[6]

—In novelistic literature, God's point of view is conveniently replaced by the point of view of the police: it is the police who see and know everything (Chesterton, Orwell, Colrado Alvaro, Graham Greene, the novels of the *nouveau roman*, Robbe-Grillet, Uwe Johnson). Today, the enigma is not attributed to the inner self but conceived of as a public enigma. When everything is revealed, something still escapes [*se dérobe*].

Has the possibility of total destruction brought about a change in the notion of violence? What is the revolutionary meaning of violence, granted that it can always transform itself into radical destruction? Is this question at the origin of de-Stalinization?

—Studying de-Stalinization from the point of view of language. What changes did it introduce in political language? There were some new words, the cult of personality, peaceful coexistence, Khrushchev's more concrete language, but was the official language modified?

—The role of the radio in Germany, that is to say, the possibilities and the temptations that it offers the German writer, a situation that one finds neither in France nor in Italy. England, America?

—The decline of the myth of the unknown soldier through its persistence. The unknown soldier is the antihero, the unnoticed, obscure revenant who remained forgotten in the memories of peoples. The memorial of nonremembrance, the apotheosis of namelessness.

—Reflections on the idea and the form of what is called a "review." Several points: (1) A short historical study; maybe we would have something to learn about the evolution of this form of publication in different countries of culture; (2) the surrealist review was one of the authentic creations of this movement; (3) criticism of every review. Collective publication, but without real collective structure, or instead a dogmatic review, an instrument of protest and combat, an organ of a party or a school, but not any type of research. Periodicity, a purely arbitrary condition: How to reintroduce "worklessness" (*désoeuvrement*), insouciance about time into a periodic publication? How can literary texts, irreducible to any unity, take part in the holistic arrangement that is a review (etc.)?

—Critical texts: the situation of Bloch in contemporary German thought. An unpublished text by Bloch.

—Cultural isolation in France and Italy.

—The structure of French publishing . . .

The Course of the World

—J[ean-Emile] Charon's theory.

—The conquest of space—the information transmitted by too many satellites to be exploited (knowledge more complex than the real).

I.—De-Stalinization: several texts in a series or not (established by international exchange).

a. Theoretical aspect: according to which principles was it led? Stalin and Stalinism. According to the [sayings] of Stalinists, Stalinism supposedly consists first and foremost in a few "errors:" the aggravation of class relations, the sharpening of the contradiction between capitalist and non-capitalist countries, to the degree that a socialist society realizes itself; the inevitability of war; proletarian dictatorship instead of the proletariat, the absence of democracy in the party; the abuse of planning. This, roughly put, is Stalinism. And Stalin is responsible for it. But making Stalin the only one responsible for Stalinism (which appears as an unexplained superstructure or else one that can only be explained by one man's excess, itself unexplained) is to perpetuate Stalin by giving a decisive importance to his personality.

Nonetheless, implicitly, by questioning pure authority, voluntarism, the organization of moral fraud, scams and mystifications instituted by dictatorial necessities, an entire system is undermined, the movement by which, even in a regime based on socialism, legal society comes to establish itself over and against real society.

Moreover, the decisive change in perspective comes from the change in meaning that the possibility of total destruction—nuclear war—has brought to the notion of *violence*. Here too, the quantitative change provoked a qualitative one, which is difficult to measure. In other words, what is the revolutionary meaning of violence, in the perspective in which it always risks turning into radical destruction? Is it still a possibility? Until now, such a line of questioning has only been very cautiously broached and not been thought through at all. It is nonetheless at the heart of the principle of "de-Stalinization" and perhaps the principle of a change in the future.

b. De-Stalinization and the myth of the Pharaoh. The fact that Stalinist dictatorship is publicly contested in its moral aspect underlines the fear of having to explain, to analyze, and to pass from the implicit to the explicit—a strange apprehension of analysis. One would rather condemn than analyze. This is because a critique of Stalin is not a critique but sacrilege. They want his name to be erased from the earth. But all sacrilege remains a sacred act, etc.

c. One could study de-Stalinization yet again from the point of view of language. What changes in political language did this contestation introduce? Some new words, the cult of personality, peaceful coexistence (the right to a more concrete language from Khrushchev), but the official language seems to have remained the same "doublespeak" [*langue de bois*]. Italian Communism.

II.—The situation of the German press. The role of the German radio.

III.—Cultural barriers in France and Italy.

IV.—Rossif's film: *Le temps du ghetto.*

V.—The Eichmann case. Eichmann constitutes a problem. As a real individual, he is without any importance; he is nothing, and what he says, what he thinks means nothing. Whatever his reaction may be, it is without value. It is equally vain whether he regrets what he did or refuses to regret it. In other words, Eichmann no longer exists as a private person. Hence his own death, his death sentence, does not constitute an event that is still personally destined for him but belongs to the truth of the Trial. Here, in the very movement [*jeu*] of justice, there is a remarkable suspension of all ethics. This private inexistence of Eichmann is something like a correlative to Jewish misfortune, a relation to this misfortune, when the Jew of the ghetto was deprived of an "I," of any possibility for first person presence.

VI.—A secret chronicle of disarray. It would perhaps be good for disarray to be directly or indirectly expressed in the review. I would even say that one of its tasks would be to reflect on events by considering them from the point of view of "disarray" . . .

VII.—Utopia: the sociology of utopia. Literature as counter-utopia. (The book; a book on the three cities of utopia; an issue devoted to Diogenes).

VIII.—The situation of Algerians in France, the reproduction of certain texts that have appeared in the press or in reviews.

IX.—Heidegger and the political texts of 1933 (published in part by Guido Schneeberger in the original language in 1960, recently translated and commented on in *Méditations*). What seems essential in these texts is not that Heidegger could have pronounced himself in favor of the Nazi party on two or three occasions but rather that he did so in the very language of his own philosophy, that he could have "spoken Nazi" with the gravity, the beauty, and the profundity of his own language; such that it is truly this language that he compromised and perhaps perverted. If he had flatly turned himself into a Nazi propagandist in the vulgar language of the Nazis, this would be much less serious, in my opinion; his responsibility would not exceed a failing of character or a mental aberration. At least this reminds us at what level our responsibility as "philosophers" is situated: at the level of one's language.

The Conquest of Space

Man does not want to leave his place. He says that technology is dangerous, that it threatens relations to the world, that true civilizations are fixed, and that the nomad acquires nothing. Who is this man? Each one of us, in those moments when we are weighed down. This is the man who felt a shock the day Gagarin became a spaceman. While the event is almost forgotten, the experience will take on other forms. Here, we must believe the man of the street, the one who does not reside. He admired Gagarin; he admired him for his courage, for the adventure, and also because of progress, but someone stated the right reason: "It's fantastic, we have left the earth." That, indeed, is the true meaning of the experience: man broke with place. This is what must be considered decisive, at least momentarily: out there, in an abstract out there of pure sciences, subtracted from our common condition symbolized by gravity, there was someone, not even in the sky, but in space, space without being and without nature which is nothing but the reality of a measurable quasi-void. Man, but man without horizon. A sacrilegious act. Upon his return, Gagarin made some bad jokes: he had been to heaven, but he didn't meet God. The Catholic press protested. But wrongly. For the profanation had taken place: the old heavens, the heaven of religions and contemplation, the sublime and pure "up there," was effaced in an instant, emptied of the privilege of inaccessibility, replaced by another absolute, the space of scientists, which is nothing but a calculable possibility. All the same, more than the Christian, Gagarin's victim was the man in us who is eternally fascinated by paganism, the one who wants nothing other than to inhabit the earth, dwell, found, lay down roots, unite himself ontologically with biological race and ancestral soil, the possessive man who wants to have the earth and whom the earth has, the one who appropriates and latches onto it, forever encrusted, wherever he is, in his tradition, in his truth, in his history, the one who does not want us to touch sacred sites of the beautiful landscape and the great past, and, finally, the melancholic who consoles himself for the cruelty of men by spending time with trees. For a moment, Gagarin freed us from this man and lightened us of millennia of clutter (so well represented by

Ionesco in *The Tenant* [*Le locataire*]). A technical victory? To be sure. Such a liberty acquired (be it in an illusory way) in relation to "place," this kind of alleviation of man-substance, of man-essence, obtained by the break from "locality" has only prolonged and momentarily accomplished the task of technology, uprooting sedentary civilizations, destroying human particularisms, leading man outside the utopia of childhood (if the man-child, in each one of us, seeks to return to place). We were immediately able to recognize how difficult it is to leave these regions and to arrive at a formulation of the problems of maturity. For hardly had this Gagarin broken with original powers and become engaged in a movement of pure dislocation, starting to become a separate man, than Khrushchev hurried to reestablish him in his own lineage by greeting him in the name of the earth, his fatherland: an astonishing interpellation, a memorable misunderstanding that we could have equally expected from the statesmen named Kennedy and de Gaulle, all heirs ready to lay claim to the benefits of technics for their own prestige, but incapable of accepting or welcoming its consequence, which is to ruin all belonging and to call all places, and place itself, into question.

—Let's admit this. But shouldn't we say that Gagarin's exploit, on the one hand, did nothing other, in its political and mythic developments, than allow the Russians to inhabit Russian soil more concretely, while, on the other hand, the relation to the Outside does not at all appear to be modified physically in a radical way? Naturally, this must be said, and also that the superstition of place can only be torn from us by committing us to a momentary utopia of some nonplace. The condition of the cosmonaut is pitiful in many ways: the man who bears the sense of freedom and who has never been more of a prisoner to his situation, freed from gravity and the heaviest of beings, on the way toward maturity and swaddled in his scientific languages, like a newborn from the olden days, feeding himself, moreover, with a bottle and wailing more than talking. Still today I hear this poor speech, a speech that, when faced with the unexpected, utters nothing but banalities, a speech that is, moreover, devoid of guarantee and that we are free to relate (as Nixon did) to some sort of mystification. Nonetheless, in this chatter there is something frightening and moving: the fact is that it does not stop, it must not stop; the smallest hole in the rumor already means the void forever; any lacuna, any interruption introduces into discourse something much more than death: it introduces external nothingness itself. And so it is necessary that out there the man of the Outside speak and speak constantly, not only to reassure us and to inform us, but because he has no other links with the old Place besides this incessant speech, which, against a grating background, far from the harmony of spheres, says nothing but insignificant clichés, at least to whoever understands it badly—but to those who understand it better, it also says that truth is nomad.*

*Here one should cite Emmanuel Levinas, to whom we owe many of these reflections and who puts it strongly: "Technology is dangerous, but less dangerous than the genius of Place." [Blanchot's quotation combines two phrases by Levinas from a text entitled "Heidegger, Gagarin, and Us," first published in *Information juive* in 1961 and later included in *Difficult Freedom*, trans. S. Hand (Baltimore: Johns Hopkins University Press, 1997).]

Berlin

For everyone, Berlin is the problem of division. From a certain point of view, it is a strictly political problem, for which we must keep in mind that there are strictly political solutions. From another point of view, it is a social and economic problem (still political, but in a broader sense), for this is where two systems and two socioeconomic structures meet. From another point of view, it is a metaphysical problem: Berlin is not only Berlin but the symbol of the division of the world: even more, a "point in the universe," the place where reflection on the necessity and the impossibility of unity occurs in each person who lives there and who, living there, has the experience not only of a dwelling place but of the absence of dwelling. That's not all. Berlin is not a symbol, it is a real city where human dramas are experienced that other cities cannot know: here, division means being torn apart. That is not all. Berlin poses the problem of two opposing cultures within the same cultural whole, of two unrelated languages within an identical language, unusually, and therefore calls into question the intellectual security or the possibility of communication that belonging to the same language and the same historical past deceptively affords human beings living together. That's not all.

To treat or to interrogate the problem of Berlin as a problem of division does not mean exhaustively enumerating the diverse forms in which it can be grasped. As a problem of division, it must be said that Berlin is an indivisible problem. This is why, when we momentarily isolate a particular element of the "Berlin" situation, even for the clarity of presentation, we may be distorting not only the question as a whole but even this particular element, which, however, can only be grasped if it is considered separately.

The problem of division—of fracture—as Berlin poses it, not only to Berliners, not only to Germans, but, I believe, to any thinking human being, and which it poses in an imperious, I mean painful, way, is a problem that one can only formulate adequately, in its *complete* reality, by deciding to formulate it in a *fragmentary* way (which does not mean in a partial way). In other words, every time we evoke a problem of this kind—there are others, after all—we should remind ourselves that to speak about it fittingly means speaking of it while letting our sudden lack of words and thought speak, and thereby letting speak our impossibility of speaking of it in a supposedly exhaustive way. This means: (1) that omniscience, even if it were possible, would not apply here: here an all-knowing god would essentially miss the situation; (2) that in general, one cannot dominate, survey, or comprehend the problem of division at a glance, no more than, in this case and others, a panoramic vision could be an accurate vision; (3) that the deliberate choice of the fragment is not a skeptical retreat, the tired renunciation of a complete grasp (which it could be), but a patient-impatient, mobile-immobile method of research, and also the affirmation that the sense, the entirety of sense, could not be immediately within us and in what we write, but that it is still to come and that, questioning the sense, we grasp it as the becoming and what will come [*devenir et avenir*] of the question; (4) this means, finally, that one must repeat oneself. Every fragmentary word, every fragmentary reflection demands this: an infinite reiteration and an infinite plurality.

I would add two (fragmentary) remarks. The frantic political abstraction that Berlin embodies found the height of its expression with the building of the wall, which is nonetheless something dramatically concrete. Until August 13, 1961, the absence of a visible separation—even though regular and irregular checks prefigured the enigmatic approach of a line of demarcation—made the nature and the meaning of partition ambiguous: What was there? A border? Certainly, but it was also something else, something less than a border, since each day people could cross it en masse by slipping through the security checks, but also, much more, because crossing it meant crossing not from one country to another, from one language to another, but, within the same country and the same language, from "truth" to "error," from "good" to "evil," from "life" to "death," and thus to undergo, as if unconsciously, a radical metamorphosis (yet without being able to decide, except by a partial reflection, where exactly this brutally divided "good" and "evil" were located). The almost instantaneous building of the wall replaced this still undecided ambiguity with the violence of decisive separation. Outside of Germany, it was understood with more or less intensity, more or less negligence, what dramatic human, economic, and political changes this event announced. But I think there is something that has escaped us (and perhaps escaped even the Germans): the reality of this wall was intended to strike the unity of this great moving city with *abstraction*, a city that was not and is not in reality—this is its deepest reality—neither one city alone nor two cities, neither the capital of a country, nor merely a random major city, nor the center, nor anything other than this absent center. Now, the wall tried *abstractly to concretize* the division, to make it visible and tangible, that is, to force one to think Berlin henceforth, in the very unity of this name, no longer under the sign of lost unity but as the sociological reality of two absolutely different cities.* The "scandal" and the importance of the wall is that, in the concrete oppression that it embodies, it is itself essentially abstract and that it thus reminds us—we who forget this constantly—that abstraction is not simply a faulty mode of thought or an apparently impoverished form of language but rather our world, the one we live and think in on a daily basis.

There has been an infinite amount of writing about the situation in Berlin. I am struck by the fact that, at least for non-Germans, it is in two novels that one finds the best approach to this situation, two novels that are neither political nor realistic.[1] I will attribute the merit not solely to Uwe Johnson's talent but to the truth of literature. The very difficulty and, more precisely, the impossibility of the author's writing these books in which division is at play, that is, the necessity for him to recapture this *impossibility* in and through writing—that is what has brought the literary work close to the strangeness of "Berlin," in the very hiatus between reality and the literary grasping of the sense of this reality, a hiatus that it was necessary for him to maintain with a dark and relentless rigor.

Perhaps the hurried reader and critic will say that in such works the relation to the world and to the responsibility of a political decision concerning this world remains distant and indirect. Indirect, yes. But, precisely, one must ask whether, to reach "the world" with speech and above all through writing, the indirect is not the straight or even the shortest path.

*The wall claimed to substitute for the sociological truth of a situation, its de facto status, the deeper truth of this situation, which one could call, but only by simplifying excessively, dialectical.

Part II

The Student-Writer Action Committee, the Review *Comité*, 1968

Tracts of the Student-Writer Action Committee (Sorbonne-Censier)

[The solidarity that we assert here]

The solidarity that we assert here with the student movement throughout the world—this movement that in a few explosive hours has shaken the so-called welfare society perfectly embodied in the French world—is first of all a response to the lies by which all the institutions and political formations (with very few exceptions), all the institutions of the press and communication (almost without exception) have sought for months to alter this movement, to pervert its meaning and even to try to ridicule it.

It is scandalous not to recognize what is being sought and what is at stake in this movement: the will to escape, by any and every means, an alienated order, but one that is so powerfully structured and integrated that simple contestation is always at risk of being placed in its service. And it is scandalous not to understand that the violence for which certain forms of this movement are blamed is a response to the immense violence behind which most contemporary societies seek to protect and preserve themselves, police brutality being merely the most overt manifestation of this violence.

This is the scandal that we want to denounce without delay, and we want to state at the same time that, faced with the established system, it is of capital and perhaps decisive importance that the student movement, without making promises and, on the contrary, rejecting any premature affirmation, oppose and maintain a power of refusal that we believe is capable of opening up a future.

May 8, 1968

[A government does not govern]

A government governs only with public trust.

Without trust, a government only governs by force.

It is clear that public trust was betrayed in the Châtelet negotiations.[1]

It is clear that the government can no longer govern without the looming specter of civil war.

It is clear that the government, since it is no longer an interlocutor, since it is nothing but the guardian and owner of repressive force, *must resign.*

The Student-Writer Action Committee

[By the power of refusal]

By the power of refusal that it possesses and through an incessant movement of struggle in a close relation of solidarity with all workers, the student uprising has decisively struck the system of exploitation and oppression that rules this country. Through this very movement, it has decisively contributed to our withdrawal from political death, going so far as to overturn the apparatuses of traditional parties and groups.

Thus everything must be done to preserve the meaning of this upheaval, the originality of the action that it denotes, the new liberty that it has already won for all. No organization today could claim to represent the revolutionary demand on its own.

This is why—at a moment when government power, through measures that are, moreover, without any legal justification and are based on defamatory arguments that could also ban every opposition group, seeks to impede the student struggle alongside the workers—the signatories of this text declare that any case against the members of the organizations targeted by the statute of dissolution[1] must also be made against those who hold themselves responsible for the actions incriminated. They will support the accused with all the means at their disposal.

Crime

At the same time as it violently set out to liquidate the student movement, General de Gaulle's regime decided to discipline the people as a whole. The illegal dissolution of opposition movements was clearly decided on only so as to allow searches without warrants, arbitrary arrests (more than a hundred arrest warrants), as well as the reactivation of special courts, with the ultimate goal of preventing any meetings or gatherings, in other words, as the president of the Republic declared, so that nothing more will happen in the streets or in public buildings (universities, parliaments). Which amounts to decreeing *political death*. As for foreigners, they have been and still are being threatened by the hundreds [in violent conditions that have even moved governments to respond], hunted down, expelled, and sometimes handed over for persecution to their countries of origin. The threat of rescinding military deferment is exercised against students suspected of any activity hostile to the regime. Following the traditions of political police in dictatorial regimes, they try to fabricate various pieces of "evidence" for a supposed "international plot," while in police headquarters files are kept with the names of people who are now becoming the targets of increasing levels of political terrorism: surveillance, warnings, investigations, interrogations, and arrests. Everything indicates that a powerful apparatus of insidious repression and brutal force has been put into place.

Therefore, by insisting on the extreme gravity of the situation, we call all citizens [and first of all intellectuals, teachers, artists, scientists, and researchers] to unite against the Gaullist system of police oppression, and since power [notably in taking over the universities, faculties, fine arts academies, and cultural institutes by force or by cunning] attempts to break the freest and most determined movement, the very movement that promises one of the rare chances for a future, we declare that we above all hold the head of State personally responsible for this crime.

Student-Writer Action Committee (June 25, 1968)

[Letter to a representative of Yugoslav radio-television]

48 rue Madame, Paris (VI)
June 6, 1968

Dear Sir,

Sorry to answer you in writing, but as you anticipated, I am associated as far as I am able with the current movement of upheaval, so that I do not feel inwardly available to deal with the questions that you are asking me about "literature"; in any case, I can do no more than try to show you why these questions are foreign to me.

However, out of friendship for the Yugoslav people and in recognition of their own efforts for liberation, I would not want to leave your request for clarification entirely without a response. First, I would like to say that, whatever the immediate political consequences may be (which have little importance in the end), what happened is such that neither from a theoretical point of view nor from a practical point of view will existence here or elsewhere ever be the same.

During the entire month of May—and particularly from May 18 to May 30—the revolution took place as [if it were] possible, and it would have taken place as [if it were] real (momentarily real), if the French Communist Party (I am referring here to the organization and the apparatus and not to the ever-admirable activists), by shirking its tasks, afraid of causing fear and because they are themselves afraid of the word *communism*, had not done everything to stop the movement and to contribute to reinstalling a Gaullist power that was falling apart, and with it the society that it represents.

Allow me to tell you here what a deplorable and ideologically reprehensible error our Eastern friends—and first of all the Soviet leaders—have made regarding de Gaulle and the Gaullist regime. This regime, for us communist intellectuals, represents the worst there is: for ten years it has imposed a state of political death on us, suppressing all real political life, having no other aim than a preposterous nationalism, reawakening it not only in France but in Germany, laying claim to an anachronistic and morally abject grandeur, maintaining a system of economic exploitation and oppression, finally, confiscating every true possibility of speech and decision in order to profit one extraordinarily authoritarian and arrogant person alone. (For if the right to speech was apparently left to us, it was on condition that this right should remain ineffectual).

For ten years we have undergone this state of political death, and de Gaulle himself was nothing other than the delegate of this death, the representative of a nothingness at once distinguished and vulgar.

On the one hand, there is political death; on the other hand, a latent state of war. For during all this time, in this supposedly tranquil French society—admired (how ridiculous!) by various peoples who are working toward socialism—all the progressive forces represented by the workers, students, and intellectuals were continually in a state of war, living here as in an occupied region, in revolt against the false law imposed and introduced ten years ago by a coup de force.

One might have expected that the immense constraint borne consciously and unconsciously by the new forces—the worker and student youth—would bring about this movement of uprising with such prodigious suddenness, though of course it was impossible to predict it exactly; a movement with an extraordinary dynamism and power of political invention, a movement both of freedom and of refusal. The moment has not come to qualify its features, to name them, that is, to restrain it by depriving it of its force of presence. But what we must indicate already today is that, if this movement constitutes a global movement of contestation aimed at bourgeois society, it is first of all the rupture with the Gaullist regime, with Gaullist society, and with General de Gaulle that it pursues and will pursue by any and every means. This is also why one of its first characteristics should be its antinationalism, in an effort to revive internationalist Marxism and to affirm or reaffirm the essential scope of the international exigency, unfortunately unrecognized for decades by traditional communist parties. This movement is a movement of radical, certainly violent rupture, but it is a very controlled violence, with a communist goal, while it also calls the authorities and all forms of power into question through incessant contestation. It thus appears essentially as a movement of refusal, keeping itself from all premature statements or programs, because it senses that in any statement formulated in a necessarily alienated or distorted discourse there is a risk of being recuperated by the established system (that of industrialized capitalist societies), a system that integrates everything, including culture, however "avant-garde" it may be.

To make my sentiment clear, I am attaching two texts[1] to this letter that we drafted at the beginning of the events with some friends and that, signed by numerous writers (from Sartre to Lacan), show the meaning of our approbation (which is active for some of us): an agreement that is, moreover, linked to our intention as writers and, thereby, excluding all established value. Excuse me once again for this hasty note and with all my best wishes,

Maurice Blanchot

The astonishing feature of the event that distinguishes it from all analogous movements is, of course—and I must content myself with repeating this—that this student uprising could spontaneously and suddenly incite a revolutionary social crisis in an apparently calm and satisfied society, a crisis that translated itself into an active wildcat strike, mobilizing and immobilizing ten to twelve million workers, and this despite the union leaders, despite the advice of all the opposition parties. In a few days, an entire modern society fell into dissolution; the great Law was shattered; the great Theory collapsed; the Transgression was accomplished; and by whom? By a plurality of forces escaping all the frames of contestation, coming literally from nowhere, unlocalized and unlocalizable. This is what I believe is decisive.

Comité: The First Issue

Bulletin Published by the Student-Writer Action Committee in Service of the Movement (October 1968)

[The possible characteristics]

The possible characteristics of this publication:

It too will strive to bring about the rupture; that is, to bring it about in a mode of rupture; hence the necessity of breaking with the traditional habits and privileges of writing.

1. The texts will be anonymous. Anonymity aims not to remove the author's right of possession over what he writes nor even to make him impersonal by freeing him from himself (his history, his person, the suspicion attached to his particularity), but to constitute collective or plural speech: a communism of writing.

2. Thus the texts will be fragmentary: precisely to make plurality possible (a nonunitary plurality), to open a place for it and at the same time never to arrest the process itself—always already ruptured and as if destined to be ruptured, in order to find their meaning not in themselves but in their conjunction-disjunction, their being placed together and in common [*mise en commun*], their relations of difference.

3. Since meaning is given by such a placing in common (the continuity of a series of always discontinuous and even divergent texts, of essentially different forms and "genres"), there are no reasons to differentiate between texts already published elsewhere and texts written for the publication. Often these already-published texts contain a latent possibility of citation, that is, they belong already to the fragmentary or, more simply, to fragments, sentences, paragraphs, which, when put into relation with others, can take on a new meaning or further our research. Abandon any preconceived idea of originality or the privilege of being previously unpublished.

4. Similarly, such information collected as is, in its brute force and without commentary, sparsely or densely punctuating the discontinuous series of texts will also belong to this same research.

5. Thus in this review those who are without words, who are not writers, the very people whom the discourse does not reach—even though it is in this discourse that they believe they can best make themselves heard—must have a place in which to express themselves or to find themselves expressed, whether directly or indirectly.

6. In short, language is given not in the content of the texts nor in their form but through their relations, the necessarily disharmonious ensemble that they may constitute. With this discontinuity that they preserve, through this nonclosure, there will be a search for a more radical language that is situated outside of discourse, outside of culture, and that, while being declarative, should continue to maintain the incessant work of questioning.

7. An essentially irregular publication, bound to a temporal irregularity, just as much as an irregularity of format and formulation.

Thus, there will be three perpetually decentered centers:

—movement as the demand for rupture (the original forces of rupture);

—the possibilities of rupture in the work space (worker-student relations);

—the international exigency (relations with foreigners).

But everything belongs to us, that is to say, we belong to everything and to nothing.

In A State of War

Remain mindful of this truth:

Here (in the French world), where we can say everything, almost everything, we can only speak in enemy territory, in a space where all speech captured by the adversary will be put at his service—a friendly, well-meaning, ferocious enemy. We will never be sufficiently aware of this: we belong to a society against which we are in a state of war; we live in an occupied zone. From 1940 to 1944, quite a large number knew, from instinct and reflection, what needed to be done to live, act, and think in dissidence against the imposed law. But liberation did not come, except in a few places during the days when everything rose up to create a vacancy of the State. If it is true that de Gaulle's first words were "*There won't be a Revolution; its hour has passed,*" then he truly said exactly what he had to say in order to designate himself the new enemy from then on, at the very moment when the old one had just disappeared. What's more, he was too visible, especially beginning in 1958, so much so that one of his most dangerous traits was to have personalized the unseemliness of the regime to the point of caricature, and at the same time to have provided a decent alibi for all the opposing forces.

This situation is relatively new. A century ago and up until the collapse of 1914, when bellicose nationalism absorbed everything, capitalist society held those it dominated on the margin and outside of itself, but it did so by using them. When Marx recommended permanent revolution as a battle cry, when he demanded that workers be armed and then organized into an autonomous proletarian guard, when he encouraged them to form illegal groups (through elections) alongside official groups—sometimes in secret, sometimes openly, in the form of municipal councils or as clubs or workers' committees—it was this very situation of war that he had in view and that must be the everyday truth, the very possibility of living and thinking. This truth, incontestably, was lost, at least in our so-called peaceful societies. If the most important event of 1967 (in addition to the war in Vietnam, the expansion of the guerilla war in Latin America, the proletarian Cultural Revolution in China) is the black uprising in the United States, this is because the last has, precisely, introduced war, open and declared war, within the largest capitalist society. This is what is decisive. A black leader said: "*We will have more and more allies among white progressives because white people will begin to feel black.*" This was said in a very clear and direct sense. The new truth is that here too we must feel (behave) like blacks in a white society: black against our whiteness, black in the struggle against those who dominate, even if it means organizing segregation at their expense, that is, turning it against them, and against ourselves. Segregation: a painful word, an untenable decision. But despite the unease, we must understand clearly that when the bars are made invisible, by ruse and by general consent, the prison not only remains in place but becomes a prison for life, since no one has any notion to struggle and escape from it, and the first task thus becomes to show the bars and even to paint them red. What is class struggle? It is not the struggle to open the ghetto that is the lower class and allow it access to a better class in a satisfying harmony. On the contrary, it is to employ the closure of the ghetto to one's advantage, to forbid any contact between classes that is not disruptive, violent, and destructive, and thus maybe, one day, to change the very law of class structure.

We must understand the demand of this new segregation: it consists in conceding everything to those who already have everything. Yes, all values, truth, knowledge, honorable privileges, beauty, including those of the arts and language, humanity itself—we abandon them to those who feel themselves attuned to the established society: it belongs to them; the Good is on their side. Let them live with this good as with God or with what they call humanism: it is theirs, it only has worth for them, it does not allow them to communicate except among themselves. And for the others? For the others—that is, if possible, for us—penury, speechlessness, the power of nothing, what Marx rightly called "the bad side," that is, the inhuman. This would be another ideology, to be sure, but one that is already radically other, such that to attain it we will need always and ever again to free ourselves from values, including those of freedom as a value already acquired. In other words, and in great seriousness, but not without difficulty: the destruction of the category of the universal.

This will lead to a kind of unreason? True. But one must also understand that the collective mode of thinking in our modern societies is still a dissimulated mode, be it schizophrenia or paranoia or both, and that if we were to accept healing, as we are amicably encouraged to do, we would find ourselves behind invisible bars without knowing it. Some time ago, on French state television a powerful American journalist called Fidel Castro "*the white-faced monkey.*" One must answer him: that's right; the man, the human of capitalist society, is you.

Affirming the Rupture

1. The ultimate goal, which is also to say the immediate and evident goal, that is, the hidden, direct-indirect one, is to affirm the rupture. To affirm it: to organize it and make it ever more real and more radical. What rupture? The rupture with the powers that be, thus with the notion of power, thus with all places where power predominates. This certainly holds for the University, for the idea of knowledge, for the relation determined by a speech that teaches, that leads, and perhaps for all speech, etc., but this holds even more for our very conception of the opposition to power, every time this opposition constitutes itself as a party with power.

2. Radically affirming the rupture: this amounts to saying (this is its first meaning) that we are in a state of war against what exists, everywhere and always; that we exist only in relation to a law that we do not recognize, within a society whose values, truths, ideals, and privileges are foreign to us; that we have to do with an enemy all the more formidable in that he seems to be accommodating, but with whom it should be understood that we will never collude in any way, not even for tactical reasons.

3. Taking on this rupture involves not only extricating, or trying to extricate, forces that tend toward rupture from their integration into established society but also acting so that in reality and each time that it is exercised, without ceasing to be an active refusal, refusal is not merely a negative moment. Politically and philosophically, this is one of the most important features of the movement. In this sense, radical refusal, as it is carried on by the movement and as we also must carry it on, goes far beyond simple negativity, if it is to be the very negation of that which has not yet been posed and affirmed. Clarifying what is peculiar and singular in this refusal is one of the theoretical tasks of the new political thinking. The theoretical obviously does not consist in elaborating a program or a platform but, on the contrary, outside of any programmatic project and even any project, in maintaining a *refusal that affirms*, in releasing or maintaining an affirmation that does not come to any arrangement but that undoes arrangements, even its own, since it is related to dis-arrangement or disarray or even the nonstructurable. This decision of refusal is not a power, nor a power to negate, nor negation in relation to an always already posed affirmation. This decision is what we name when we inject spontaneity into the "revolutionary" process, with the proviso that this notion of *spontaneity* is subject to caution in many respects, as it traffics more than one dubious ideal—for example, a sort of vitalism, natural auto-creativity, etc.

[Today]

Today, the refusal to collaborate with all the cultural institutions of Gaullist power must impose itself as an absolute decision—just as it did during the war from 1940 to 1944—on every writer and every artist in opposition. Culture is the place where power always finds accomplices. By means of culture, it recuperates and reduces all free speech. We must struggle against this complicity of culture; we must show that in culture there is a relation of possession through meaning and a use of repressive forces functioning independently of the social game.

[Political death]

When we happen to say, speaking of someone, as if out of forgetfulness, "he is politically dead," we know that not only does this judgment affect the other, it affects us all, or very nearly so. We must accept this, even welcome and endorse it. Political death keeps vigil in us, "a light in the tomb," to save us from every distraction, every journalistic rumination, every word of facile recrimination—more precisely, from every possibility of survival. Political death, which makes the unacceptable acceptable, is not an individual phenomenon. We participate in it whether we want to or not. And in French society, the higher one goes, the more death grows, reaching, at the top, a ridiculous excess: a presence of petrified humanity. If today there is a politically dead man in this country, it is the one who carries—does he carry it?—the title of President of the Republic, a Republic to which he is just as foreign as he is to any living political future. He is an actor, playing a role borrowed from the oldest story, just as his language is the language of a role, an imitated speech at times so anachronistic that it seems to have been always posthumous. Naturally, he does not know this. He believes in his role, believing that he magnifies the present, whereas he parodies the past. And this dead man, unaware that he is dead, is impressive with the great stature of death, with the dead obstinacy that passes for authority, and at times with the obnoxious, distinguished vulgarity that signifies the dissolution of being-dead. A strange, insulting presence, in whom we see an old world persevering and in which, let us not forget, we feel ourselves dying splendidly and laughably.

For he himself is nothing, he is nothing but the delegate of our own political death; he is a victim too, a mask behind which there is nothing.

The first task is thus to make the higher alibi disappear, then, on every level, the alibi of alibis. Let us not believe that we are politically alive because we participate with moderation in legal opposition. And let us not believe we are intellectually alive because we participate in a highly developed culture where contestation is the rule, where criticism and even negation are still a sign of belonging. Some time ago, a Parisian minister declared—with the lack of intelligence that comes with vanity—that the fate of the world will not be played out in Bolivia. It is played out there just as much as it is in France, here where the only principle of government is stability and the only change expected is the death of a spectral old man who always seems to wonder whether he is in the Pantheon or not and whether his memory, which doesn't forget anything, has not simply forgotten the imperceptible event of his end: which is to say, the end of a simulacrum.

If he survives, let us take advantage of his survival to gain consciousness of the living-dead state that we share with him, but in keeping the supplementary right to denounce our destruction, even if it is by means of words that are already destroyed themselves. From this, here and there, today, tomorrow, others will perhaps derive a new and strong power to destroy.

Tomorrow was May: the infinite power of destruction-construction.

[The streets]

Just as it undertook the violent elimination of the student uprising, General de Gaulle's government decided to discipline the people as a whole.

The dissolution (lacking any legal foundation) of opposition movements has only this goal: to allow searches without warrants, to facilitate arbitrary arrests (more that a hundred arrest warrants), as well as to reactivate the special courts—an indispensable tool of all State terrorism—and, finally, to prevent any meetings or gatherings. In other words, as the president of the Republic declared in a formula that everyone should remember because it clearly shows what he is and what he wants: nothing should happen anywhere, neither in the streets nor in public buildings (Universities, Parliaments). This amounts to decreeing POLITICAL DEATH.

An unmistakable sign: the invasion of the street by plainclothes police. They are not there only to surveil declared opponents. They are everywhere, in every place that attracts their suspicion, near cinemas, in cafés, even in museums, coming closer as soon as three or four people gather, having an innocent discussion; invisible, yet very visible. Each citizen must learn that the streets do not belong to him any longer but belong only to the regime, which wants to impose muteness and suffocation there.

Why this frightened mobilization?

Since May, the streets have awakened: they speak. This is one of the decisive changes. They have become alive, powerful, and sovereign once again: the place of all possible freedom. It is against this sovereign word of the streets that the most dangerous apparatus of insidious repression and brutal force has been put into place, threatening everyone. Each one of us should understand what is at stake. When there are demonstrations, these demonstrations do not concern only the small or large number of those who participate in them: they express the right of all to be free in the streets, freely to be a passerby and to make something happen in the streets. This is the first right.

July 17, 1968

[Communism without heirs]

One must recall simple things that are always forgotten: there is nothing that distinguishes the movements of patriotism, chauvinism, and nationalism except that nationalism is the consistent ideology of which patriotism is the sentimental affirmation (as obnoxious declarations still show: "*I married France*").[1] Everything that through values and through feelings roots men in a time, in a history, and in a language is the principle of alienation constituting man as privileged in his particularity (French, the precious French blood), imprisoning him in a contentment with his own reality, and leading him to propose it as an example or to impose it as a conquering affirmation. Marx said with calm force: the end of alienation only begins if man is willing to come out of himself (out of everything that institutes him as interiority): out of religion, out of the family, and out of the State. This call to the outside, an outside that is neither another world nor a hidden world, is the only movement that can oppose all forms of patriotism, whatever they may be.

- Patriotism is the most prodigious power of integration, being that which, in the intimacy of thought, in everyday practice, in political movement, is at work to reconcile everything—works, men, classes —to prevent all class struggle, to found unity in the name of values that particularize (national particularism promoted as universal), and to set aside the necessary division of an infinite destruction. The day when, through a tactical ruse, international communism agreed to serve the national community and was ashamed to be considered the foreigner's party, it lost what Lenin called its soul. Even speaking of the fatherland of the revolution, of the homeland of socialism, is the least felicitous metaphor, the most likely to awaken the need to be home somewhere, to subject oneself to the Father, to the law of the Father, to the benediction of the Father. A single word, and the man who wanted to free himself is reconciled. The party [*parti*] becomes, in turn, the fatherland [*patrie*]. The socialists (who are no more ridiculous in this than other intransigent progressives) say with an emotion that is no doubt very touching: the party is family for us, and, of course, we sacrifice everything for the survival of the family, beginning with socialism. I would say that, if the glorious call "fatherland or death" did not privilege the word *death* and consequently the word *life*, it would risk leading only to a kind of awful mystification, for the fatherland is precisely death, the false life that perpetuates dead values, or else the tiresome tragic death, the death of heroes, detestable heroes.

- Communism is what excludes (and excludes itself from) any already constituted community. The proletarian class, community without any common denominator other than penury, dissatisfaction, and lack in every sense of the term.
- Communism that accommodates: whereas Lenin, not shying from this word, said that the soul of communism is what makes it intolerable, intractable. To reflect on the error of humanism is to reflect on the error of comfortable communism, when the latter, not wanting to lose anything, comes to be reconciled with everything, including values that are human, all too human: national values.
- Communism cannot be an heir. We must be convinced of this: it is not even the heir of itself and is always called upon to allow the loss, at least momentarily, yet radically, of the legacy of centuries, however venerable this legacy may be. The theoretical hiatus is absolute; the rupture, in fact, is decisive. Between the liberal capitalist world, our world, and the present of the communist exigency (present without presence), there is only the dash [*trait d'union*] of a disaster, an astral change.

[For a long time, brutality]

For a long time, brutality, at times of language, at others of action, has remained the only point by which the so-called communist parties and socialist states believe they remain in contact with the revolutionary force of rupture. The more their political, ideological, and social practice is conservative and tends only to maintain the status quo, the more this practice is imposed by domination or intimidation. In a traditional communist party, the elements that are called "hard" are always the weakest, which is to say, the most mediocre. Why? Their function is to set aside any true decision and to impede the production of new concepts. This mediocrity is not even the fault of an apparatus or the effect of bureaucracy; it does not come from individual psychology; it is not personal mediocrity. It is the necessary support of dogmatism, that is, a theoretical and practical void that needs "hardness"—"rigidity" (ossified *praxis*), both as an alibi and as a vector. Which does not mean that these states will not be capable of resorting to considerable actions, but that these actions: (1) are always repetitive; they never innovate; they reproduce the same "erroneous" solutions through a false comparison of situations; (2) are always repressive. One initiates movement only so as to show immobility: impeding, arresting, and closing off the dangerous future.

One must not be content to remark that these parties or these states would be reformist or revisionist, their only nonbourgeois feature being their methods of terror: they are neither reformists, nor revolutionaries, nor terrorists (in the revolutionary sense), nor even—this, after all, is the structural modification—capitalist. They are frozen in a noncapitalist and nonsocialist order and ethic that are translated into a repressive state apparatus of management and into a state superpower. Why this is so and what the exact characteristics of this situation are, as well as the possibilities for modifying it, that is what we should be looking for.

[Tracts, posters, bulletins]

Writing *on* . . . is, in any case, inappropriate. But writing on the event that is precisely destined (among others) no longer to allow us ever to write *on* . . .—epitaph, commentary, analysis, panegyric, condemnation—is to falsify it in advance and to have always already missed it. We will never write on what took place or didn't take place in May: not out of respect, nor from a concern not to restrain the event by circumscribing it. We admit that this refusal is one of the points where writing and the decision of rupture coincide: both are always imminent and unpredictable.

- Dozens of books have already been published dealing with what happened, or didn't happen, in May. They are generally intelligent, partially right, and maybe useful. Written by sociologists, professors, journalists, and even activists. Naturally, no one expected that the force of the movement, which in a way blocks it, would make the reality and the possibility of the book disappear: that is, its end and completion, its fulfillment.
- The book has not disappeared; this must be acknowledged. Nonetheless, we can say that everything that in the history of our culture, and in history tout court, incessantly destines writing not for the book but for the absence of the book has continued to announce the upheaval, by preparing for it. There will still be books and, what's worse, beautiful books. But mural writing, this mode that is neither inscription nor enunciation, the tracts that are hastily distributed in the streets

and are the manifestation of the haste of the streets, the posters that do not need to be read but are like a challenge to every law, words of disorder,[1] the speech outside of discourse that marks our steps, political cries—and bulletins by the dozen, like this one, everything that disturbs, calls, threatens, and finally questions without expecting an answer, without resting in certainty, never will we enclose it in a book, which, even when open, tends toward closure, a refined form of oppression.

- In May, there is no book on May—not due to a lack of time or due to the necessity "to act," but because of a more decisive obstacle: it is written elsewhere, in a world devoid of publication; it is distributed with the police and in a certain way with their help, violence against violence. This arrest of the book [*arrêt du livre*] is also an arrest of history that, far from leading us back before culture, designates a point well beyond culture, and this is what most provokes authority, power, and the law. May this bulletin prolong this arrest, while preventing it from being arrested, suspended, ended. No more books, never again a book, so long as we maintain our relation with the upheaval of the rupture.
- Tracts, posters, bulletins, words of the streets, infinite words—it is not through a concern for effectiveness that they become imperative. Effective or not, they belong to the decision of the instant. They appear, and they disappear. They do not say everything; on the contrary, they ruin everything; they are outside of everything. They act and reflect fragmentarily. They do not leave a trace: trait without trace. Like words on the wall, they are written in insecurity, received under threat; they carry the danger themselves and then pass with the passerby who transmits, loses, or forgets them.

Letter to Ilija Bojovic

Dear Ilija Bojovic,

I am terribly sorry for my incapacity to answer your questions directly. A remark before everything else: if I am not mistaken, I think I have always refused to get taken in by the play of questions. Why? One can respond only to the interlocutor, and yet it is clear that the one who succeeds in asking a good question, a true question, has accomplished his duty and there is nothing left but to withdraw. But if there is in fact a response, it can elicit a new question or still refer to the initial questioning. Writing is linked to the demand of an always indirect and unformulated question, a demand so strong and accusatory that one takes responsibility for it even before responding to it.

With this affirmation, I think I have already said everything. I would like to add another general comment in order to better justify my reservations concerning the particular questions you are asking me. Indeed, books are continually published in all countries and in all languages. Some are considered critical works, while others are called novels or even poetry. These differentiations will probably be maintained for a long time, or they will yield to new differentiations. The book will always exist, even long after the notion of the book will have been exhausted. It is nonetheless necessary to add an observation. Since Mallarmé (let us take this name as a reference), these differentiations have become sterile, for it is through them that a complete understanding about what we continue to call literature came to light, but with a revivified seriousness and responsibility. In other words, one might say that essays, novels, and poems exist and are written only to make literary work possible, to pose and spread the following question, thanks to this work: What is at stake for contemporary man in the statement that something like art or literature exists? This is an extremely urgent and historically necessary question, which was and will be veiled by the secular tradition of aestheticism.

I do not mean to say that this moment is over; that would be a senseless statement. The magnificent experiment of the Surrealists showed that literature takes hold of what we do or write, and we continue to belong to the civilization of the book. But literary work in itself, as well as its quest, contributes to shattering the principles and truths that literature protects. This work has appeared (this is not the first time), for it is correlated with the global movement of science and is borne by the entire history of philosophy. The question of language has been posed by diverse works in the most original and imperious ways, and likewise through this question another question arises, which perhaps cancels it (the result of the action) and which is summed up in the word *writing*, "this insane game of writing." As if the epoch of literature had to be followed, outside of time, by the time of writing.

Writing, the demand of writing (not only the writing that was always put at the service of the spoken word or ideological thinking but, on the contrary, writing gently liberated by its own force as if it gave itself over to the questioning that it alone conceals), gradually frees all other possibilities, an anonymous way of being in relation and communicating (which puts everything into question, first of all ideas concerning God, the Self, Truth, and then the Book and the Work themselves), so that this writing considered in its enigmatic austerity should not have its finality in the Book, somehow a mark of the end, but writing that one could envisage outside of discourse, outside of language.

Excuse me for these severe remarks; they are necessary. What I am trying to say (and to problematize) is this: writing, as I have conceived of it, seems to suppose a change of epoch and, to speak hyperbolically, the end of History, and in this sense it goes beyond the advent of communism. The latter is recognized as supreme; it does not leave anything in peace, for communism is still on the other side of communism. In an invisible way, writing is called on to destroy, to annihilate a discourse in which we were so unhappy, comfortably settled, enclosed. From this point of view, writing is the greatest force, for it inevitably violates the Law—all laws, as well as its own law. Writing is fundamentally dangerous, innocently dangerous. It is to this, in the end, that I wanted to draw your attention.

Maurice Blanchot

[That the immense constraint]

That the immense constraint consciously and unconsciously borne by the new forces—the worker and student youth—would bring about this movement of uprising with such prodigious suddenness was foreseeable, though of course it was impossible to predict it exactly: a movement with an extraordinary dynamism and power of political invention, a movement both of freedom and of refusal. The moment has not come to delineate its characteristics, to name it, that is, to restrain it. But what we must remind our Eastern friends is that if this movement constitutes a global movement of contestation aimed at bourgeois society, it is first of all the rupture with the Gaullist regime, with Gaullist society, that it has asserted in such a striking fashion and that it pursues and will pursue by any and every means. This is also why one of its first characteristics is antinationalism, in an effort to revive internationalist practices and to affirm or reaffirm the essential scope of the international exigency, unfortunately unrecognized for decades by traditional communist parties. This movement is a movement of radical, indeed violent rupture, but it is a very controlled violence, with a communist goal, while it also calls the authorities and all forms of power into question through incessant contestation. It thus appears essentially as a movement of refusal, keeping itself from any premature statements or programs, because it senses that in any statement formulated in a necessarily alienated or distorted discourse there is a risk of being recuperated by the established system (of industrialized capitalist societies), a system that integrates everything, including culture, however "avant-garde" it may be.

[Exemplary acts]

There is no Revolution without "exemplary acts." But it is Revolution itself, this suddenly decisive change by which a society confounds itself with its own rupture, which gives any act its explosive force, its potential to be an example, which is to say, without example.

I think that at certain moments the revolution of May, after being clarified by several demonstrations in which it seemed to be present, developed a dangerous tendency—and thus became too methodical—to seek systematically for ways to embody its mobilizing potential in somehow significant acts, as it were. Thus we ended up with the burning of the Paris Bourse, a dull symbol, whereas the stock market itself cannot be burned. Similarly, the storming of the Odéon, however joyous, made it too easy to believe that culture had thereby been liberated, while it was decaying in that place, where it performed only the delectable enjoyment of its own decay (which is the ultimate sign of bourgeois culture).[1] One comes to think that the thesis of *symbolic efficacy* (Lévi-Strauss) was applied in many cases without rhyme or reason and showed its limitations.

The storming of the Bastille and the death—which is to say, the condemnation—of the king were prodigiously exemplary acts; likewise the constitution of the Petrograd commune by Trotsky and the storming of the Winter Palace by the Baltic seamen, but not the obscure death of the czar, a simple practical precaution.

The night of the barricades, the occupation of the Sorbonne, the "No" to the Grenelle agreement, the active strikes, Flins—among others—were moments when revolutionary possibility not only was present but was affirmed in a negation that, while opening a void and stopping time, also pointed toward the future. In each case, there was a transgression: an innocent transgression.[2] The law (the law of power: a weak law; the law of the Party: a more serious authority) was overthrown or, better yet, neglected—or else, it was Transgression itself, as an impossible possibility, that alone still gave a little meaning to the otherwise erased Interdiction.

We will have to come back to all of this. Let us say briefly that an "exemplary act" is such because it goes beyond itself while coming from very far away, superseding itself and in an instant, with a shattering suddenness, exploding its limits. The barricades were exemplary because they meant: (1) we will stay here, we have freed up a space of nonlaw; (2) from now on, it's war, we are fighters and not demonstrators; (3) we have crossed over to the other side of fear; (4) we raise barricades through a common effort by which the new community, the Commune II, is affirmed; (5) the objective being an occupied Sorbonne, this poor building, where obsolete knowledge was taught for a millennium, suddenly became once again, in an extraordinarily unusual way, a sign exalted by interdiction: the sign of new knowledge to be reconquered or reinvented, knowledge without law, freed from law, and, as such, nonknowledge—henceforth, an incessant speech. I would also say that perhaps what makes for an exemplary act, what makes it vertiginous and overwhelming, is that it bears the necessity of violence, does violence, discloses violence that has been suffered for too long, suddenly intolerable, and responds to it with a decision of infinite violence, which is sometimes terrible, sometimes calm. And so, the highest violence was no doubt in an instant of nonviolence, when, to reject the ban (the banning of Cohn-Bendit was the pathetic "exemplary act" of the powers that be[3]), thousands of workers and students—revolutionaries then in an absolute sense—stamped their feet and chanted: "*We are all German Jews.*" Never had this been said anywhere, never at any moment: inaugural speech, opening and overthrowing the frontiers, opening and disrupting the future.

[Two characteristic innovations]

Two characteristic innovations in the vocabulary, and thus the ideology, of the P.C.F.,[1] in the course of the month of July:

1. For the first time, the general secretary of the party (in a report to the central Committee) uses the words *subversive* and *insurrection* in a violently reproachful sense, a sense reserved until now for the language of the grande and petite bourgeoisie.

2. An important member of the central Committee of the party, François Billoux, denounces what he calls "*anti-authoritarian propaganda*" as reactionary. Why? Because this propaganda hurts the Communist Party, which is to say, its "apparatus" and its "organization," which can function only in an authoritarian manner.

Hence the following consequence, among others: it is recommended, from now on, no longer to accuse General de Gaulle's regime of authoritarianism (a sickness of authority).

[A rupture in time: revolution]

As soon as, through the movement of forces tending toward rupture, revolution appears possible, in a possibility that is not abstract but rather historically and concretely determined, it is in these moments, at these instants, that revolution takes place. The only mode of presence of revolution is its real possibility. Then there is a state of arrest and suspension. In this suspension, society undoes itself entirely. The law collapses. Transgression occurs: for a moment, there is innocence; interrupted history.

Walter Benjamin: "The conscious desire to rupture the continuity of history belongs to the revolutionary classes in the moment of action. Such a consciousness was asserted during the July Revolution.[1] On the evening of the first day of fighting, the clocks in towers were fired upon, simultaneously but independently, from various places in Paris."[2]

[For Comrade Castro]

Let us set aside our feelings, let us try to think outside of the moral space that is left, whether we want to or not, the space of our habits and our dependency, and let us search, along with others, for the conclusions we must reach concerning the military intervention in Czechoslovakia.[1]

1. Neither the communist exigency nor revolutionary reason is at all implicated in this crude demonstration of force, which is as politically unbearable as it is ideologically misplaced. The fact that Castro approves of it only shows that Castro, even if he thinks he speaks in the name of the Cuban communist party, is capable of speaking against the Cuban revolution, which is to say, of allowing himself to be misled by a false conception of internationalism.

2. Violated borders, misunderstood sovereignty, demolished institutions: if the international movement has been contravened, it is not by these events but by the perfectly inappropriate claim that international demands can be repressive and that national armies, the most brutal affirmation of bellicose nationalism, can invoke the sort of revolutionary necessity presupposed by the process of world communism. Only speech—and even then speech that is never given, but must be sought—can carry forth international reason on the basis of the structures that make it possible. International practice is the practice of a language that seeks out its common space—violently, at times—whenever productive

forces, in their discrepancy with the conditions of production, have delineated this space as the interplay of struggling social forces, or else by proposing its elaboration through politics and ideology.

3. Let us admit (a hypothesis that stems from the most mediocre journalistic speculation and not from "solid analysis") that Czechoslovakia, as Castro claims, was threatening to fall "into the hands of capitalism."[1] The primary means, if not to send it rushing in that direction, then at least to slow down communist progression indefinitely, is to identify socialism[2] with military repression and, consequently, nonsocialism with a certain form of independence.

4. The Soviet Union's policy is an unprincipled combination of superpower strategy (a glacis policy, a justifiable anxiety toward other powers) and of ideological pretension. The result is that the Soviet Union uses internationalism, which it dares to call "proletarian," for ends that contradict it and by means that ruin it.

5. The notion of "Stalinism," the system that this notion supports, the moral character that is implicated within it (the perversions of a superpowerful individual) cannot allow us to dispense with all explanatory efforts to account for the state of things, every time there is an "alteration of the revolutionary ideal." What is clear is that the Revolution never happens once and for all. As soon as it happens, the struggle by which it perpetuates itself threatens to further distance it from itself, impeding all linear progression in its movement.

6. Revolution is terrible. But martial invasion can in no way be assimilated to what is necessarily excessive—impossible—in revolutionary terror, when it is called upon to derange and transgress all law. The Napoleonic armies liberated peoples by overthrowing governments and then subjected them in the name of crowned universal liberty, "the world soul" passing back and forth beneath the Philosopher's windows.[3] Here we are very far removed from Jacobin ideology. Let us consider how many communists (Soviets, Poles, Hungarians, Bulgarians, and East Germans), especially if they are part of the occupation forces, have felt themselves brutally ejected, because of the role of oppressors that they were made to play, from the revolutionary possibility to which, like the Czechs and like us, they have devoted their right to live and die.

7. The Czech resistance must be understood not as a national resistance but as a revolutionary resistance. Everything must be done to preserve this meaning, especially here, to the extent that we are able to use the means of struggle, whose prodigious subversive efficiency this resistance has recalled to us, against Gaullist and capitalist oppression.

8. The process of liberalization underway since January 1968 in Czechoslovakia poses certain risks; this cannot be denied. The questioning, in a liberated speech, of an order that has been fixed prematurely and imposed by the police under the false title of socialism can tend toward either a facile liberalism, whose future is the bourgeois society of the past, or a dissolution of the state leading to revolutionary explosion. The USSR does not accept these risks. It is ideologically weak; this is why it resorts to military force. Castro knows this. He also knows that, if Cuba were situated on the Russian border, it would have been "liberated" from Castro a long time ago. Why, then, such an error in judgment? Is he, by some strange anomaly, confusing guerilla warfare and war, military intervention and revolutionary violence? Comrade Castro, do not dig your own grave, and if you are so tempted, let yourself slip into it from the natural exhaustion of power. Let us write on the walls of Havana, as was magnificently written on the walls of Prague: LENIN WAKE UP!

[Ideological surrender]

Force belongs to the state. It has law and legitimacy to itself, and with them it protects itself in order to monopolize all means of domination. Violence is either individual, popular, or class based. Violence becomes revolutionary whenever it tends ideologically toward rupture, shaking up an order based on privilege and a government based on inequality. There have been three demonstrations of force in the history of Czechoslovakia:

1. the threat, Soviet armies operating in "friendly" territory;
2. declared attack, military invasion, armed occupation;
3. the murderous Moscow treaty, the constraint accepted, that is, consent granted to the intolerable: finally, ideological surrender (the auto-critique of certain Czech leaders, qualified, it is true, by the frankness of other declarations), which, even if it is devoid of all credibility, goes to destroy the possibility of language by turning it into the spoils of war seized by power.

This is obviously the worst. The Soviet State is without force despite its force so long as it remains unable to freeze the revolutionary word, to depreciate it by subjecting its perilous freedom to servile morality. The rest is almost nothing: it is the hereditary charnel house.

[Clandestine resistance out in the open]

Clandestine resistance out in the open—the manifesto of two thousand words,[1] which some of us criticized, contains the sentence: "*Nonetheless we are speaking.*" This movement of possible speech would have sufficed to establish ardent and rigorous relations between the May of Prague and the May of Paris. The same infinite, uncontrollable speech has since spoken through secret radios, been written on walls, on trees, on shop windows, on the dust of pathways, on Russian tanks, and is now speaking through a silence that lets it seep through. It was to be expected that this would not be tolerated by a State without language, the Soviet State, any more than it would have been tolerated by a State that pretends to monopolize language, the Gaullist State. And let us understand thoroughly that this is not simply an issue of the freedom of the press. Something entirely different is at stake: an excessive, irrepressible, incessant movement, the impetus of outrageous speech, always speaking beyond, going beyond, spilling over, and thus threatening everything that contains and everything that limits; the very speech that transgresses. And it is not at all capable of being assimilated to this procedure of "dialogue" that liberal stupidity and hypocrisy offer as the final term of free power, whereas dialogue, in its binary structure, destined for the propriety of an exchange of compromises, tends to reduce to indifference a plural speech that must always remain different, speaking out of difference, to the point of rupture, without stopping, always and ever again.

Members of the Czech resistance have said that, during the days when they had no law other than enemy military power, they were never freer through words and through writing than they were then. May this freedom before the enemy—clandestine resistance out in the open—be ours along with them.

[Reading Marx]

In Marx, and always coming from Marx, we see three kinds of speech taking form and gathering force, all three of which are necessary, but separated and more than opposed, as if they were juxtaposed. The disparity that holds them together designates a plurality of demands, to which everyone who speaks and writes since Marx cannot fail to feel subjected, unless he feels himself to be failing at everything.

1. The first of these kinds of speech is direct but lengthy. In it, Marx appears as the "writer of thought," in the sense that it emerges from the tradition, makes use of the philosophical *logos*, helps itself to major names borrowed from Hegel or not (this is without importance), and is elaborated in the element of reflection. Lengthy, insofar as the entire history of *logos* is reaffirmed in it, but doubly direct, for not only does it have something to say, what it says is an answer, inscribed in the form of an answer. These formally decisive responses, given as final and as if introduced by history, can only take on a truth value at the moment when history is arrested or ruptured. Giving a response—alienation, the primacy of need, history as a process of material practice, the total man—it nevertheless leaves the questions to which it responds undetermined or undecided: depending on how today's or yesterday's readers formulate differently what, according to them, should take the place of such an absence of question—thereby filling a void that should instead be rendered ever emptier—this speech of Marx is interpreted at times as humanism, or indeed as historicism, and at times as atheism, antihumanism, or even nihilism.

2. The second kind of speech is political: it is brief and direct, more than brief and direct, because it short-circuits all speech. It no longer carries meaning but is a call, a gesture of violence, a decision of rupture. It does not say anything as such; it is the urgency of what it announces, linked to an impatient and always excessive demand, for excess is its only measure: thereby calling to the struggle and even (what we ourselves hurry to forget) positing "*revolutionary terror*," recommending "*permanent revolution*," and always designating revolution not as an eventual necessity but as *imminence*, for it is characteristic of revolution to brook no delay, if it opens and crosses time, giving itself to be lived as an ever present demand.

3. The third speech is the indirect (and therefore the lengthiest) speech, that of scientific discourse. In this respect, Marx is honored and recognized by other representatives of knowledge. He is thus a man of science, responds to the scientist's ethic, and agrees to submit to every critical revision. This is the Marx who appropriates the maxim *de omnibus dubitandum* and states: "I call 'vile' any man who tries to accommodate science to interests that are foreign and exterior to it." And yet, *Capital* is an essentially subversive work. It is less so because it would lead, through paths of scientific objectivity, to revolution as a necessary consequence than because it includes a mode of theoretical thinking, without explicitly formulating it, that upsets the idea of science itself. Neither science nor thinking emerges intact from Marx's oeuvre, and this in the strongest sense, insofar as it designates science as a radical transformation of itself,

a theory of a mutation always at work in practice, as well as, in this practice, an always theoretical mutation.

Let us not further develop these remarks here. Marx's example helps us to understand that the speech of writing, the speech of incessant contestation, must constantly develop and break away from itself in *multiple* forms. Communist speech is always *at the same time* tacit and violent, political and scientific, direct, indirect, total and fragmentary, lengthy, and almost instantaneous. Marx does not live comfortably with this plurality of languages, which always clash and come apart in him. Even if these languages seem to converge toward the same end, they could not be translated into one another. It is their heterogeneity, the gap or the distance that throws them off center, that make them noncontemporary and that, producing an effect of irreducible distortion, oblige those who must embark on a reading (a practice) to submit themselves to an endless reworking.

The word *science* becomes a key word once again. Let us admit this much. But let us also remind ourselves that, if there are sciences, there is not yet science, because the scientificity of science always depends on ideology, an ideology that no particular science, albeit human science, could reduce today, and, moreover, let us remember that no writer, even a Marxist, would be able to set himself to writing as to a form of knowledge, for literature (the demand to write, when it takes charge of every force and form of dissolution and transformation) only becomes science by the same movement that leads science to become literature in turn, an inscribed discourse, which falls, as usual, into the "insane game of writing."[1]

On the Movement

May, a revolution by idea, desire, and imagination, risks becoming a purely ideal and imaginary event if this revolution does not renounce itself and yield to new organization and strategies.

In other words, the "movement" (insofar as this term has any meaning and does not conceal a restless form of immobility), rather than being sheltered in academic contestation, must try to express itself through a *primarily social struggle*, an always collective struggle involving every oppressed category, mobilizing every form of popular energy. Everything must thus be done so that conflicts that modern society has always avoided and that have now become everyday public reality may express themselves up to the breaking point. An extremely difficult struggle, *which is why small isolated acts*, as well as all initiatives *that tend only toward spectacle* and that cannot be taken up by the entirety of the struggling classes *must be cast aside*. A battle that is all the more difficult given that, in some way and on a representative level, a victorious outcome has already occurred without having been politically and institutionally effective, since the issue outstripped the usual political possibilities, and entirely so.

Thus, the first danger to avoid is that the movement should seem reduced to a student movement, that it confine itself to universities and schools. What was its force in May? The fact is that students never acted as students in this so-called student action, but as those who unveiled a collective crisis, as the bearers of a power of rupture questioning the regime, the State, and society. The University was only a point of departure; we should not look to use it as a shelter out of ease, complacency, and habit. Let us prepare and organize ourselves for other, much more serious, and, admittedly, far more violent battles, for which patience, discipline, and daily and nightly work, in view of a common praxis, will be necessary.

Critique of the Movement

I consider it necessary to begin radically and critically to question what we call the movement. This is both necessary and possible. No party would tolerate such questioning, above all if it were a party whose theoretical and practical struggle is meant to transform the world. The Communist Party would do so less than any other, because it believes it embodies the seriousness and intransigence of a new law that demands and comprehends everything.

1. The weakness of the movement was also its force, and its force is to have succeeded prodigiously, in conditions that made its success brilliant but left it without any future political means, without the power of institution. Very many observers, including well-meaning ones, say that it was important, but that it failed. This is false. It was important and it realized itself in a sovereign manner. We speak of revolution, a very equivocal term, but one must accept that we speak of it and say: it's true, there was a revolution; the revolution took place. The movement of May was a REVOLUTION, with the searing intensity and brilliance of an event that was accomplished and thereby changed everything.

2. A revolution unlike any other, incapable of being incorporated into any model. More philosophical than political; more social than institutional; more exemplary than real; destroying everything without any destructive element, destroying, rather than the past, the very present in which it was accomplished; and not seeking to give itself a future, extremely indifferent toward the possible future, as if the time that it sought to cleave open was already beyond its usual determinations. This took place. The decision of radical, one might say absolute, DISCONTINUITY was made, separating not only two periods in history but history and a possibility that already no longer belongs to it directly.

3. It must be added that all the features that seemed to mark what has been called the failure of May were, on the contrary, signs of its accomplishment. *From the point of view of ideas*, this would be easy to show. But *politically, too*: the regime crumbled; de Gaulle disappeared in a manner much more disastrous for himself and for the order he asserts and pretends to maintain than if he had, indeed, never returned from his trip to Germany and had been buried there somewhere in Frederick Barbarossa's cave.[1] The electoral victory of Gaullism, which was *fabulous* in the strict sense of the word, justly confirmed the ruin of an entire system behind the illusion and saved appearances. A simple fact: it is the political security that such a victory seemed to guarantee to the party of Order, causing the upheaval of the whole to be entirely forgotten, that precipitated the financial collapse of the whole, which was technically unjustified. We are living off appearances. Everything is a sham. Another example: poor Mr. Faure's reform; reform of what, for what?[2] We must say what the lucid teachers already know: there is no more university; there is a great and

venerable, barely camouflaged hole, a game of ceremonies, occasionally traversed by savage forces or by a savagery that is both ritualistic and spectacular. Rectors, deans, professors, students, dissidents, counter-dissidents, all move in order to cover over the void, a void that is governed by the rules of dead time.

4. The fact that May took place, accomplishing its work, this is what needs to be questioned and what, moreover, poses the greatest difficulties to the movement itself: a kind of everyday impossibility that is full of danger (and perhaps promise). I will only articulate some of these dangers, leaving the task of pursuing or contradicting this analysis to others.

(a) The temptation to repeat May, as if May had not taken place or as if it had failed, so that it might someday reach its conclusion. Thus we see the same tactics of agitation that had meaning and effect in February-March-April poorly and painfully retried, with only a supplement of gestures and resources inexhaustibly provided by the errors of a regime that is incapable of realizing that it no longer exists and yet is conscious of its own impotence.

(b) The temptation to continue May, without noticing that all the force of originality of this revolution is to offer no precedent, no foundation, not even for its own success, for it has made itself impossible as such, leaving only a trace that divides everything, sky and earth, like lightening. NOTHING WILL BE AS IT WAS. Thinking and writing, organizing and disorganizing: everything is posed in other terms, and not only are the problems new but the problematic itself has changed. In particular, all the problems of revolutionary struggle, and above all of class struggle, have taken a different form.

(c) The worst aspect (not the most dangerous, only the most tiresome) is that in the destruction of the traditional, a new tradition is being constituted, which is respected, even sanctified, in turn. Here again, only a few suggestions: it suffices that certain key words be uttered—such as *spontaneity*, *self-management*, *dual power*, *symbolic action*, *open general assembly*, *action committee*—for the "movement" to be reassured of itself, certain, then, of prolonging itself without losing any of its original truth. The same holds for the prestige (which must be deemed ill considered) of the word *student*, implicitly considered equivalent to the word *revolutionary* (which is misused no less), to the point that no matter what campus disturbance, wherever in the world it may be—even if it is a pathetic uproar about a thesis or a student procession for Saint Nicholas Day—seems to be a prodigious enterprise of subversion to both the opponents and the bearers of power. And, of course, it is the group in power, equally idiotic and excessively authoritarian, haunted by the memory of terror with which May has left it, that falls into the trap of repetition each time, locking itself inside, along with its adversaries, and tumbling around with them in an immobile movement in which everything is repeated without being renewed. And yet this struggle forces repetition to exhibit its power of death, a dead power that at length can provoke the invisible dissolution of the whole.

5. These remarks are only projects for reflection. The conclusion toward which some of them tend is that the May revolution, because it was global, because it changed everything, also left everything intact. I do not believe this, but from now on I will hold onto an exigency: to become fully conscious, and always anew, that we are at the end of history, so that most of our inherited notions, beginning with the ones from the revolutionary tradition, must be reexamined and, as such, refuted. The discontinuity that May represented (no less than produced) strikes language and ideological action equally. Let us admit that Marx, Lenin, and Bakunin have come closer together and come farther apart. There is an absolute void behind us and before us—and we must think and act without help, without any other support than the radicality of this emptiness. Once more, everything has changed. Even internationalism is different. Let us not be mystified. Let us put everything into question, including our own certainties and verbal hopes. THE REVOLUTION IS BEHIND US: it is already an object of consumption and, occasionally, of enjoyment. But what is before us, and it will be terrible, does not yet have a name.

December 1968

Paranoia in Power

(The Dialectics of Repression: A Small Contribution to Research)

How did Gaullist power account for the events of May? Through two contrary explanations that were nonetheless put forth together and that were only made coherent by an unformulated ideology. First, there was the exclamation: "They were rogues," a cry of the heart. Here we are in the intellectual dregs of Gaullism where de Gaulle (*chienlit*), ferocious stupidity (Poujade, Vivien, Fanton) and simple minds like Fouchet cohabit.[1]

Then there is the explanation meant to alert the ailing part in every possessor of power that watches and wakes every time this power feels itself incomprehensibly shaken: "*It was a conspiracy organized by an international power.*" Pompidou said this, as did Grimaud, as did de Gaulle in turn.[2]

Certainly, nothing is more unintelligent, of an almost prodigious mediocrity. And so one has to choose: either this, or else it was the lowlifes, these famous unknowns gone "out of control," scum of the streets and paving stones, delinquents with criminal records, misfits, *Kantangais*, lawless beings incapable of discipline, rebelling against any and all organization, marvelously unorganizable.[3] But then how is the international conspiracy thesis defensible, as it presupposes at least highly trained armed groups destined to control and "enlist" the masses?

Nonetheless, the two theses have their sense and deserve to be examined. Rogues, boys with "dirty hands," long hair, and strange outfits, are beings of another species: moreover, they are young, that is, doubly foreign. They frighten because they are other. What's more, they represent the streets, and the streets, when they speak, are terrible. They are the place of liberty, and maybe sovereignty. Whereas de Gaulle—it must be said—is afraid of the streets. And the word *fear* is intellectually and physically justified here: de Gaulle was afraid of May. From here on, whatever he does, he will always be frightened, with this racist fear that leads to the extermination of the *other*, always considered without place, without right, depraved: a rogue?

The other theme is the one that activates paranoid delirium. It is entirely certain that the Gaullist system has entered into the active phase of psychosis. Whether de Gaulle and his ministers believe the thesis of an externally organized shadowy conspiracy or not (Baumel[4] suspending flights to Cuba and thus making Gaullism tag along with Johnson) is unimportant: his system believes it. And a system is powerful; a system organizes aggressiveness through a delirium that has always explained everything via reason and that ends up forcing reality in turn to organize itself in response to it. The myth of conspiracy, created entirely out of the difficulties of a sick Self (sick of suddenly feeling inferior, the object of contempt, ridiculous in the eyes of everyone, and having almost collapsed for a few days), leads to police and judicial measures. Thus (without any effort of the imagination) we come to declare the dissolution of small opposition groups, some of which do not even exist or have not existed for many years. Marcellin[5] says that "we must lay the ground for the legal possibility of misdemeanor." In other words, the law is designed only to create "crime," to make it emerge from the imaginary. This is the paranoiac procedure. Social or individual paranoia, through the irregular reactions of the subject it affects, circumscribes a space where everything takes on an air of irregularity, where every gesture, every word, every manner of being draws suspicion.

Let us follow the development of the psychotic process. In the beginning, the government is still shy; it says the decree will lead to no indictment; all the same, searches take place; there are lockdowns, and people are arrested (especially Frank[6]) and placed in police custody; and above all foreigners are targeted. "The foreigner" is the choice victim of the paranoiac; he is not like the others; he does not speak like the others; he "plots," which soon means that he is part of a plot, thus of a terrible conspiracy. When the foreigner is pursued, we can be sure that the passion of persecutory delirium has come into force. And then things go very quickly. There is only a hint of suspicion concerning the disbanded organization that is regrouping. Members of nonexistent small groups, once they are on file (and these days opportunities to create files were innumerable, the arrests during the demonstrations never having had any other end; the very word *arrest* is meaningful: I arrest you, I single you out, I denounce you, from now on and forever you are listed somewhere in my register) obviously have no other means of proving that they have ceased to belong to an organization that does not exist as such. If, by misfortune, one of them happens to leave his place of residence, it becomes evidence: he is an illegal immigrant (consider Pompidou's declaration against illegal immigrants). If he behaves normally, *continuing* to meet his usual friends and possibly continuing to say what he thinks, then it is worse; it amounts to a confession: he continues; that is literally the crime. He is immediately arrested. And just as quickly society starts *bustling* [s'agite]; mysterious information is spread; a judge gets to work; good people protest; certain protestors even demonstrate; the police beat, again arrest, and put people on file. Hence the conclusion that there was nonetheless "something," since it is talked about. Such is the eternal and indigent madness. How do you stop being Krivine?[7] How do you stop being Jewish?

The dialectic of police repression develops according to a well-known method. It has its own power of organization, which means that, whatever its initial intentions may be, it is carried out precisely to organize any social and political reality through a conspiracy that it later denounces. Everything is a sign; everything is evidence. If in the course of a search one finds *Gramma*, the Cuban journal, Cuba thus becomes the conspiracy. All address books are suspect, just as it is enough that Krivine shakes a passerby's hand for the latter to be immediately arrested, put under police custody, and labeled: after which, if he is released, he is always under surveillance, throwing suspicion in turn on his relations; it is a raging epidemic. But in sickness there is a decisive complication, indicating, by a double development, the approach of the critical moment. Let us briefly describe this double symptom: (a) the invasion of the streets by plainclothes policemen; (b) support for the police and collaboration with them by "patriots of civic action."[8] From here on, everything goes even faster. Anyone can suspect anyone. The paranoia of power, of police, and of justice sets in motion countless little private manias, which the great events have first repressed, then brought to light. From now on, daily life changes. The police are in the streets, without anything to differentiate them; this means: they are everywhere, all the more visible because they want to be invisible; look carefully, you will discover them first near cinemas, in front of drugstores, better yet, in the cafés of a certain neighborhood or another, at times even in museums (for illegal immigrants are supposed to meet there); finally, the police is you. For it does not fail to occur that, when the police dress as civilians, civilians—those who have a shared interest with the government and are officially recognized, constituted by it—become policemen (recall what Sartre rightly termed General de Gaulle's "*call to murder*": "At the summit, it is the politics of cowardice, but at the same time a call to murder is sent out, for de Gaulle's call for the creation of committees of civic action is exactly this. . . . The old man . . . saw red, and told his partisans: 'THE FUN IS OVER, NOW IT'S TIME FOR

BLOWS'" [*Le nouvel observateur*, June 1, 1968, p. 27)]. But specialized civilians organize themselves in turn. Some have worked in the student communities; they will listen, maintain surveillance notebooks, and at times provoke (the extraordinary spread of the term *provocateur* is one of the striking phenomena of the current sickness). Others establish relations with special sections of the police; they are called "the sportsmen" and, given that some police units are composed of agents specially trained in violent disciplines, the mix occurs easily. Finally, the SAC and the CDR try to recruit militants within the police itself.[9] It's an excellent strategy. Policemen, turned militants, do not feel themselves bound by the orders of their commanders, if the latter happen to forbid certain procedures: if they commit "regrettable excesses," it is out of pure civic passion and without compromising the regular police. But at the same time they have access to all the information and all the arms of the official bodies. Note, however, that a good part of the police, if only out of esprit de corps, disapprove of this mixture (this has been seen) and denounce these practices, which they themselves call fascist.

Let us conclude without concluding. There is a great paranoia: it is the paranoia of reason as such, of a reason that raves as a fanaticism of reason, wanting to subject everything to reason, to force everyone to reason and to give reasons, and to reduce everything, the whole, to reason. There is the paranoia of old people: it is more fragile, less systematic, irritatingly shaky, and senile from the repetition of themes. It would not be defamation to state that de Gaulle is very old and the society that he represents is very old. But State paranoia is always powerful, and the system that it organizes ignores its limits. It is thus up to us to choose: Will we use the repression that is developing to force all the—tolerant or intolerant—repressive functions at work in society to spread and thus become more apparent? Or will we respond to paranoia, which always takes itself excessively seriously, by a strategy of unseriousness, by undoing a game that escapes the spirit of play, or are we entering a war, a war that is certainly new and whose rules even the regime does not suspect? There is a question. Let us not expect—and such is our contribution to the myth of mysterious conspiracy—to find a clear answer here.

Part III

Interventions, 1970–1993

Refusing the Established Order

How can I respond to your questionnaire, when the writer is always in search of a question that he has not been asked in advance and that obliges him, when he is content with an answer, to put himself slowly, patiently, into question in the face of the lost question, which is no longer the same and which turns him away from himself? Committed literature: I have the impression of going back thirty years into the past, when Sartre, more out of polemical defiance (a defiance he addressed to the classical writer he thought he was) than theoretical conviction, gave this expression a charge that made it unquestionable, put it beyond all discussion. In a general way, almost all writers, I mean writers of the left, were opposed to and irritated by it, whether André Breton, Georges Bataille, or Roland Barthes (if one may be allowed to make the dead speak—however alive they may be within us). To limit myself to the story I know, Sartre himself was very surprised when the most important postwar decision, the one that had the most influence on events (before May 68), by which I mean "The Declaration of 121" on the right to insubordination in the Algerian War, appeared to be the work of writers who could be considered noncommitted and who nonetheless could only affirm, and not without risk, the need to refuse, at a time when the government was tending toward an abhorrent form of oppression. With characteristic authority, he immediately rallied to it, but I think he was led (so he told me) to question the excessively simple formulas with which he wanted to shock (and with reason) literary good conscience.

What is there to add? Perhaps cultural power exists, but it is ambiguous, and it always runs the risk, should it lose this ambiguity, of putting itself at the service of another power that subjugates it. Writing is, at the limit, that which cannot be effected, thus always in search of a nonpower, refusing mastery, order, and the established order above all, preferring silence to the speech of absolute truth, thereby contesting things and contesting them incessantly.

If I had to cite texts that evoke what committed literature might have been, I would have found them in the ancient period, when literature did not exist. The first, the one closest to us, is the biblical story of Exodus.

Everything can be found there: liberation from slavery, wandering in the desert, waiting for writing, that is, for legislative writing, of which one always falls short, so that the only tablets received are broken, ones that cannot make up a complete response except in their breaking, even their fragmentation; finally, the necessity of dying without completing the work, without attaining the Promised Land, which, however, insofar as it is inaccessible, is always hoped for and thus already given. If, in the ceremony of Passover, it is traditional to save a cup of wine for the one who will precede and announce the messianic coming of the just world, it is understandable that the vocation of the (committed) writer is not to consider himself a prophet or a messiah but to save the place of the one who will come, to preserve absence from all usurpation, and also to maintain the immemorial memory that reminds us that we were slaves, that even liberated we remain and will remain slaves as long as others remain so, that there is thus no freedom (to put it too simply) except for others and through others: certainly, an infinite task that risks condemning the writer to a didactic, pedagogic role and, in so doing, of excluding the demand he carries within him and that constrains him to lack a place, a name, a role, and an identity, that is, never yet to be a writer.

Thinking the Apocalypse

I prefer to write you a letter, rather than a text designed to pretend that I have any authority to speak about what has become the H. & H.[1] affair (just as there was the Luchaire affair, the Chaumet affair, etc.)[2] in the media. In other words, journalistic vertigo has taken hold of an extremely serious "cause," one that has already been dealt with many times but that, of course, remains interminable and has reduced us to the basest kinds of passion, vehemence, and even violence. I understand that Victor Farias is being talked about; he brings up some undisclosed facts, although with a polemical intent that does not help in evaluating them. But how is it that Philippe Lacoue-Labarthe's book, which came out six months ago, was received with a silence that I am perhaps the first to break?* It is because he sets anecdote aside, while also citing and contextualizing most of the facts that Farias mentions. He is severe and rigorous. He places before us the essential questions.

I will not summarize this text (one does not summarize a philosophical text, even though Lacoue-Labarthe rejects the philosopher's status). Heidegger too used to say: there is no philosophy of Martin Heidegger, for he claimed that metaphysics had reached its end, an end that Nietzsche had already anticipated but to which he still belonged. And yet it is undeniable that, by adhering to National Socialism, Heidegger returned to ideology and, what is more disconcerting, without realizing it himself. Each time he was urged to recognize his "error," he maintained a strict silence or expressed himself in such a way that it aggravated the situation (for it would seem that Heidegger could make no mistake: it was the Nazi movement that had transformed itself by renouncing its radicalism). Lacoue-Labarthe, however, reminds us (I did not know this) that Heidegger admitted *in private* that he had committed "the greatest blunder of his life"

---

*Published by the University of Strasbourg. I would also mention *La poésie comme expérience* (Paris: Christian Bourgois, 1986); *Poetry as Experience*, trans. Andrea Tarnowski (Stanford: Stanford University Press, 1999), dedicated to Paul Celan. [Blanchot is referring to *La fiction du politique* (Paris: Christian Bourgois, 1987); *Heidegger, Art and Politics*, trans. Chris Turner (Oxford: Basil Blackwell, 1990).]

in the precise situation of the political commitment from 1933 to 1934 (a "blunder," nothing more).* But a year ago we learned from a testimony offered by Karl Löwith that in 1936 (two years after his resignation from the rectorate), Heidegger affirmed his continued faith in Hitler, with the same certainty that "*National Socialism was the right path for Germany*."† It would be worthwhile to cite this troubling testimony, the testimony of a man whose intellectual and moral probity is unquestionable (moreover, a disciple of Heidegger—or, more exactly, his student—and his close acquaintance, as he was very often the caretaker of Heidegger's children). While Heidegger was in Rome for his lecture on Hölderlin, Karl Löwith, who had taken shelter in a desolate house, nearly without any books (which moved Heidegger—no, this man did not burn books, as Farias suggests he did) took the opportunity of a stroll together to try to question Heidegger on the incendiary topic that everyone had avoided until then. I quote: "I brought the conversation to the controversy in the *Neue Zürcher Zeitung* and told him that I agreed neither with the manner in which Karl Barth had attacked him nor with the way Steiger had defended him, because my opinion was that his partisanship in favor of National-Socialism agreed in essence with *his philosophy* [my emphasis]. Heidegger agreed with me without reservation and developed his thought by saying that his concept of historicity—*Geschichtlichkeit*—was the basis of his political commitment." I interrupt the quotation to emphasize that Heidegger did accept the assertion that there is a philosophy of Heidegger, which confirms Lacoue-Labarthe's sense that it is the political commitment that transformed this thought into *philosophy*. But this "philosopher's" reservations and doubts, as they were then expressed to Löwith, are nothing other than mediocre political opinions. I will continue my quotation: "Yet, he underestimated two things: the vitality of Christian churches and the obstacles encountered by the *Anschluss*. What made him reflect, moreover, was the excessive organization [the administrative structuring, I suppose] at the expense of vital forces." To which Löwith adds this commentary:

---

*To be fair, or to try to be fair, one must take into account the few reservations that Heidegger put to use (even as he veiled them) in order to attenuate the glorification of National Socialism. As I wrote a long time ago in *The Infinite Conversation*, it is undeniable that the courses on Nietzsche, delivered during National Socialism's triumphant period, constitute an increasingly aggressive critique of the vulgar way in which "official philosophy" claimed to use Nietzsche.

†Karl Löwith, *My Life in Germany before and after 1933*. (Urbana: University of Illinois Press, 1994). The text on Heidegger and Husserl, entitled: "The Last Time I Saw Husserl in 1933 and Heidegger in Rome in 1936," was written in 1940 and not intended for publication, being an "account" for himself. The belated publication in 1986 by a Stuttgart editor was decided upon by Mrs. Löwith.

> The destructive radicalism of the entire movement and the petit-bourgeois character of all the organizations like "Strength through joy" had not even occurred to him, for Heidegger himself was a radical petit-bourgeois. Upon my remark that I understood many things about his attitude except one, namely, that he agreed to sit at the same table as a character like Julius Streicher[3] (at the Academy for the German Right), he at first remained silent. Finally, there followed the well-known justification (brought out very clearly by Karl Barth), which amounted to saying that "everything would have been much worse if certain men of science had not gotten involved" (thereby designating himself). And with a bitter resentment toward people of culture (*Gebildete*), he concluded his declaration: "If these men had not considered themselves too refined to commit themselves, it would have been quite different, but I had to stay there on my own." To my retort that there was no need to be very refined in order to refuse to work alongside a Streicher, he responded: it is useless to waste words about Streicher: the *Stürmer* was nothing more than "pornography." Why didn't Hitler free himself of this sinister individual? This he could not understand. Perhaps he was afraid of him.

Löwith adds, after a few remarks on Heidegger's pseudo-radicalism: "In reality, the program of what Heidegger called 'pornography' had been applied entirely in 1938 and became a German reality. No one can deny that Streicher and Hitler were on this point one and the same person."

What is one to conclude from this interview? First, that it was a conversation, but Heidegger was not a man who expressed himself lightly, even in conversation. He thus admitted that one could speak of *his* philosophy and that this was the basis of his political commitment; this is 1936, Hitler is fully in power and Heidegger has resigned from the rectorate but has not distanced himself from Krieck, Rosenberg, and all those for whom anti-Semitism was the expression of a biological or racist ideology.[4] Now what does he write in 1945?* "I believed that Hitler, after having taken the responsibility for the entirety of the people in 1933, would dare to disengage himself from the party and its doctrine and that the whole would come together on the grounds of renovation and of gathering, aiming toward a Western responsibility. This conviction was an error that I recognized from the events of June 30, 1934 onwards." (The Night of the Long Knives, the assassination of Röhm and the dissolution of the SA). "I

*Cited by Jacques Derrida in *Psyché* (Galilée). [Jacques Derrida, "La main de Heidegger (Geschlecht II)," in *Pysché*, vol. 2, (Paris: Galilée, 2003); "Heidegger's Hand (Geschlecht II)," in *Pysche*, vol. 2, trans. Peggy Kamuf (Stanford: Stanford University Press, 2008), 32.]

had already intervened in 1933 to say yes to the national and to the social but not at all to nationalism—and not any more so to the intellectual and metaphysical foundations on which the biologism of party doctrine was based. . . ." If this was indeed his thinking on the matter, he said nothing of it to Löwith in 1936, kept his confidence in Hitler, wore the Nazi sign on his lapel, and found merely that things were not going quickly enough, but that it was enough to bear it and to hold firm.

That he preferred the national to nationalism does not amount to substituting one word for another. This preference is also the foundation of his thinking; it expresses his profound attachment to the land, that is, to the native land (*Heimat*), his decision for rootedness (not that distant from Barrès's hatred of the "uprooted," a hatred that led him to condemn Dreyfus, who belonged to a rootless people), similarly his hatred of urbanity.

I will not develop these points, which are in fact well known, but they make me think that a kind of anti-Semitism was never foreign to him and that this explains why, despite multiple requests, he never agreed to express himself on the Extermination. Lacoue-Labarthe (and not Farias) reproduces a terrible text that one has trouble copying out. What is there to say about this text? "Agriculture is now a motorized food industry, the same thing in its essence as the production of corpses in the gas chambers and the extermination camps, the same thing as blockades and the reduction of countries to famine, the same thing as the manufacture of hydrogen bombs."[5] This is a scandalously insufficient phrase, says Lacoue-Labarthe, because it points to nothing in the Extermination except for a certain use of technics and mentions neither the name nor the fate of the Jews. It is true that, at Auschwitz and elsewhere, the Jews were treated as one treats industrial waste and that they were considered the refuse of Germany and Europe (in this sense, each one of us is implicated in our responsibility). What is unthinkable and unforgivable about the event of Auschwitz, this absolute caesura, collides with Heidegger's determined silence, or else the only time he speaks of it, to my knowledge, is in the manner of the "revisionists," placing on the same level the destruction of the East Germans killed during the war and the Jews also killed during the war: if we replace the word *Jews* by *East Germans*, it will balance the account.* That the Jews, who committed no crime other than being Jewish, were condemned to final extermination—this, writes Lacoue-Labarthe, is something that has

*This was said in a letter solicited by Herbert Marcuse and addressed to him. Since Marcuse does not reproduce the letter, however, we cannot be sure of the terms that were used.

no parallel in history. And he adds, "The God of the Greco-Christian West died at Auschwitz,—and it was not at all by chance that the victims of that attempted annihilation were the witnesses, in that West, of another origin of the God who was venerated and thought there—if not indeed, perhaps, of another God—one that had remained free of its Hellenistic and Roman capture . . ."[6]

Allow me to withdraw after these words, emphasizing that Heidegger's irreparable fault is his silence concerning the Extermination, his silence or his refusal, faced with Paul Celan, to ask for forgiveness, a refusal that threw Celan into despair and made him sick, for Celan knew, that in the face of the West, the Shoah was the revelation of its essence. And that it was necessary to preserve its memory in common, even if it meant losing all peace, but in order to preserve the possibility of a relation to others.

P.S. Some more words about my own case. Thanks to Emmanuel Levinas, without whom I could not have begun to understand *Being and Time* as early as 1927 or 1928, reading that book provoked a true intellectual shock within me. An event of primary importance had just occurred: impossible to attenuate it, even today, even in my memory. This is doubtless why I took part in the homage for Heidegger's seventieth birthday; my contribution: a page of *Waiting, Forgetting*. Now, a little later, Guido Schneeberger (to whom Farias owes a lot) sent me or had his editor send speeches Heidegger made during his rectorate in favor of Hitler. Speeches that are equally frightening in their form and in their content, for Heidegger invoked this very writing and this very language—through which, in a great moment of thought, we were invited to the highest interrogation that could have come to us from Being and from Time—to call for votes in Hitler's favor, to justify Nazi Germany's secession from the League of Nations, or to praise Schlageter.[7] Yes, the same sacred language, maybe slightly cruder, slightly more emphatic, but it would make itself heard up to the commentaries on Hölderlin and would alter those, but for different reasons still.

Faithfully yours,
Maurice Blanchot
November 10, 1987

Do Not Forget

Allow me to write to you, without pretension, in the form of a letter, rather than trying to join you in an interview, which I am unable to give.

In a certain way, Judaism is so close to me that I do not feel myself worthy to speak about it, except in order to make this proximity known. (But can I even say this much?) Isn't there some presumption in the hope of saying it one day? The answer: not in what is to come, but perhaps in the future (cf. Levinas, in the review *Spuren*, no. 20).*

I think all that I owe to Emmanuel Levinas is well known. Today he is my oldest friend, the only one with whom I feel authorized to use the familiar address [*tutoiement*]. It is also known that we met at the University of Strasbourg in 1926, where so many great teachers made it impossible for us to think of philosophy as something mediocre. Did this meeting happen by chance? One could say so. But the friendship was not random or fortuitous. Something profound carried us toward one another. I won't say that it was already Judaism that brought us together, but I would say that, besides his gaiety, it was his indefinably serious and beautiful way of envisaging life, a way of deeply examining it without the slightest pedantry. At the same time, I owe him a first approach to Husserl and even to Heidegger, whose courses he had attended in Germany, which was already stirring with perverse political movements. We left Strasbourg for Paris at about the same time, but even though we never fell out of contact, it took the misfortune of a disastrous war for our friendship, which had become distant, to become closer—all the more so when, after being taken prisoner in France, he entrusted to me, through a kind of secret request, the care of looking after some of his loved ones, who were being threatened, alas, by the perils of a heinous political program.

I will not enter any further into these biographical detours, whose memory is nonetheless very present to me. It was obviously the Nazi persecution (it was carried out from the beginning, contrary to what some

*You will recall what Levinas told you one day during an interview: "*Judaism is an essential modality of every human*," an essential modality but one most often misunderstood, buried, or, even worse, perverted and finally refused.

philosophy professors would have us believe, in order to persuade us that in 1933, when Heidegger adhered to it, National Socialism was still a respectable doctrine that did not merit condemnation) that made us feel that the Jews were our brothers and that Judaism was more than a culture and even more than a religion, but rather the foundation of our relations with others. I will not return at length to Levinas's work, which you have spoken about in the best way, except to repeat that it demands to be studied and meditated upon with the greatest vigilance. This is what it teaches us first: reading does not suffice; understanding and assimilating does not suffice; what matters is to stay awake and be alert. We believe we respect the other by parsimoniously leaving him his place, but the other demands (without demanding it) the entire place. Just as the other is always higher than me, closer to God (that unpronounceable name) than I am, so the dissymmetrical relation from him to me is what founds ethics and obliges me, through an extraordinary obligation that weighs upon me. (Levinas's ethics still belongs to the philosophical, as in Kant, where practical reason takes precedence over pure reason.)

You also asked me about Martin Buber, who woke Judaism at a time when assimilation threatened to make it disappear. We love Martin Buber for all that he gave us, in an enchanted style that at times approaches Chagall. Correctly or incorrectly, there is this ray of Hassidism in him, with all his marvelous stories in which humor is enriched by teaching. But one must not forget that Hassidism, which has little to do with that of the Middle Ages, marks the renaissance of Judaism, after the catastrophe represented by the apostasy (conversion to Islam) of the false messiah Shabbetai Tsvi[1] (as the esteemed David Banon transcribes it).

Here I would like to indicate that, in the nineteenth century above all, Christians and non-Christians who were interested in Judaism were looking for a secret doctrine within it, the mysticism that the name of the Kabbalah embodies, and thus, without meaning to do so, they made the Jews the bearers of an interesting but perhaps harmful mystery. Hence the feeling that the Jews are separate and that they can live only among themselves, which in turn justifies every ghetto, the prelude to the sinister concentration camps where there was nothing but waiting for death.

Martin Buber has taught us the excellence of the relation between I and the Other by unveiling to us the richness and the beauty of the familiar address [*tutoiement*], through the emotional movement of affectivity (but also through the demand of reason). The relation of I to you [*tu*] is privileged; it is essentially differentiated from the relation between I and this.

It is the encounter that precedes every possibility of a relation, an encounter in which unanticipated and unexpected reciprocity is accomplished in a flash that we still doubt, although we are sure of it. But doesn't this reciprocity make us forget that the I can never be in a relation of equality to the Other, when the Other is an Other [*l'Autre est Autrui*]? This is precisely what Levinas has taught us—knowledge that is not merely knowledge. He leads us on a more difficult path, because we find ourselves on it only because of a philosophical upheaval that puts ethics at the beginning and even before any beginning. Thus we discover the Other not only in the happy or rough equality of friendship but in the extreme responsibility that constitutes each of us as obliged, even as a hostage, revealing the dissymmetry between You [*Toi*] and me. A me without me—without ego—that no longer has the sufficiency of its subjectivity, that tends to strip itself of what it is and even of being, not for a purely personal askesis, but in an attempt to rejoin the ethical obligation that I recognize in the face and the invisibility of the face. This is not the face with the clear outline of the *figure*, but rather the weakness of the Other exposed to death, or what I recognize in the "Saying" [*Dire*] by which I speak to the Other, in which I call to him, an interpellation, an invocation in which what is invoked is out of reach, since it is always beyond me, outstripping and towering over me.

These are rather insufficient statements, which I will try to supplement, with permission from Jean Halpérin to repeat along with him once again: "What is enunciated or rather announced with Levinas is a surplus, a beyond of the universal, a singularity that one could call Jewish and that still remains to be thought. And in this it is prophetic. Judaism as what outstrips perennial thought for having always already been thought, but which nonetheless carries the responsibility of a thinking to come, this is what the other philosophy of Levinas gives us, a burden and a hope, a burden of hope."[2]

This is what makes it difficult for me to return to this somber Heidegger "quarrel" you ask me about. There is nothing to say that does not incite some sort of horror. Certainly, the book that puts Heidegger into question is unsatisfying, worthy of the noise in the media by which we have been deafened, but perhaps also awakened. Nonetheless, the central question of Heidegger's responsibility in adhering to National Socialism continues to pose the most serious problems in relation to his thought itself. Was it a decision that events imposed upon him, in such a way that the man who wrote *Being and Time* did not recognize himself in this decision, thus leaving his thought intact? Now, concerning this essential point,

Heidegger clearly responded to Karl Löwith in 1936, two years after he resigned from the Rectorate. And what was this response (never mentioned in Farias's book)? "It is my concept of historiality [*Geschichtlichkeit*]—(or one could speak more simply of historicity) that was the foundation [*die Grundlage*] of my commitment [*Einsatz*]." I would add: this was a political but also and equally a philosophical commitment. In this interview, Karl Löwith does not question his former teacher any further. One can suppose that, according to his distinct handling of the German language, historiality is not the simple succession of time but a response to a call of destiny, and whether one responds to this call or not determines whether or not one contributes to the radical change of epoch. In the posthumous *Spiegel* testament, Heidegger himself recognized that with the advent of Hitler he had saluted the grandeur and the splendor of a beginning. For him, that which begins is always the most important: it is the irruption of absolute renewal, the interruption that suspends our relation to established laws and values and perhaps to the "gods." In a sense, this was true. But this interruption—which for Heidegger was the promise of a Germany as heir to Greek excellence and, in this capacity, as the nation called upon to enlighten the world by dominating it, whatever the price may have been—was also for us and above all for the Jews the interregnum when all rights, all recourse ceased, when friendship became uncertain and the silence of the highest spiritual authorities left us without guarantee, not only threatened but anxious about not responding as one should to the silent call of others.

The disaster that followed touched Heidegger, for, when he began his courses again, he invited his listeners to go and meditate on the exhibition on German prisoners of war mistreated by the Russians that was being inaugurated; meditations on victims for whom Hitler was partially responsible, to the extent that the war against Russia was his work. Absolute silence about other victims, the six million Jews, whose only crime was to have been born Jewish and who represented the whole of Judaism, which was what one wanted to annihilate. A silence that some doctor of philosophy recommends that we should not break today; in other words, we should not invoke Auschwitz or make an argument or a mechanical term out of it—a respect that would thus lead to making respectable Heidegger's unpardonable silence.*

*Your readers will recall Levinas's Talmudic reading (on pardon—1967) in which he says that one could pardon many Germans but not Heidegger, because of his mastery (he is the Master), because of his "*perspicacity*" and his "*knowledge*." But what if it were his "*knowledge*"

Must we say once again (yes, we must) that Auschwitz, an event that makes a ceaseless appeal to us, demands, through testimony, the inexhaustible duty not to forget: Remember, beware of forgetting and yet, in this faithful Memory, *never will you know*. I emphasize this, for what is said here sends us back to that for which there is no memory, to the unrepresentable, to unspeakable horror, which, however, is always, in one way or another, and always in anguish, the immemorial.

Hence you may permit me this quotation, because it lets us hear the unknown name that Auschwitz still is (holocaust, extermination, Shoah, a word outside of nomination): "*The holocaust, the* absolute *event of history—which is a date in history—that utter-burn where all history took fire, where the movement of Meaning was swallowed up, where the gift, which knows nothing of forgiveness or consent, shattered without* giving *place to anything that can be affirmed, that can be denied—gift of passivity itself, gift of what cannot be given. How can it be preserved, even by thought? How can thought be made the keeper of the holocaust where all was lost, including guardian thought?*"[3]

I do not feel I have the power to add anything, except to salute you, in this language and in another, and to thank you for greeting and welcoming me, in these declining years of my life.

Maurice Blanchot

NB This is not the place for me to pursue further an interrogation of Heidegger's work, which has exerted such fascination—a term that already calls into question a thinking held under the sway of a language that the play of etymology perhaps leads outside the field of philosophy and that never affirms anything except through the artful reservations of a necessarily concealed denegation. Hence an important sociologist, who is at the same time very distant from Heidegger's "discourse," can arrive at the following suggestion: "It is perhaps because he never realized what he was saying that Heidegger was able to say what he did without really having to say it. And it is perhaps for the same reason that he refused to the very end to discuss his Nazi involvement [we have nonetheless seen that, speaking to Karl Löwith during Nazism's triumphant period, he recognized and accepted the agreement between his thinking and his radical

---

that had closed his eyes and had made him incapable of any confession? What redoubled responsibility then perhaps might also weigh on us? [The Talmudic reading Blanchot is referring to actually dates from 1963 but was published in 1968: Emmanuel Levinas, "Envers autrui," in *Quatre lectures talmudiques* (Paris: Gallimard), 56; "Toward the Other" in *Nine Talmudic Readings*, trans. A. Aronowicz (Bloomington: Indiana University Press, 1990), 25.]

engagement]. Really to do so would have been to admit that essential thinking had not thought the essential, the social unthought that was expressed through it." This is Pierre Bourdieu's conclusion.[4] He would not accept our saying that he implicitly exonerates Heidegger (he denies that he is putting him on trial) by calling into question all philosophical activity, whose possibilities (beginning with expressive possibilities) Heidegger would merely have pushed to the extreme.

But we must also read the very recent book by Lyotard entitled *Heidegger and "the jews"* (he explains the quotation marks without being entirely convincing). He shows that Heidegger is very close to the terrible anti-Semitism of the young Hegel. Heidegger's silence "betrays" the mistaken way in which all "knowledge" confronts the Other in the name of the truth of Being. Finally, concerning Granel,[5] who attempted to extract from Heideggerean National Socialism a "truth," a "grandeur" more true and greater than Heidegger himself thought them to be (disciples are like that), he writes that he thus gravely defaults on the debt that is our only lot (namely) to forget neither that there is something forgotten nor what horror the mind is capable of in its frenzy to make sure it is forgotten. "Our" lot, whose lot? That of this nonpeople of survivors, Jews and non-Jews, called "jews" here, whose being together depends not on the authenticity of any primary root but solely on this debt of a first anamnesis. Reminiscence, memory of the Law that is forgotten only if time is not granted for studying it and for acting in such a way that I never feel myself free of my responsibility toward others, in whom the trace of the one who is never there, the one who has already left, uncovers itself: God, perhaps, but not the God of power, promise, and salvation, whose retreat Auschwitz marks.

Yes, Silence Is Necessary for Writing

Yes, silence is necessary for writing. Why? *Pace* Wittgenstein (at least as he is superficially understood), I would say that what we cannot say is precisely where writing finds its resource and its necessity. It follows too that the author as an I must make the greatest possible abstraction from self. He should not survive, and if he does, in principle no one knows it and perhaps not even himself.

For almost sixty-five years now, I have been bound to Emmanuel Levinas, the only friend whom I address familiarly [*tutoie*]. I owe him a lot, if not everything. An unmerited benediction.

"Factory-Excess," or Infinity in Pieces

Factory-Excess: at first it was a manuscript in my hands. And the reading of a manuscript can only be faulty, since it is not disinterested. The editor's concerns impose precautions and demands. They impede the objectivity that, happily and in any case, is impossible. Impossible objectivity clouds the view that wants to be too clear-sighted. And the book is not yet a book. Incomplete, will it ever renounce being incomplete in order to attain the status where it will be protected by respect: the respect of the book?

But *Factory-Excess* almost immediately stopped being a manuscript, stopped being a book. From the very first page, it said what could only be said by tearing us away from saying. Simple words, short phrases, no discourse, and on the contrary the discontinuity of a language that interrupts itself because it reaches an extreme limit [*touche à l'extrémité*]. Perhaps it is poetry, perhaps it is more than poetry.

Other remarkable books have described the work done by a factory and in a factory. But here from the very first words we understand that, if we enter into working in the factory, we will belong henceforth to the immensity of the universe ("the great factory universe"), there will no longer be any other world, there has never been any other: time is finished, succession is abolished, and "things exist together, simultaneously." There is no more outside—you think you're getting out? You're not getting out. Night, day, there's no difference, and you have to know that retirement at sixty and death at seventy will not liberate you. Great lengths of time, the flash of an instant—both are equally lost. This is the "structure" of being, to the point of vacating being. It is perhaps the there is [*l'il y a*]. Yes, you have to know that whatever you do, you're always doing ("one never stops doing"). It's incessant: eternity that has suppressed once and for all the happiness of an end. You are the wretched gods condemned to immortality without a future.

The impersonality is all the more impersonal given that it is experienced in the feminine. A factory of women. As if anonymity had generic characteristics. "We're sitting . . . we're crazy, that's how it is" ["*On est assise . . . on est folle, c'est normal*"] The "*On*" is the mark of an "I"—a subject without subject—that has renounced singularity without achieving anything in common. And the worst is that the unbearable opens up into something wonderful: "Most of the women have a wonderful toothless smile." Just as the work consists in making holes in paper (holes in things, holes that are only things added to things), so the wonderful perfection of the smile grows from what it lacks—the toothless mouth's flaw is its very perfection. This does not mean that in this desolate and empty space there would be nothing beautiful except what is already ruined, but that the distinction of beauty is to undo itself, not to refer to a model or an ideal (Platonic) idea.

Why excess? The "this" [*cela*] that one lives through in the factory exceeds the words belonging to discourse, but words, however neutral they may be, are always excessive in turn—they are too much, what they say is extraneous. And yet they remain just, even opening onto the infinite and into infinity. One can always say: "God exists," for the factory is God. There is no other, as there is no other history. You would think: "This is terror." Yes, this is endless terror, without distraction, possibly without terror.

In *Factory-Excess*, one speaks little of the factory. Outside the factory, one is not outside. One looks at oneself in a little mirror: one looks, one looks and yet there is no image. One eats without hunger, desire is satisfied by excluding satisfaction. "Where's the taste?" It's with the teeth of the other that one chews, interchangeable, and without any solidarity being affirmed.

The factory is immense, but the immensity is in pieces; we are in an infinity divided into pieces. This is what Leslie Kaplan teaches me, far from Pascal: the infinite, but the infinite in pieces. Discontinuity has done its work. One lives, one dies: Is this "true" death? Only fatigue, useless work, the truth disarticulated at every moment.

The most inhuman aspect is that one does not become dehumanized. Just as one sits, all alone, among everyone else, likewise one makes holes so that the object, the beautiful object, can be manufactured, just as one would make children—children of the factory and for the factory, the lovable birth of something already used up ("the baby is gray"), destined for an end that will be nothing but beginning again.

However, the factory is not the universe of the concentration camp.[1] Hell has its circles. One crosses them. One believes with naive terror that the terrible has its limits. What awaits us will remain without testimony. We have no premonition of it. Let us at least save the words given to us, on this side of all culture, by a woman who knew how to express "divided space," what without origin has always already destroyed memory: "Factory, the factory, the first memory." The immemorial.

In the Night That Is Watched Over

It is slowly, in those nights when I sleep without sleeping, that I became conscious (this word is inappropriate) of your proximity, which is distant nonetheless. I persuaded myself that you were here: not you, but this repeated phrase: "I am going far away, I am going far away."

I immediately understood that Robert, so generous, so little concerned about himself, was not speaking to me about or for himself, but of all the places of extermination, of which (if it was him speaking) he listed a few: "Listen to them, listen to the names: Treblinka, Chelmno, Belzec, Majdanek, Auschwitz, Sobibor, Birkenau, Ravensbrück, Dachau."

"But," I say, speaking, not speaking, "do we forget?"—"Yes, you forget; you forget all the more for remembering. Your memory does not impede you from living, from surviving, nor even from loving me. But one does not love a dead person, because then the meaning escapes you, the impossibility of meaning, the nonbeing and the impossibility of nonbeing."

When I reread these lines, I know that I have already lost sight of Robert Antelme, the incomparable friend I knew. He was so simple and at the same time so rich, with a knowledge that the greatest minds lacked. In the experience of servitude that was his, even if he shared it with others, he kept the human truth from which he knew not to exclude even those who oppressed him.

But he went even further: not recognizing a companion (K.) he had come to see in the infirmary, who was still alive, he understood that there is a nothingness in life itself, an unfathomable void against which one has to defend oneself, even while acknowledging its approach. We must learn to live with this void. We will maintain plenitude even in nothingness.

This is why, Robert, I still have my place next to you. And this "night watched over" in which you come to see me is not an illusion where everything would disappear but my right to make you live, even in the void I feel approaching.

November 1993

For Friendship

The thought of friendship: I think we know when friendship comes to an end (even if it still lasts), in a disagreement that a phenomenologist might call existential, a drama, an unfortunate act. But do we know when it begins? There is no friendship at first sight; instead, it develops little by little, in a slow labor of time. We were friends and did not know it.

I came to know Dionys Mascolo at Gallimard. I used to see him from afar; he seemed very young to me. I was much closer to Raymond Queneau (from before the war), on the one hand, and Jean Paulhan, on the other—though the two of them were rather distant from each other.

One day (during the war . . .) Dionys told me that Gaston Gallimard wanted to publish as a book the literary chronicles (or some of them) that I was sending to the free zone through special channels. "But," I said, "I don't have them, I don't keep them (out of laziness or maybe out of prudence)." But the publishing house had found them all, or the majority of them. I am persuaded that the work of collecting and conserving them was undertaken and carried out by Mascolo alone.

This is not the place to express the shock mixed with irritation that I felt. I was working—if it was work—at a loss, in uncertainty and without expectation—and here I was, face to face with myself and with a decision I had to make. (Writing is perhaps testimonial; it is the message in a bottle that always returns).

I won't say any more about this. I wanted simply to point out that, if the book *Faux Pas* exists, it is due to Dionys Mascolo—and of course to Gaston Gallimard, who took the initiative or at least the responsibility for it. And not without difficulties: the censors banned the publication of the manuscript twice. "You're going to have problems," Raymond Queneau told me. I think (one is never sure) that my commentary on *The Marble Cliffs*, where I had drawn attention to the dark character of the "Head Forester," so close to the sinister figure that could not be named—yes, this commentary frightened the scribes of censorship. Ernst Jünger was protected by the highest medal that could be awarded to a "hero," but vengeance could be unleashed on others.

I emphasize that friendship did not begin then—an effusion of heart and mind. Without a doubt a certain complicity and a regret, too, for I thought that *Faux Pas* really was a faux pas. At the time I was close to Jean Paulhan, who used to advise me. I recall that, during a trip in the metro, he came close to me and said in my ear: "Watch out for so and so, watch out for this other one." Nothing more; I did not need explanations, and I refrained from asking. An epoch of silence, a period of mute trust. I will only briefly recount the responsibility that was almost invested in me, had I agreed to be the editor in chief of the *N.R.F.*, for which Drieu was responsible, but he had grown tired of it.

Why this proposal? I had met him before the war because of a literary column on the *Rêveuse bourgeoisie* [Dreaming Bourgeoisie], then at the beginning of the Occupation, when I withdrew from "Jeune France" by resigning with a few friends.[1] A rumor spread; he will know how to resist, Drieu said to himself. But why this resignation? The situation was too ambiguous. "Jeune France," which had been founded by unknown musicians who would later become famous, was subsidized by Vichy, and our naive project to use this association against Vichy (I recall the presence of Jean Vilar, who was writing more than he was playing), failed because of this contradiction. Paul Flamand also found our conception of "culture" too lofty.

Thus, Drieu's proposal: "I will remain the director," he told me, "vis-à-vis the Germans, but you will have complete freedom, on the condition that you avoid any political texts." I immediately saw the trap, which perhaps escaped Drieu. I pointed out to him that, being an unknown writer, I was not a sufficient barrier against the occupiers and that a directorial committee needed to be formed with writers who would be too well known and respected to be toyed with. Drieu did not say no. Jean Paulhan gave me his consent, but, even more, took things into his own hands once again and did all the work, gaining the agreement of Gide, Valéry, Claudel (Claudel's very correct remark: "But who is Blanchot, this unknown?"), and Schlumberger. We knew, nonetheless, that all these writers (including Paulhan, of course) would protect us (one couldn't dispose of them silently) but would also compromise themselves by agreeing to be the guarantors of a dubious, even impossible, enterprise.

It was then that Paulhan, with his ingenious subtlety, found a way out by inviting François Mauriac to attend a short interview, in which everything was said in hushed voices and half words. He knew that Mauriac was unacceptable to Drieu, and when I presented Drieu with the list of names to be called to constitute the directoral committee, he became furious ("Mauriac has never belonged to the *N.R.F.* and never will"). Then he returned to his first proposal, according to which he would entrust to me, to me alone, the direction of a neutral review, one purely literary. To which I answered (this happened in a café on the Champs-Elysées): "Let's be frank. I cannot invite people to contribute to a journal in which I would not myself want to be published."

And so the tragicomedy came to an end. One of the oldest founders of the first *N.R.F.*—it wasn't Gide—had still insisted, without seeing the unspeakable character of the proposal: "If B. agrees to compromise himself, we will repay him later." "How abject," I said to J.P. "Yes, he said, we're in a state of abjection, and we have to put a stop to all of this. You'll see, Drieu will be able to extricate himself from it only by killing himself."

I never had much to do with Gaston Gallimard. He might, on the whole, have hoped that the review would continue, sacrificing it to save the publishing house.

At the beginning of the Occupation, he had wanted to give up everything, at the risk of abandoning so many writers who had trusted him. But then he had a certain friendship for Drieu, who was a friend of Malraux.

I realize that what I am writing here (maybe I will erase it) is not a chronological story. The attempt and failure of the *N.R.F.*, like my participation in "Jeune France," took place at the beginning of 1941. The occupiers wanted it to seem that they were leaving us a certain freedom, which we knew would be merely a sham. *Thomas the Obscure* had been published and deemed a work of Jewish decadence. And *Faux Pas* appeared a year or two later, when the war with Russia was giving us new hope (1943).

I interrupt this account. Some unknown malaise has always distanced me from any account that would claim to be historical, as if what we considered true were also fallaciously reconstructed according to the play of memory and forgetting. I know that Dionys Mascolo was present, in an uncertain way (he joined Gallimard in 1942), and yet I do not see him distinctly. He was very close, I think, to Brice Parain, whom everyone respected and whose theses on language masterfully inaugurated a new era.

Some time has to pass: the time in which we also meet the death that awaits each of us and only barely misses us. I was living very far away. The "I" is already incongruous and inappropriate. I don't think I exchanged many letters with D.M. (none, upon reflection, until the publication of *14 juillet*). I was silently absent. It was political responsibility and exigency that somehow made me return and turn toward Dionys, who, I was certain (or had the sense) would be my recourse. Receiving *14 juillet*, I heard the call and responded to it with my resolute agreement. From then on, there would be together—"between us"*—what we would refuse with a refusal that was expressed with reasons but was more firm and also more rigorous than what can be called reasonable. The second issue of *14 juillet* published a fairly long text, entitled "The Essential Perversion" ["La perversion essentielle"]. René Char made me aware of his agreement.[2]

But I would like to say that it was then without a doubt that I met Robert Antelme. I remember the circumstances. I was sitting in D.M.'s office (at Gallimard). The door opened slowly, and a tall man appeared but hesitated to enter, undoubtedly out of politeness, so as not to disturb our conversation. He was almost timid but certainly intimidating. He was simplicity embodied but also reluctance, even in his speech, which was firm and created authority. I won't say that I knew from that moment how precious his friendship would be to me. That would be romantic. In Montaigne's considerations of his friendship with La Boétie, he writes: "Because it was him . . . because it was me." I have always been less moved than disturbed by this. It was later, with the passing of time, after Montaigne had abandoned the idea of introducing the *Discourse on Voluntary Servitude* into his writings (though it was supposed to be its central point), that he returned to more just, less exalted feelings, allowing us to understand the complexity of friendship and the discretion that it requires when we speak about it.

Why was I there? Unable to tolerate what was intolerable in current events (the Algerian War), I called D.M.: "Something must be done . . ."—"But we are precisely working to do something." Hence the innumerable, almost daily meetings and the elaboration of what would become, with everyone's contribution, the "Declaration of the Right to Insubordination in the Algerian War."

I never had the intention, and neither did Dionys and Maurice Nadeau, or the Surrealists or so many others, to turn the elaboration of a text that was an event in itself into a story. What took place then (it took months) belongs to everyone, and as Victor Hugo says about maternal feeling,

---

* *Entre nous* is the title of a recent book by Emmanuel Levinas [*Entre nous: Essais sur la pensée de l'autre* (Paris: Grasset, 1991); *Entre Nous: On Thinking-of-the-Other*, trans. Michael B. Smith and Barbara Harshav (New York: Columbia University Press, 1998].

"Each one has his share, and everyone has it entirely." The responsibility was common, and even those who refused to sign did so for important, considered reasons, transcribed in long letters. At times this was very intense. I will thus exclude names as well as anecdotes. I will only say—this is a necessary exception—that if Georges Bataille did not sign (against his will), it was at my request: he was already very sick then, and we knew that we were all heading for hard times. But this is not the essential motive. What would have made his "case" particularly unfair is that his daughter Laurence was already in prison: no doubt she had carried suitcases (as our adversaries put it with contempt).[3] Later freed, she explained everything to me, but her father, who was not in on the secret then, would have been mixed up with a dreadful intrigue, from which it was our duty to keep him at a distance.

What followed is well known. As soon as the Declaration of the 121 was published (in only two reviews, Nadeau's *Les lettres nouvelles* and Sartre's *Les temps modernes*, which were immediately suspended, censored, muffled—it would be better to say that the Declaration was published but did not appear), and as no newspaper, including the largest ones, would print any passages (the risk was too great), we were prosecuted, accused, condemned, without knowing why. I then learned what an investigating magistrate [*juge d'instruction*] was, his privileges, and his concern to impose his law rather than represent it. A remarkable and awkward judge nonetheless. On two points, we clashed heatedly. When I pointed out that the current prime minister, Michel Debré, in a speech delivered two to three days earlier in Strasbourg, had announced that we would be severely punished, so that the verdict had already been pronounced, thus rendering the judge's task useless, for we were condemned in advance, he became furious. I recall one of his phrases: "There are things that one does not say here."—"Your office is thus a sacred space where one cannot express oneself freely, albeit respectfully? A little like the oak tree where a king dispensed justice: at least that was out in the open."—"Do not forget that I can put you in prison for such words."—"I ask for nothing else." He then turned to my lawyer (a friend of Trotsky) and muttered between his teeth: "How useless these upper-class types are."

Our other subject of disagreement was more serious, putting into question a custom that was never abolished, even if nothing imposes it and everything ought to impede it. Once my deposition was over, the judge wanted to dictate it to the stenographer: "Oh no, I said, you won't substitute your words for mine. I am not questioning your good faith, but you a have a way of speaking that I cannot accept." He insisted. "I won't sign."—"We will do without your signature, and the trial will be moved to a different place." Finally he gave in and let me repeat strictly the words that I had uttered.

I am not mentioning this out of a love for anecdote. There is a seriously deficient point in this intrigue, which is a debate between a man well versed in juridical knowledge and another who perhaps has few words and does not even know the sovereign value of his speech, of speech itself. Why does the judge have the right to be the only master of language, dictating (it is already a *diktat*) the words according to his liking, reproducing them, not as they were said, stuttered, poor and unsure, but aggravated, because more beautiful, conforming more to a classical ideal and above all more definitive? The lawyer can intervene, but at times there is no lawyer, or else he does not want to bother the judge or break with the connivance that, as Kafka showed, unites magistrates, lawyers, the defense, and the accused in the world of justice.

I would like Jean-Denis Bredin's story "A Culprit" ["Un coupable"] to be read and thought about.* Bredin, a law professor, a lawyer and a good writer, moves and instructs us. He does not paint a rosy picture. The guilty-innocent man in his story is educated; he is a first-year law student. His crime: participating, at a friend's invitation, in a peaceful demonstration that ended badly: beer bottles versus clubs. He didn't do anything, but he was there. This is his fault, which he cannot accept. He is French, born of a Breton father (a tax inspector) and an Algerian mother. His father is dead, and his mother, back in Algeria, part of the administration there, sends him money. His mother must not know. Justice follows its course, with its prejudices and habits. The certainty of his innocence impedes him from defending himself; his lawyer defends him too well, with the eloquence of the lectern, which burdens his case. Condemned less than the others, and not tolerating his lost innocence, he kills himself with the shards of a beer bottle that he was falsely accused of using against the authorities.

Bredin explains that Ali's guilt was somehow inside him and that the law only declared it, while keeping him from defending himself through the perversion and the rectitude of the judicial machine. This is another version of Kafka's *Trial*. Maybe Ali lacked the strength that political convictions bring; the conviction of one's innocence is not enough.

---

*It was published by Gallimard [Jean-Louis Bredin, *Un coupable* (Paris: Gallimard, 1987)], who also published Georges Bataille's *Le coupable* [Paris: Gallimard, 1961); *Guilty*, trans. Bruce Boon [Venice, Calif.: Lapis Press, 1986]).

I'll resume the story of the 121. Sartre, who had been traveling, declared upon his return that he was no less responsible than we were. He was not prosecuted. Why? He was too famous. We know de Gaulle's verdict, according to a rumor: "One does not imprison Voltaire." What a strange confusion and what a regrettable exclusion. De Gaulle forgot—was it disdain for culture or the momentary lack of it?—that Voltaire precisely was imprisoned in the Bastille for close to a year because of satirical verses attacking the Regent, who well deserved it.

We were thus charged, not judged, not condemned, perhaps forgotten or pardoned.

I take no satisfaction in recalling this distortion of justice. One need not shrink from the apparent ridiculousness of recalling for this small case (perhaps there are no small ones) the death of Socrates, who chose to die in obedience to an unfair sentence in order to restore justice, the essence of justice, by accepting as just what was unjust. In his view, everything happens as if the city could never be wrong, even if it is not right. It is a death that is not tragic and that should not be mourned. For it is an ironic death, just as his trial is perhaps the first Stalinist trial (ah, there have been others, as there will be others, whenever community lays claim to the absolute).

I hasten to the end. The Declaration of the 121 was soon better known abroad than in France. A dear friend—a very recent friend for me, a perennial friend for our group—Elio Vittorini, was there to support us and even to train us. What joy, what good fortune to hear him, to see Italo Calvino and later Leonetti with him. Invaluable messages came to us from Germany, first from Hans-Magnus Enzensberger, then from Günter Grass, Ingeborg Bachmann, and Uwe Johnson. Who first had the idea of an international review? I think it was Vittorini, the most ardent and the most experienced. Only recently the review *Lignes* published some of the documents (thanks to Dionys Mascolo, who had kept them) concerning this attempt, which was not vain, even if it failed. On the French side, Louis-René des Forêts—and this turned out to be most precious—had brought us more than his participation, for he agreed to be the secretary for the review to come, a guarantee of vigilance and reserve in relation to so many passions. Maurice Nadeau brought us his experience and Roland Barthes his fame; he worked a lot, and the failure so upset him that he suggested looking for causes and identifying those responsible. He wanted to erect a tomb and turn our deception into an oeuvre. If we refused, it was both to preserve the future and not to accuse some people rather than others, thus escaping the misfortunes of groups that survive through their explosive quarrels.*

Very quickly, it seems to me, there came the most unexpected movement, which felt, however, like the most inevitable one. It was bound to happen. The March 22 movement, the May 1968 revolution. The initiative certainly did not come from us, nor even from those who created the impetus and seemed to lead it. Wildfire, effervescence where we were carried along and where we stopped being together, but in a new way. I will not recount what has already been told many times; instead I will limit myself to evoking the barely conscious difficulties that may have affected us, but without dividing us. I know I felt it: we had become a group of friends, united even in our disagreements. (Which ones? I have forgotten.) Now, in the Action Committees of May 1968, there were no friends, but comrades who addressed each other with the familiar *tu* and did not allow for age differences or the recognition of prior fame (as Sartre realized very quickly). Among the prohibitions written on the walls, there was one that was brought up from time to time and that no one knew was from the Talmud: *It is forbidden to grow old* [Il est interdit de vieillir] (see *The Burnt Book*). During this time, I was closer to Robert and Monique Antelme, letting Dionys spent his days and nights in struggles that were as symbolic as they were real. I recall the day spent at Flins with Marguerite Duras, when we had the feeling that something decisive was going to happen. (There was a death.) It was with Robert and Monique that I went to the Charléty stadium to hear Mendès-France, who was there only to affirm his solidarity and bring his support to a movement that was nothing but movement, undoubtedly to protect demonstrators who did not want to be protected and whom nothing could threaten, outside of fatigue, the absence of a goal, interminable revolt.[4] Despite our precautions, in the Action Committees and elsewhere, we kept inciting reservations, because friendship does not easily yield its place to comradeship. We addressed comrades as *tu*, but as friends we did not address each other as *tu*. Sometimes I ended up blaming Dionys in order to distance myself from friendship. How it cost me; but a little later, with his incomparable generosity, he told me: "I understand you very well." The last demonstration, the one we organized—students, writers, and workers—was forbidden. (I received an official notice from the police that very morning at home: how did

*The responsible party was the Berlin Wall. This event touched us all, but it overwhelmed our German friends. Enzensberger, who was closest to the project, the friendliest too, withdrew to Norway; everyone dispersed. The project of the review continued; it wasn't dead, but it had entered its death throes.

these civil servants know us so well?) It left me with a memory of Michel Leiris: we were walking, arm in arm, with Marguerite between us, to protect each other, and Claude Roy had the honor of being taken and thrown into the van, where the police needed victims so that order would not be so excessively scorned.

Friendship, comradeship, I would have liked, dear Dionys, to interrogate myself from afar with you who are so present, as with those who are even more present, because, having disappeared, they can respond to us only through their disappearance: the dead we let depart and who put the blame on us, for we are never innocent of their deaths. We feel the certainty that we are guilty of not holding them back and not accompanying them all the way to the end. I had a naive plan to have a discussion with Aristotle, with Montaigne, on their conception of friendship. But what for? Sadness lets me only cite these lines, which could just as well be from Apollinaire or Villon and which speak about the time of friendship, what is fleeting about it, up to the moment beyond the end.

> Que sont mes amis devenus . . .
> Je vois qu'ils sont trop clairsemés
> Il ne furent pas bien semés
> Et sont faillis
> Ce sont amis que vent emporte*
>
> What have my friends become . . .
> I see that they are scattered too widely
> They were not well sown
> And fell
> They are friends the wind carries away.

Moving verses, but they lie. Here I contradict my beginning. Fidelity, constancy, endurance, and perhaps continuity, such are the traits of friendship or at least the gifts it gave me.

Greek *philia* is reciprocity, exchange of the Same for the Same, but never opening onto the Other, discovery of the Other as responsible for

---

*Rutebeuf, as quoted by Maurice Roche (éditions Point Hors Lignes). [Rutebeuf (ca. 1245–85) was a medieval French troubadour. This particular poem was adapted into a popular song by Léo Ferré in 1955.]

him, recognition of his pre-excellence, the awakening and the dis-intoxication through this Other who never leaves me in peace, enjoyment (without lust, as Pascal says) of his Highness, of what makes him always closer to the Good than "me."

This is my salutation to Emmanuel Levinas, the only friend—ah, distant friend—whom I call *tu* and who calls me *tu*; that happened not because we were young but out of a deliberate decision, a pact that I hope never to breach.

Our Clandestine Companion

Around twenty years ago, Levinas wrote: "For everyone, this century will have been the end of philosophy,"[1] but he ended his sentence with an exclamation point, which inflected its meaning and perhaps inverted it. This punctual addition was particularly well placed, for our era, destined to give philosophy its burial, will perhaps be described as one of the richest in philosophers (if the word *rich* can still be considered pertinent), marked throughout by philosophical investigations and by an unmatched rivalry between science, literature, and philosophy, in which the latter necessarily has the last word, which does not succeed in being the last.

All, Shamefully, Gloriously

Shamefully, gloriously, by error or by default, we are all philosophers, above all when we submit the philosophical (a term chosen to avoid stressing philosophy) to a questioning that is so radical that all of philosophy is necessary to support it. But I would add (while repeating Bacon and Kant's warning: *de nobis ipsis silemus**) that, as soon as I met Emmanuel Levinas, more than fifty years ago—a happy meeting, in the strongest sense—it was through a sort of manifest obviousness that I persuaded myself that philosophy was life itself, youth itself, in its unbound passion, yet reasonable nonetheless, renewing itself continually and suddenly by the brilliance of entirely new, enigmatic thoughts or by still-unknown names that would shine forth prodigiously much later. Philosophy would be our companion forever, day and night, even in losing its name, becoming literature, knowledge, or nonknowledge—or becoming absent. Our clandestine friend, about whom we respect—we love—that which did not allow us to be linked to her, while having a premonition that there was nothing awake in us, nothing vigilant, including even sleep, that was not due to her difficult friendship. Philosophy or friendship. But here philosophy was precisely not an allegory.

---

*"We are silent about ourselves": Jean-Luc Nancy reminds us of this in his remarkable *Logodaedalus* [*Le discours de la syncope: 1. Logodaedalus* (Paris: Flammarion, 1976)]; *The Discourse of the Syncope: Logodaedalus*, trans. Saul Anton (Stanford: Stanford University Press, 2008)].

Invincible Skepticism

Levinas writes (I will cite from memory at times, thus unreliably) that skepticism is invincible. Skepticism is easily refuted, by a refutation that leaves it intact; does it contradict itself when it presents itself using the reasons that it ruins? Contradiction is also its essence, just as it fights all dogmatism, bringing dissatisfied or onerous presuppositions to light (origin, truth, authenticity, the exemplary, the proper, values), but also, implicitly, by referring to a "dogmatism" so absolute that all affirmation is threatened. (This is already notable in the ancient Skeptics and Sextus Empiricus.) This does not mean that one should play at the maniacal and pathetic nihilism that Lyotard so rightly denounces and for which, once and for all, nothing is *valid.* That would be rest and security once again. The defect of nihilism—a term without vigor, without rigor—is not to know itself as lacking and always to stop itself prematurely. The invincible skepticism that Levinas recognizes shows that for him philosophy and metaphysics, these easily decried names, do not affirm anything that is not surveyed by an indefatigable refuter, to whom he does not yield, but who obliges him to go further, not outside of reason, into the facility of the irrational or of mystical effusion, but toward another reason, toward the other as reason or exigency: this is what appears in each one of his books. Without a doubt he follows the same path; nonetheless, the unexpected things revealed make the path so new or so ancient that, in accompanying him, we are struck as with a blow to the heart—the heart of reason—that makes us think inside: "but I have thought this too, I *must* think it."

Valéry: "The Other Man, a Capital Conception"

There are perhaps thinkers who are more naive than others: Descartes more naive than Leibniz; Plato more naive than Plato. Heidegger, this thinker of our own time, is so bereft of naïveté that he needs disciples to put him into perspective and disciplines; he cannot, moreover, invoke naïveté to excuse him for what occurred in 1933. (But this last point is so serious that one couldn't be content with an episodic allusion: Nazism and Heidegger, this is a wound to thought; each one of us is deeply wounded; we will not deal with it through paralipsis.) Philosophical naïveté is perhaps inseparable from philosophical evidence, because the novelty (the most ancient newness) brought forth by the latter and what it says or *advances* necessarily lends itself to criticism; what advances is vulnerable, yet it is the most important thing. When Levinas asked whether ontology was fundamental (excluding other issues here, and for other reasons, preceding Heidegger, who came to reject the two terms, just as he crossed out the word *being*), he posed a naive question in a certain way, unexpected and unheard of, because he broke with what seemed to have renewed philosophy, something that he was the first to have contributed to understanding and transmitting, thus breaking with himself. Similarly, and in the aftermath of this movement, when he pronounced the word *other* and the relation of I to the Other [*Autrui*] as an exorbitant, infinite, or transcendent relation, one that could not be grasped within a reflection on being and beings, such that all Western philosophy had traditionally turned away from it via the privilege accorded to the Same, to the Self-Same (My-Self), or, more abruptly, to identity, critique would judge this affirmation as naive, accumulate objections, refute it (as is said of K. in *The Castle*: he has always refuted everything). Nonetheless, it is critique that was naive, not understanding what was decisive as well as difficult about this demand, which made reason, including practical reason, ill at ease, but without dismissing it.

I take from Valéry's notebooks (this writer who was hardly naive, who nonetheless is naive, sometimes happily, sometimes unhappily, especially when he tries to demean philosophy, which he does not know well, as when he says: "the systems of the philosophers, which are largely unknown to me, seem generally negligible"), the following presentiment concerning the importance of the Other, even if he expresses it insufficiently: "The Other, a similar other, or perhaps a double of me [but the Other cannot, precisely, be an *alter ego*] is the most mesmerizing abyss, the most recurrent question, the most cunning obstacle. . . . Thus," adds Valéry remarkably, "the other man . . . remains a conception of capital importance."

Questioning Language

I am sure that Levinas does not worry about philosophizing against the prevailing currents. Philosophy is never anything but untimely. The epithet *new* is what suits it the least. However, while restoring to metaphysics and ethics an eminence that, with a facile thoughtlessness, was no longer considered relevant, Levinas walks ahead of, or accompanies—along his own paths—the preoccupations that are par excellence (or *par indigence*) those of our time. For example: he does not fail to question the domain of language in a non-naïve, crucial manner that has been neglected for such a long time by the philosophical tradition. Valéry, to mention him again, thought he was creating difficulties for philosophy by claiming that "philosophy and the rest are nothing but a peculiar use of words," and, further on, "all metaphysics results from a poor use of words." A remark that is clarified when he explains his conception—which can be called existential—namely, that what counts as a "real internal experience" is something that is hidden by a bound system of concepts, or a system of notations or conventions, going beyond "the very particular and personal phenomenon," and presents itself as having, outside this singular phenomenon, the general value of truth or law. In other words, Valéry reproaches philosophy for being what he will demand that literature and poetry should be: a possibility of language, the invention of a language in the second degree ("thinking in a form that one would have invented"), without the "silly and invincible pretension" of assuming that one could get out of this situation by passing this language off as thought. It is true that Valéry would add (and this warning still holds for the best linguists when they deal with poetics) that "all research on Art and Poetry tends to render necessary what is essentially arbitrary"; he thus denounces all temptations or "mimological perversions,"—so long as one understands this necessity as a semblance or an effect of necessity, which is, after all, an enigmatic attempt to transform discourse.

Irreducible Diachrony

What matters to Levinas is different, and passes (should I say fortunately?) only indirectly through linguistic research. If there is an extreme dissymmetry between "me and the other person" (expressed by the impressive phrase "the Other is always closer to God than me," which retains its power whatever one may understand by the unnamed name of *God*), if, however, the infinite relation between me and the Other can be a relation of language, if it is permitted me, me who am barely myself, to have a relation with the extremely Other—the closest and the farthest—through speech, then certain demands that might reverse or overturn speech itself would not fail to result, even if only the following: Others or the Other [*autrui ou l'autre*] cannot be thematized, which is to say, I will not speak of the other or about the other, but I will speak—if I speak—to the Other (the stranger, the one who is poor, the one, precisely, who is speechless, even the master who is without mastery), not to inform him or to transmit knowledge to him—a task for ordinary language—but rather to invoke him (this other so other that his mode of being addressed is not "you" [*tu*] but "he" [*il*]), to testify to him through a manner of Saying that does not erase infinite distance but permits speech through this distance, the speech of the infinite.

In each of his books, Levinas continually refines, in an ever more rigorous reflection, what was said on the subject in *Totality and Infinity*. But precisely, it was *said*, that is to say, thematized, thus was always already said instead of remaining to be said (hence one of the most persistent and insoluble problems of philosophy: How can philosophy say, expose, or present itself without thereby, in using a certain language, contradicting or compromising itself? Must the philosopher not be a writer and thus renounce philosophy, even if it means denouncing the philosophy implicit in writing? Or—must he claim to present a teaching, to exercise mastery—that is, to undertake the venture of the unmastered oral word, while occasionally stooping to *put out* a book? How are we to preserve the dissymmetry, the curvature of space qualified [mistakenly] as intersubjective, the infinity of the speech of the infinite?). Levinas goes the furthest in a text entitled "The Saying and the Said,"[2] a text that speaks to us as if the extraordinary were speaking to us. I have neither the intention nor the ability to repeat or summarize it. It must be read and meditated upon. I can, certainly, evasively recall that, if the said is always already said, Saying is always only yet to be said, which does not privilege the future (the future present of what is to come), nor is it even—at least this is how I interpret it—a prescription in the form of an edict. It is what no I can take upon itself by keeping or safeguarding it, but rather only by giving it. Saying is giving, loss (yes loss), but, I would add, loss within the impossibility of loss pure and simple. Through the said, we belong to order, to the world (the cosmos); we are present to the other with whom we can deal as equals—we are contemporaries. Through Saying, we are torn from that order, but without order quietly disappearing into disorder: noncoincidence with the Other, the impossibility of being together in simple simultaneity, the necessity (the obligation) of assuming a time without present, what Levinas will call "irreducible diachrony," which is not the temporalization that we live but is marked as a lapse of time (or absence of time)—this is what Saying commits us to in our responsibility toward the Other, a responsibility so excessive that we are given over to it passively, at the extreme limit of all patience, rather than being capable of responding to it in our autonomy, in our pretension as Subjects. On the contrary, we are subjected, laid bare (in a laying bare that is not presence or unveiling), a risky laying bear of *oneself*, obsessed or besieged through and through, to the point of "substitution"—one that almost does not exist, existing only for the other—in the "one for the other" relation. This relation must not be conceived as identification, for it does not pass through being, nor is it simply nonbeing, for it measures the incommensurable. It is a relation of absolute impropriety, of strangeness and interruption: nevertheless, a *substitution* of one for another, difference as nonindifference.

Indiscretion with Regard to the Unsayable

I recall several of Levinas's phrases, whose resonance is a philosophical resonance, a call of reason for the awakening of another reason, a reminder of Saying within the said, this ancillary language that nonetheless does not claim to subjugate *the ex-ception*: "indiscretion with regard to the unsayable, which is probably the very task of philosophy."[3] Or again: "Philosophy is perhaps but this exaltation of language in which the words, after the event, find for themselves a condition in which religions, sciences and technologies owe their equilibrium."[4] From here we can glimpse the exigency toward which language is raised, enunciating Saying, which is activity only in appearance, if it prolongs—sustaining without containing—the most extreme passivity. Enigma of a Saying like that of a God speaking within man, this man who counts on no God, for whom there is no inhabiting, who is exiled from every world without a back-world, and who finally does not have even language as a dwelling—at least no more than he would have language merely to affirm or to negate. This is why Levinas, returning to the thought about invincible skepticism, will also say (if I am not mistaken): "Language is already skepticism,"[5] where the accent may be placed on the *already*, and not only because language would be insufficient or essentially negativity, or even because it would exceed the limits of thinking, or else perhaps because of this relation with the excessive, insofar as it carries the trace of the past without presence, a trace that has not left any traces, always already erased, bearing it, nonetheless, outside of being. Thus language would already be skepticism, certainly as a language that does not allow us to hold onto certain knowledge or does not allow transparent communication, but, because of this, a language that exceeds all language by not exceeding it: a language of the *epochē* or, according to Jean-Luc Nancy, a language of the *syncope*. The skepticism of language therefore withdraws from us, up to a certain point (an undetermined limit), all guarantees; and for this reason it does not enclose us in what it would claim as a necessary precaution or a condition.

The Divine Comedy

I do not think that a good approach to Levinas's thinking would be to fix it under titles that it does not refuse, but that justify cursory interpretations or arrest the extreme questions that it incessantly asks us: for example, is it a philosophy of transcendence or a metaphysics of ethics? Perhaps such an approach is bound to fail because we no longer know how to understand such words, weighed down as they are by traditional meanings. The word *transcendence* is either too strong—immediately reducing us to silence—or, on the contrary, maintains itself and us within limits that it should explode. It was Jean Wahl who used to say, in his distinct way, that the greatest transcendence, the transcendence of transcendence, is finally immanence, or the perpetual referral of one to the other. Transcendence within immanence, Levinas is the first to question this strange structure—sensibility, subjectivity—without allowing himself to be satisfied by the clash of such contrarieties. Yet his procedures are striking: to begin or pursue an analysis (most often inspired by phenomenology) with such faithful rigor and knowledge that it seems that everything has thus been said and he is disclosing truth itself—until we arrive at a small remark, introduced (for example) by an "unless" that might easily escape our attention but that imperceptibly fissures all the preceding text and disturbs the solid order that we have been called to observe, an order that remains important nonetheless. This is perhaps the distinctly philosophical movement, not a philosophy by force or with a hammer, but one that was already a resource for Plato in his dialogues (his probity, and also his ruse). We are not dealing with a hermeneutics, and yet because in a certain sense Levinas severs and breaks with a tradition that he knows well, this tradition still serves as a springboard and remains a reference. It is in contrast to this reference that *philosophical invention* renders concrete our indiscretion toward the unsayable, as it does—in a way that is anything but schematic—the call to a beyond of essence, to an "excess" that is neither irrational nor romantic. Thus, by a kind of respectful parricide, he proposes that we should not trust the *presence* and identity of Husserlian *consciousness*, but rather substitute for phenomenological (or ontological) reason reason understood as vigil, as incessant waking, as *vigilance*. This is not a state of the soul—and while it is not the ecstasy of intoxication, it does not remain within lucidity; rather, it makes the heart of the "Ego" beat within its enucleated interior, the other in me outside of me, which can no longer grasp itself in an experience (neither event nor advent), since all manifestation (indeed even the nonmanifestation of the unconscious) always ends up giving itself over to *presence*, which holds us within being. Thus we are exposed, through responsibility, to the enigma of the nonphenomenon, the nonrepresentable, within the ambiguity of an indecipherable trace, a trace to be deciphered.

In the same way (the same way?), if Levinas pronounces, writes the name of God, he does not thereby enter into religion or theology, nor does he conceptualize it, but he makes us intuit that, without being another name for the other (always other than the other, "other otherwise"), the infinite transcendence, or transcendence of the infinite, to which we try to constrain God, will always be ready to slide into absence, "to the point of possible confusion with the incessant bustle of the *there is* [il y a]." But what is it exactly that Levinas calls the *il y a*, beyond any reference to Heidegger's *es gibt* and even well before the latter offered us his entirely different structural analysis of it? The *il y a* is one of Levinas's most fascinating propositions: but it is also his temptation, since, being the inverse of transcendence, it is also indistinct from it. It could be described in terms of being, but as an *impossibility* not to be, the incessant insistence of the neuter, the nocturnal rustling of the anonymous, which never begins (thus an-archic, because it eternally escapes the determination of a beginning), the absolute, but as absolute indetermination. A bewitchment, it attracts one toward an uncertain outside, speaking infinitely outside truth, in the manner of an Other we cannot get rid of simply by considering him deceitful (the evil genius), a mere mockery and derision, for this speech is nothing but laughter treacherously withheld; it gives out signs even as it escapes all interpretation; neither gratuitous nor cheerful, it is serious, but it is also like the illusion of seriousness, which is what disturbs us the most—this speech then is also the movement most likely to deny us the resources of being as place and light. It is a gift of literature, perhaps, and we do not know whether it intoxicates by sobering up or whether its speaking, which both charms and disgusts, does not ultimately attract us because it promises (in a promise that it keeps and does not keep) to clarify what is obscure in all speech, that which in speech evades revelation and manifestation. It is still a trace of nonpresence, the opacity of the transparent.

That God, by his highest transcendence, as the Good above being, must give himself to this inextricable intrigue, and that he cannot directly resolve (except by the unheard call to rectitude) what Hegel might have termed bad infinity, the repetitiveness of what does not return—this is what leaves us before a demand that is necessarily our own, because it exceeds us, a demand that, in the ambiguity of the sacred and the holy, of the "temple" and "theater," makes us spectators-actors-witnesses of the

Divine Comedy where, if we end up laughing, "our laughter remains stuck in our throat."

I would like to add an obsessive reminder to these notes. The book that Levinas entitled *Otherwise than Being, or Beyond Essence* is a philosophical work. It would be difficult not to take it as such. Philosophy, even when it breaks and ruptures, nonetheless solicits us philosophically. And yet the book begins with a dedication, which I transcribe here: "To the memory of those who were closest among the six million assassinated by the National Socialists, alongside the millions and millions of humans of all confessions and all nations, victims of the same hate of the other man, of the same anti-Semitism." How can one philosophize, how can one write in memory of Auschwitz, of those who told us, sometimes in notes buried closed to the crematories: know what happened here, do not forget, and at the same time you will never know.

This is the thought that traverses, and bears, all of Levinas's philosophy and that he proposes to us without saying it, beyond and before every obligation.

The Ascendant Word; or, Are We Still Worthy of Poetry?

(Scattered Notes)

When Mallarmé says: "Only the Poet can speak," when Valéry says: "The true writer is a man who cannot find his words so he seeks them,"[1] I am prepared to give an assent that nonetheless leaves me far from what is at stake, for me, in what we call poetry (we call it, it does not answer). But when I read at the end of a text by Vadim Kozovoï: "Between two points of pain, the shortest path is poetry. So short that, from its solitary blow, time falls decapitated,"[2] I feel questioned by the torment of an enigma whose first effect is to make me feel—confusedly, clearly—that there is no "defining" when it comes to poetry, that, exhausting any definition, it sends me (not in my mind alone but in my life-writing-mind) toward a definitive crisis, because of the indefinite, which it endlessly provokes.

Who could say "I am a poet," as if the "I" could attribute poetry to itself, as if poetry could be one of its many rich possibilities, something that would glorify it and depend upon it, without this subject being, rather than elevated, immediately disqualified and desubjectified [*désassujetti*] by this inappropriate attribution? The old *poète maudit* is nothing other than this impossibility of being recognized in anything other than a bad saying, bad in relation to common, socially admitted language, which, disturbing nothing and no one, can easily be forgotten.

On the one hand, the poet is honored; poetry deserves reverence: "Only the Poet [with his essential capital letter] can speak." On the other hand, he is the placeless wanderer, the pursuer who is persecuted, the one who fails and falters, grounded in nothing but his own refusal (to which all certainty is alien), the multiple solitary vainly in search of solitude, his uninhabitable dwelling. No, he is not the victor; if he turns his distress into courage, if from fear he receives the perpetuation of the unfinished, he finds no richness in being denuded, he who is considered obscure because he brings the generosity of a new day to the "night for nothing."

It falls to the poet to sense the relation between terror and speech, and in this he is always the ancient Pythia, who embodies the horror specific to any saying, the monstrous one who chokes on an impossible voice, incapable of uttering anything, and in doing so gives voice to what precedes all speech, this terrible antecedence that calls for and devastates expression, until expression takes it into itself in order to temper it, to regulate it according to its rhythm—but rhythm, always maintaining a relation to its furious origin, extends this origin through scansion itself, so that no ultimate meaning may escape or settle there. This is poetic untranslation, not in the difficult passage from one language to another, but in the heart of the original language itself, that which escapes from it while being at work within it, which is to say, the untransmissible aspect of the anterior trace, which always erases itself. (Let me recall Jules Renard's witlessly witty phrase: "Mallarmé is untranslatable, even in French." I would add: "above all in French."[3]) But what does Mallarmé himself say about this? Nothing that would immobilize him. He does not escape the national language, but goes toward the *strangeness* that it harbors, as ancient as it is new: ancient because "innate" (the generative idiom), and more than modern, for it uncovers itself in unheard intonations or frees itself through new harmonies: "To endow the voice with intonations entirely unheard even by oneself . . . and to provide the national instrument such harmonies, new but recognized as innate, constitutes the poet, in the extension of his task and his prestige."[4] A disappointing phrase, perhaps, if it did not refer to the poet who is henceforth instituted, and belongs to the institution that builds a tomb for him. But what about the one who does not belong to anything, the one who does not yet have a language "except in the abolition of the text, subtracting the image from it"? Perhaps it is carried by a transnational, indeed translinguistic rhythm that undoes the linear sentence—the syntactic space—to the point of bringing out the fragmentary energy "in which everything becomes suspension," just as (just as?) it interrupts time by replacing it with "the shipwreck of eternal circumstances" or with the short circuit of what escapes measure—metrics—: the shock of "decapitated" expectation. Thus poetic language is never that of a patrimony or the hope of an abstract or fulfilled universality, but the rupture of a Saying refractory to the already said, without which there would not even be silence.

I nullify all this. I will merely add: when Mallarmé points out what his aim is, the reply comes, decisively: "I call it Transposition"[5]—certainly, first the transport of what *is* in the other of a language, but also, in this language that is never given as a mother tongue would be, the punctuated trajectory where only passage, tension, and modulation count, but not the points one passes through, the terms that do not terminate anything. Thus poetry would be the demand for a translation that it renders impossible, or else the perpetual transfer that it calls for while missing or denying it. Hence, perhaps, the answer that Joyce is supposed to have given: "Untranslatable? Nothing." This means that there is nothing that should not already be the work of a laborious translator, just like the insolent Commentator, all the indefatigable Passers-on and Passers-by—hence Vadim Kozovoï's injunction: "Clear the path, all of you." (Must we recall René Char's morning-time affirmation: "We are passers-by *striving* to pass, trying to stir up trouble, to inflict our warmth, to say our exuberance"?[6])

Mallarmé—him again—: he took time to renounce the distinction between prose and verse, that is, to recognize that this division should be placed elsewhere—where? This will remain problematic. In 1893, writing to Charles Bonnier, he robustly defined the poetic deed: "The poetic deed consists in grouping, rapidly, in a certain number of equal traits, in order to adjust them, otherwise distant and scattered phrases, but ones that nonetheless—this is explosive—rhyme together, so to speak. One must thus, above all, lay out the common measure, which is what must be applied; or the Verse. The poem remains brief, multiplies itself, into a book." Of course, Mallarmé adapts his thought to poems that he is reading (Bonnier's); hence, despite the politeness, the exclusion of the *emotional notation* that is audaciously declared to be not poetry but prose . . .: "The poetic operation of the common measure is [thus] lacking there, or is not in play."* And yet (it is well known), after the "memorable crisis" ("Such a case has never been seen. Verse has been violated"),[7] he says: "In the genre called prose there are sometimes admirable verses, every sort of rhythm."[8] And this, at the limit, suppresses poetry and, above all, dissolves these hybrid modes dubbed "poems in prose" or "free verse," whereas in 1895, with "Mystery in Letters," he institutes "the Critical poem" or "the critical poems," etc. But—thus claiming to be more of a formalist than he is, only in order to break with all romanticism and perhaps even with Baudelaire—he will reaffirm: "Above all it is a question of making music with one's pain, which itself does not directly matter." (But the word *directly* must be taken into account: the pathetic register or pathos aspires to the immediate, which refuses expression).

Always Mallarmé. The meaning of the "*Mardis*," an advanced course in poetry, should be questioned, says one of the participants. This is nothing to get excited about. But despite the charm and the enchantment, was it Mallarmé who, leaning against the chimney, let a speech unfold whose wonders were incapable of being reconstructed once outside (perhaps Lacan and his seminar)? Or was it no more than Mallarmé, he who used to say something like: I bear no relation to anyone by that name? Or, when he described how disagreeable the word *poet* was to him and declared (before Georges Bataille) his hatred for the word *poetry*, adding, according to Fontainas[9]—which is not a guarantee—: one must dream of an art that is eternal and yet continually growing, and from which man disappears; there is no Monsieur who all his life is a poet; one was a poet the day, the hour when the poem gave him a momentary existence (breaking him at the same time as he contributes to it in relation to the unknown that excludes or disperses him). "Creating: excluding oneself" (René Char). "Author, creator, poet, this man has never existed"[10] (Rimbaud).

---

*One must cite and reread the letter in context: "The poetic fact itself consists in grouping, rapidly [*rapidly*, a word to consider], in a certain number of equal traits, in order to adjust them, otherwise distant and scattered phrases, but ones that nonetheless—this is explosive—rhyme together, so to speak. One must thus, above all, lay out the common measure, which is what must be applied; or the Verse. The poem remains brief, multiplies itself, into a book; its fixity forms a norm, like verse. Such, at least, is my vision. Now, as for the proportional emotional notation, I taste it absolutely, but as prose, delicate, nude, openworked. The poetic operation of the common measure is [thus] lacking there, or is not in play." (Letter to Charles Bonnier, March 1893, *Correspondance*, vol. 6 (Paris: Gallimard, 1959–85); "Letter to Charles Bonnier, March 1893," in *Selected Letters of Stéphane Mallarmé*, trans. Rosemary Lloyd (Chicago: University of Chicago Press, 1988), 191. The translation provided here follows Blanchot's quote.

That the fury (the terror), impure pure violence, the explosive kind attributed, through image, to the beginning of the universe (the big bang) can remain in the still traditional poem, Rimbaud, of course, attests: "And all vengeance?—Nothing! . . . But yes, all of it,/We want it! . . . /This is our due. Blood! Blood! The Golden flame!/All for war, for vengeance, for terror."[11] Poetic rage to an extreme point. Artaud does not add to it, except in making syllabic language explode with spasm, arythmia, pulse without measure, a sudden dash toward the unattained form, expulsion and retention of the void. But Rimbaud will remain eternally separate through his solitary indifference, the definitive oblivion in which he cuts himself off, "surgically removing poetry from himself, alive," even in poetry itself, not because one day he leaves, but because he is always already outside: "What is my nothingness compared to the stupor that awaits you?"[12] Poetry: violence of forceful entry where language holds itself back in order to open itself, out of shock or weakness, to the enigma of its improper gap, its alien separation. "Moving ahead it can only be the end of the world."[13]

Valéry, who did not always attach great value to Rimbaud's work, says something concerning him: "The poet's work is perhaps, of all work, the one where the greatest impatience essentially requires the greatest patience." The few sketches or drafts of *A Season in Hell* show that Rimbaud needed time to achieve brevity, for tightening the rhythm, for "decapitated time." He never added but always cut away, as if brute or brutal language—and sudden bitterness—did not come first in this all too amenable and almost naturally likeable French. The draft: "Shut up, this is arrogance. Right now." The definitive text: "Arrogance." Draft: "Oh! My God, I'm afraid, have pity." Final text: "Pity! Lord, I'm afraid." Etc.

What is hard and rough (for us) in some of Vadim Kozovoï's poems—to put it better, devastating—evokes this impatient demand, the rhythmic rupture, the necessity of going fast that rejects the state of arrest, and at times an accumulation of images that, one could say, are telescoped into a single word. But just as Rimbaud's dryness, the striking violence, the nonincantatory shock maintain an inner rhythm and a premeditated vibration that, beyond lyricism and provocation, marks the impetus toward . . . (the unknown?), likewise in Vadim Kozovoï, one must intuit a rigor and a freedom, a terrible vehemence and an even more terrible softness, a furious, uncontrollable movement, controlled nonetheless, perhaps the intolerant revolt against all intolerance, that is to say, against the oppression that forbids this eternal migrant to leave, the poet, whose only task is to go away. "I have stayed awake, trying to find out why he wanted to escape so much . . . One day perhaps he would disappear marvelously . . ."[14] Marvelously? Miserably? There is no difference. "Miserable miracle": Michaux has warned us about it forever more.[15]

The poetic enigma. Take Mallarmé's most certain affirmation: "The work implies the elocutionary disappearance of the poet."[16] Whereas (in 1941) Valéry described Mallarmé's strangeness by saying exactly the contrary: "From where and how was this strange and unshakeable *certainty* born upon which Mallarmé was able to base his whole life—his renunciations, his unknown fears . . .—to make himself . . . the very man of an oeuvre *that he did not complete* and that he knew was incapable of being completed?" Put otherwise (for there is always an "otherwise"): for Mallarmé, the work is the final negation of the author, and his progressive deletion (which has the sense of a great exigency); but Valéry sees nothing in Mallarmé but an author without an oeuvre, a man certain of an unfinished oeuvre, or devoting himself all his life to the nothingness of an oeuvre (which means: Mallarmé was admirable and mad, admirable for having imparted his madness to the person who was the least inclined to it, Valéry). But isn't there, in this duplicity, the very force of the poetic enigma, which has a share in the impossible?

Valéry's judgment on Rimbaud (*A Season in Hell*, at least). The immense blaze that it set alight left him "cold." There is nothing scandalous in that. I deduce from it not that poetry is pure subjectivity but that it is not a "value" that can be recognized: it escapes anyone waiting for an *effect*. Rimbaud was far too impatient, much too foreign to others and to himself to want to exercise effects upon anyone. His books rot in a cellar. He forgets them, he forgets himself, and he leaves. He is a Hebrew, perhaps, a prophet without a people and without God, summoned by no word, attracted by the bitter risk of the unknown from which the other could never take shape—thus, the man who most neglects ordinary consideration, who is destructive of solidarity to the point that he is even deprived of solitude. Elsewhere Valéry speaks differently: "All known literature is written in the language of *common sense*. Except Rimbaud . . ." But he is clearly not overwhelmed.* Mallarmé was, intuitively, at least. Perhaps one can only love a single poet—polygamy is forbidden: in one alone, the one who would be every one, not totality, but poetic infinity.

It is here that translation, "this madness," comes back to us as an impossible necessity. To translate, above all, the untranslatable: not only when the text transports an autonomous meaning that alone would matter, but when sound, image, voice (the phonological), and especially the principality of rhythm are predominant in relation to meaning, or when they make sense in such a way that sense—always actualized, in formation, or "in the nascent state"—is indissociable from what, by itself, has no sense and is not ordered within the semantic register. And that is what the poem is. Certainly, no translator and no translation can make it pass intact from one language to another, or allow it to be read or heard as if it were transparent. And I would add: fortunately. The poem, in its original language, is always already different from this language, whether it reinstates or instates it, and it is this difference, this alterity, through which the translator comes to grasp himself or by which he is seized, modifying his own language in turn, making it shift dangerously, taking away its identity and transparency, which would reduce it to "common sense," as Valéry says. Opacity? Opacity of sense? Opacity as sense? Neither one nor the other. Opacity comes from the multiple strata of language through which wanders and is formed what finally—at infinity—will signify: strata that at the same time shine or darken in their signifying, moments that are neglected in everyday language but that of themselves transform the latter to the point of making heard another hearing, another understanding [*entente*], the unlimited hearing that breaks with ordinary commerce. This is perhaps the source of poetic solitude. (Is someone there to hear? Does hearing suffice for the infinite?) It is also the source of poetic fraternity ("sovereign conversation"), since through the poem we are called to the

*A term that it would certainly be unsuitable to apply to him. And yet he writes: "Mallarmé struck me."—struck [*frappé*] is a very strong term; he received a blow. And another morning, he would write: "I adored this extraordinary man."

exigency of an interminable relation in which the "I" is always inflected before the other and in which speech, writing, and sign collapse, without ceasing the pursuit of an anteriority that founds them and that mysteriously remains in them by way of a terrifying dispersal.

To end (but have I started?), I will quote a passing remark from Valéry: "I admit that I do not believe in the future of poetry every day." How is one to believe in it, and how is one to believe in any future without it? I will also quote René Char: "How are we to deliver poetry from its oppressors? Poetry, which is enigmatic clarity and rapid approach, in discovering them, annuls them."[17] May the poems of Vadim Kozovoï, in his language, which is unknown to us, and in our language, which is not only ours, bring us the promise that against the oppressors (they are everywhere, but their threat is not nameless) "decapitated time" is still preparing another time when, without us, hope remains for the hopeless whom we have loved, the only survival that we can never deny.

Encounters (On the Resistance and May 68)

Can the *Nouvel observateur* be twenty years old? Sometimes it seems younger to me, sometimes older: all the more so when I remember the work I did for "France Observateur," which takes me back to an even older period. That is why I think I could respond better by going back in time. For me, what counted were encounters, those moments when chance becomes necessity. Encounters with people, encounters with places. Here is my share of biography:

The encounter with Emmanuel Levinas (Strasbourg, 1925). Husserl, Heidegger, an approach to Judaism.

The encounters with Georges Bataille and René Char (1940). The call to irregularity. The limit experience. Opposition to the Occupier and the Vichy regime. The underground.

Éze-Village (1947–57). Ten years of solitary writing.

The encounter with Robert Antelme and his friends (1958). The Algerian War, the Declaration of the 121, the attempt at a *Revue internationale*.

With the same people and with everyone
May 1968

Maurice Blanchot

Peace, Peace Far and Near

In our tradition, which exhausts itself by preserving itself, it seems to me that there have always been two chosen peoples, two "miracles" or two enigmas. They are two small peoples, almost imperceptible on the map, and yet rich with a message that has educated the centuries. One of them, however, never suffered from being the model nation, the exemplary representative of that which nourishes our nostalgia. The Greeks were never the object of resentment for having transmitted logos, philosophy, beauty, and a certain idea of democracy. The Greeks, a chosen people par excellence. But for the Jews, the same election, or a superior and much more ancient election, is held to be an arrogant claim, a particularity that isolates, even if what was passed down or taught to the Jews is valid for all and is the affirmation or the promise of the Unique that is valid for all.

God would not have revealed himself only to a single people. This is what displeased many thinkers, some Christians, and even certain Jews. "Why did the Creator not communicate the secret of his Unity to all the peoples of the Universe . . .?" But maybe the idea of election was misunderstood. "From now on, if you hear my voice and if you keep my covenant, you will be a segulah to me dearer than all others, for all the earth is mine." A "segulah" (and here I am repeating a knowledge that is not my own) would not be the affirmation, the trait of "election," but a "benefit," a "precious treasure," and perhaps a "mediation." (I have doubts about this last meaning.) The point is to make it known that the Jewish people was not chosen among others because it was already most worthy of a lofty choice, but that this choice imposed a burden, an additional charge, an excess of responsibility, a blessing that could be suspended whenever the covenant was broken, for nothing is given once and for all (nor is anything definitively withdrawn).

The fact remains that the Jewish people are a people apart, not because of ethnic or racial particularities, but because they were constituted as a people by the revelation on Sinai—and until then they were a crowd, a mass, subjected to the ordeal and the lesson of the desert. Certainly, the revelation was heard or received by one man only, but the waiting was shared by all, and it consecrated them as a people, a people of priests (though the sacerdotal function is reserved for only a few), a prophetic people: "Before you were born, I had consecrated (separated, sacrificed) you, and I designated you ever since as the prophet of nations." Election is not a privilege. If the revelation of the Torah chooses a people to bear it, this was meant to tell them not that because of this choice they are the best, but rather that they are privileged to make it known that they are not: "Absolute rule for your generations: you and the stranger will be equal before the Eternal." A revelation that is unique, and also of the unique. Never were the Greeks, the bearers of logos, aware that there should be equality of speech and law with the barbarians. This is an astonishing situation. The Hebrews were drawn out from all nations (represented by Egypt) in order to recognize, in this withdrawal and in this marginalization, the opening to all and to every nation, the equality of all before the Eternal (but not the abstract and repetitive equality that excludes responsibility and fraternity). It is as if what had been revealed to the Jews was that they were other in order to be liberated from the Same, to awaken to alterity in the extraordinary concern for the other. For at the very instant when the Eternal, in seemingly untimely fashion, sets the Jewish people apart from the whole, through an ambiguous election in view of their singular vocation, but also proclaims, "for all the earth is mine," he renews the demand for universality from which Jewish singularity must not turn away but toward which it opens itself—in order to keep it open. An infinite task.

Must we recall (yes, no doubt for myself) that such was Abraham's task from the very first? Drawn away from Ur—a great, closed civilization—to respond to the call, he leaves, without knowing where he is going (his knowledge is Chaldean), through the desert, the ordeal of the unknown with the uncertain promise of the future, heading toward . . . toward himself, toward the transgression of himself, toward the other name that would finally be given to him so that his vocation as a guide and a threshold being would be signified. ("Now the Eternal appeared to Abraham, as he sat at the entrance to his tent in the heat of the day.")[1]

Conveyor [*passeur*], passage, crossing: this is the definition of the Hebrew, his vocation, but it is also the double manner in which the particular is in a relation without relation with the infinitely distant infinity, which it is not fitting to represent even metaphorically. This relation is voice or speech, a speech that does not mediate in the manner of logos and does not abolish distance, but one that can make itself heard only by the absolute gap of an infinitely maintained separation. At the same time, God is not only the God of the philosophers, withdrawn and preserved by his absence, for he accepts particularizing himself in some way in order to let himself be named the God of Abraham, Isaac, and Jacob (as Pascal still knew). He does not historicize himself, certainly, but he passes and crosses through history, teaching Israel that Israel is not a stranger to history and that it is Israel's task to appear in history in order to judge it and to pass into it through its very separation.

The universal vocation of a people separated and chosen so that this particularity may have an annunciatory value cannot occur without conflict and at the very least without a dialogue in which Jewish thought, so welcoming (the very thought that is considered closed off), not only welcomes Greek philosophy but gives it a meaning that will perpetuate it beyond itself. At other times this dialogue maintains itself through historical conflicts as a Tradition that has both universality and a specific demand for reason that can enlighten us today, at a moment when we are suspicious of both, discovering in them a form of oppression as well as a lure and a myth (reason as idol and as myth: this might be the suspicion that founds modernity, as well as the threat it poses to itself).

All the terms with which we might be content to evoke or invoke this double finality of Judaism—immanence, transcendence, eternity, history, universality, particularity, eternal Zion, and temporal Zion—are important because in being worn down they let shine through the need for a renewal that will exceed and upset all established language. It does not suffice to put philosophy into question; one must awaken a question or a meaning in it that it has not known how to bear, in spite of the effort of so many exceptional thinkers. How, for example, is one to consider the proximity of the Eternal in the Bible, which has been called his fellowship, without losing what is no less essential: the absolute distance, the retreat from all presence, the voice of absence that resounds in the distance of historical understanding? How can the Infinite—which is not a pure and simple beyond, nor a definitively superlative supereminence, but a "growing surplus of Infinity"—expose itself to the constraint of finitude without breaching it through a dangerously communionlike experience that will exclude or dissolve the sacred value of separation? In our time, we need a thinker who is extraordinary (I mean this in the literal sense, not as an indication of praise) to teach us once again that the meaning of the beyond and of transcendence may find a place in *ethics*, which would not merely be a forgotten or neglected discipline but would impose a philosophical reversal upon us, an upheaval of all our theoretical and practical assumptions (even if these are not scorned, but put back in their place). Thus, the absolute distance of God will not be signified by a movement of sensibility (religious experience), but rather "edges into my responsibility," which becomes infinite, as it were, by making itself into an always insufficient obligation toward others. It is not that the alterity of God can find its substitute or its analogue in the alterity of others to whom, liberated or expelled from myself, I am called to respond, with an unlimited responsibility. Other, certainly, "but other otherwise, other with an alterity prior to the otherness of others," transcendence unto absence that excludes itself from Being, making possible its denial or its disappearance.

Here, it may perhaps be permissible to evoke—awkwardly—Moses' singular demands, first praying to the Eternal to make him know his "goodness," both his actions and our obligations (that is, the decisions of God in the government of the world, for through them there is an indirect knowledge of God). He receives a favorable response. Such things could thus be asked for. But when Moses, going further in order to deepen his knowledge of the divine, presents the irrepressible demand, which is dangerous in every sense, "Show me your glory," he runs into eternal refusal: "You will not see my face." And if God, with infinite precautions, allows himself to be seen *a tergo*—that is, as having always passed, as a trace that guarantees no presence, it is not to attenuate the interdiction; rather, it is to privilege invisibility and prevent the perils of direct knowledge of the divine. Judaism, through the gift of the written and the oral Torah, where a unique intrigue with the Most High is inscribed, is the testimony, always to be recalled, that turns away from the temptations of Presence and the vain brilliance of Manifestation.

Messianic *impatience* is perhaps the danger of dangers. Ethics is linked to a teaching of patience within urgency itself, for the address of the other does not leave any time and demands a response from me that exceeds me, that withdraws me from myself and, in this withdrawal, opens me to something greater than myself and than any self.*

Justice demands and calls for ever more justice: in me, outside of me, and in justice itself, thus also in the knowledge and exercise of justice. All of which presupposes what we could call the tragic imbroglio of *the other* and others, hence the intervention of the social and the political, under

*However, one must not conclude—this would still be impatience—that concern for others would be a fruitful way to show a concern for the divine (he who gives to the poor does not lend to God) or that ethics could replace theology. If philosophy still maintains itself in what goes beyond it, it does so because it is called to raise logos to its breaking point, and in this rupture, to seek a field other than that of a heightened power, a coherence other than that of the system, and a beyond of the universal that cannot be diverted into or pacified by any totality.

the guarantee of the law, in the service of all that is far (first of all) and all that is near—the redoubling of the word *peace* may come from here, so that this last word may be deepened as an echo of itself in an incomparable repetition.

The long road of justice is also hard. Like the path of Abraham, who left alone, going toward everyone—from particularity to universality, under the threat of nights and in the hope of days.

P.S. In this text, although I name no commentators, I am nonetheless indebted to many. And, to one alone, I am indebted for almost everything, both in my life and in my thinking.

Letter to Blandine Jeanson

February 6, 1986

Dear Blandine Jeanson,

Do not be offended by my negative response. I have always tried, more or less justifiably, to *appear* as little as possible, not in order to exalt my books, but to avoid the presence of an author who would claim to have an existence of his own.

Naturally, this is an entirely personal exigency, which has no value for anyone else (maybe).

May Jean Gattegno's project and yours meet with success, wishing you the very best,

Maurice Blanchot

Our Responsibility (On Nelson Mandela)

How can one speak or write in an appropriate way on the segregation of Blacks and Whites? Thus what was experienced when Nazism excluded a part of humanity from life and from the right to life persists after the disaster that seemed to render such a wretched doctrine impossible or unformulatable.

And in fact, *apartheid* found its juridical form at the precise moment when the colonialist nations were collapsing, as they recognized that they did not have the privilege of embodying the diversity of the human spirit. For the Boers, everything happened, on the contrary, as if they had the task of arresting development and lending truth to Hegel's ill-considered formulation: "Africa has no history."[1] If one wanted to find excuses for them, one might say that they themselves have not changed and that they have held onto and even strengthened the prejudices of former colonizers (from the sixteenth and seventeenth centuries, during the time when Montaigne was discovering that there are cultures that are different yet equal).

Initially, these adventurers who wanted to put down roots in some unknown lands had force on their side, as well as an exclusive culture and a limited and, moreover, persecuted religion. Centuries passed. The archaic exigencies remained. They merely protected themselves with fierce yet contradictory codes. It was more or less implicitly understood that everyone (people of color and Whites) had their own culture, which could only develop through reciprocal separation. This hypocritical decision yielded almost immediately to the terror of number and the necessity of using "inferiors" for servile tasks. Whites and Blacks lived side by side, a coexistence that was indispensable, without ceasing to be dangerous. In many cases, it was necessary for Blacks to be present (to work), but not present (having no right to a purely personal or idle presence).

Apartheid thus gave way to a piece of legislation almost more unbearable than slavery. Blacks are indispensable, but they expose Whites to a dangerous contamination. Similarly, it is a great crime for a Black man to become cultured in the Western way. If this misfortune occurs, it destroys social equilibrium and may lead to communism or its equivalent. Hence the sentence imposed on Nelson Mandela. He is too well educated and too capable to be allowed to remain free. Communism, community, and democracy are excluded. In the end, the laws are insufficient, for they maintain certain guarantees. So they must be suspended. There is a state of emergency, the banning of all free information, a turning inward and self-enclosure, and, in the end, a break with the rest of the world, except when it comes to commodities, since business remains the final truth.

I do not recall the awful facts only so that they will not be erased from memory, but also so that memory of them should make us more aware of our responsibility. This barbarity, this suffering, the countless assassinations, we have a share in them to the extent that we welcome them with a certain indifference and to the extent that our days and nights are not troubled by them. It is very striking that the man who unfortunately leads the government of this country mocks what he calls our concern for a good conscience—his own is assuredly unaffected by what takes place over there, in some other world. Similarly, the inertia of the European community disqualifies the pledge of ideals and of civilization that it claims to represent. We must know that we too are responsible and guilty, if we do not make a call heard, a denunciation, a shout and a shout once more.

And let us become worthy to repeat Breyten Breytenbach's words, addressed to Winnie Mandela:

Our heart is with you.
Africa will be free.[2]

What Is Closest to Me

Whatever happens, I am with Israel. I am with Israel when Israel suffers. I am with Israel when Israel suffers from inflicting suffering.

I cannot say anything more. Certainly, I have my political preferences. I am for Peres.

I think Begin was wrong, very wrong, to encourage colonization.[1] But I do not feel I have the right to preach, when what is closest to me is at stake.

Writing Committed to Silence

For Edmond Jabès

Should we forget? Should we remember? Remember what? That which we cannot name—the Shoah, the Extermination, the Genocide. Some time ago, a correspondent of mine, responding to (among other questions) some fragments of *Writing of the Disaster*, as well as to a text that appeared in *L'Arche*, told me the following: Benny Lévy (Sartre's companion and friend in the last days) thinks that too much fidelity to testimony of the Horror exposes us to nihilism. He invokes God's warning: "Write this for a memorial in the book . . . that I will surely erase the remembrance of Amalek from under the heavens." Then, in Deuteronomy, which is perhaps only a less abrupt reprise of Exodus: "Memorize what Amalek does on the way before the exit from Mesram. . . . Amalek did not shudder before Elohim." (This absence of shuddering is the utmost arrogance, as if he wanted to put himself on the same plane as the Most High). The conclusion: "Erase the memory of Amalek from under the heavens. You shall not forget!"*

The two recommendations are close yet different. In Exodus, it is "God" (the unnamable name) who asserts: "I will surely erase the memory of Amalek from under the heavens." In Deuteronomy, it is said "Erase (yourself) the memory of Amalek from beneath the heavens." A remarkable change. But, in the two cases, if erasure is prescribed, then so too is

*Why is Amalek considered the incarnation of Evil, when there are so many other persecutors of Israel? Let us not forget the lesson of Levinas and David Banon. Amalek is not just anyone: he is the son or the grandson of Esau, the nephew of Jacob. An extraordinary lineage. Only his mother, who was of royal blood but lacked a crown, is a foreigner, who had the profound desire to convert. A desire that was not fulfilled: the patriarchs, unable to discern her vocation, merely saw a banal desire to find a husband and rejected her. Banished, she could have returned with the resentment of the spurned, to rule among her own people. But she humbly made herself a servant and concubine to Eliphaz, Esau's son, considering it "better to be a servant in this house than a queen in another country." The result was Amalek, who embodied the bitter memory of his repudiated mother. What followed was the misfortune of endless resentment, the cause of enduring but unjustified evil. Here Amalek's cruelty can be made out from the fact that he attacks the Hebrews immediately after they left Egypt (and even before they did so), while they were still a confused, disorganized, and vulnerable mass ready for peace, not war.

remembering: "Write this as a memorial in the book" (Exodus). In Deuteronomy: "You shall remember what Amalek did"—and finally: "do not forget."

Do Forgetfulness and Remembering go together? You cannot liberate yourself from remembering if you hold it in forgetting. Beyond remembering, there is still Memory. Forgetting does not erase the impossibility of forgetting. Perhaps everything begins with forgetting, but forgetting ruins the beginning, reminding us that forgetting only refers to the forgetting that torments us by refusing the absence that is irresponsibility.

Allow me to borrow from Emmanuel Levinas (what have I not borrowed from him?) Ben Yoma's scruple, which asks our sages: "Will the remembrance of the exodus from Egypt still be obligatory in the Days of the Messiah? (to which the answer is yes, even if the memory is not the same).[1] And the word of Isaiah: "Do not recall past events, do not meditate on ancient times." Are we thus freed, unburdened from what we have suffered? Quite the contrary, for Isaiah announces the war of wars, of Gog and Magog; he enjoins us not to lament the past, for the worst is yet to come, and even the past is to come. (I am simplifying excessively.)

The Shoah. Once again I transcribe what was written at Birkenau and escapes memory as it escapes thought, by way of a warning from which no thoughts and no memories are free: "Know what happened here. Do not forget. And yet you will never know." Claude Lanzmann tells us: "Do not ask *why* it took place. Here, there is no why."[2] If one questions oneself about the horror, questions how it might be possible for it to be explained, questions the possibility of this possibility, then it is altered (lost), to the very degree that something is saved (the question itself). Neither memory nor forgetting inherits the task of transmission, "for the act of transmission alone is what counts and because no intelligibility preexists transmission" (itself always uncertain, entrusted to others without the transmission releasing them, on the contrary, with it burdening them all the more). "No why, but no response to the refusal of why, either."

Nothing, then, is to be said about remembering, nothing about the past (which does not pass), nothing about the *trace*, nothing about the piercing point. It comes down to each one to remain (or to fall) in the face of the event: the event beyond answer, beyond questions. That is the pact.

Jabès: "The desert has no book."

Jabès: "There is no innocent memory."

Jabès: "Here, the end of speech, of the book, of chance."

[I think it suits a writer better]

(On Nationalism and Internationalism)

I think it suits a writer better to attempt to ask new questions rather than respond to questions that have already been posed.

However, when it comes to the questionnaire that you put before me, I would answer without hesitation:

There is no good nationalism. Nationalism always tends to assimilate and unify [*intégrer*] everything, all values; that is why it ends up being exclusive and fundamentalist [*intégral*], which is to say, the only value.

The International exigency: allow me to refer to issue 11 of the review *Lignes*, which published the dossier on the *Revue internationale* (1960–64), which lays out the concerns that were ours as French writers, Italian writers, German writers, and English writers. The failure of this project did not demonstrate that it was a utopia. That which does not succeed remains necessary. It still remains our concern.

[The Inquisition destroyed the Catholic religion]

(On Salman Rushdie)

The Inquisition destroyed the Catholic religion at the same time as Giordano Bruno was killed.

The death penalty over a book is destroying the Islamic religion.

What remains is the Bible, what remains is Judaism considered as respect for the other by means of writing itself.

To write is to hold oneself, through passivity, beyond death—a death that fleetingly establishes a search for the Other, a relation without relation to others [*autrui*].

I invite Rushdie to my house (in the South). I invite the descendent or the successor of the Khomeini to my house. I will be between the two of you, the Koran as well.

It will pronounce itself,

Come.

NOTES

FOREWORD: THE FRIENDSHIP OF THE NO, BY KEVIN HART

NOTE: I wish to thank Leslie Hill and Michael Holland for sharing some of their copies of early political writings by Blanchot and for their comments on an earlier version of this foreword. Thanks too to Claire Lyu for her careful reading. I am obliged to William Flesch for allowing me to read Blanchot's unpublished letters to him about the "de Man affair." Jean-Luc Nancy, Claire Nancy, and Leonid Kharlamov showed great kindness in allowing me to read a letter that Blanchot wrote to Roger Laporte in the 1980s about his early political life. The letter was to be included in a special issue of *Cahiers de l'Herne* on Blanchot, but the project remained incomplete, and the letter unpublished.

1. Emmanuel Levinas, "Interview with François Poiré (1986)," *Is It Righteous to Be? Interviews with Emmanuel Levinas*, ed. Jill Robbins (Stanford: Stanford University Press, 2001), 29.

2. Ibid.

3. Paul Valéry, *Reflections on the World Today*, trans. Francis Scarfe (London: Thames and Hudson, 1951), 7, 10. The English translation is of an expanded and selective version of *Regards sur le monde actuel* (1931).

4. Ibid., 26.

5. Ibid., 27.

6. See Maurice Blanchot, "Comment s'emparer du pouvoir?" *Journal des débats*, August 18, 1931, 1. The piece is signed "M.B.," not "M.Bl.," yet the identification by Michael Holland seems accurate.

7. Curzio Malaparte, *Coup d'État: The Technique of Revolution*, trans. Sylvia Saunders (New York: E. P. Dutton and Co., 1932), 250, 18.

8. Blanchot, "Comment s'emparer du pouvoir?" 1.

9. See Blanchot, "Réquisitoire contre la France," *L'Insurgé* 1, January 13, 1937, 4.

10. See Blanchot, "La guerre pour rien," *Combat* 3, March 1936, 42, and "Après le coup de force germanique," *Combat* 4, April 1936, 59. Also see "Blum provoque à la guerre," *L'Insurgé* 12, March 31, 1937, 4, esp. the final paragraph.

11. See Blanchot, "Le caravansérail," *Combat* 10, December 1936, 171.

12. See Blanchot, "La révolte contre le pouvoir," *Le rempart* 40, May 31, 1933, 1.

13. Blanchot, "La révolution nécessaire," *Le rempart* 62, June 22, 1933, 3.

14. Blanchot, "La vraie menace du Troisième Reich," *Le rempart* 69, June 29, 1933, 3.

15. On the formulation "neither right nor left," see Zeev Sternhell, *Ni droite ni gauche: L'Idéologie fasciste en France* (Paris: Seuil, 1983). I am in complete agreement with Leslie Hill in his interpretation of this matter. See his *Blanchot: Extreme Contemporary* (London: Routledge, 1997), 40–41.

16. See, e.g., Blanchot, "La vraie menace du Troisième Reich," 3, esp. the final paragraph.

17. See Blanchot, "La révolution nécessaire," 2.

18. Blanchot, "Le terrorisme, méthode de salut public," *Combat* 7, July 1936, 106.

19. Blanchot, "Des violences antisémites à l'apothéose du travail," *Le rempart* 10, May 1, 1933, 3.

20. See Blanchot, "Two Letters to Maurice Nadeau," trans. Michael Holland, *Paragraph* 30, no. 3 (2007): 19, where Blanchot writes of closing down *L'Insurgé* "the moment it allowed an article with a hint of anti-semitism in it to appear." In Blanchot's as yet unpublished letter to Laporte, the piece is called "détestable."

21. Blanchot, "Le terrorisme, méthode de salut public," 106.

22. See Blanchot, "Two Letters to Maurice Nadeau," 18. See the unsigned review of the novel in *Je suis partout*, 534, October 18, 1941, 8. Earlier, the paper had two special issues, "Les juifs" and "Les juifs et la France," both of which are fiercely anti-Semitic.

23. Levinas, "Interview with François Poiré (1986)," *Is It Righteous to Be?* 29.

24. See Paul Lévy, *Journal d'un exilé* (Paris: Grasset, 1949), 30.

25. See Paul Lévy, "La peste hitlerienne," *Au temps des grimaces* (Paris: Nagel, 1948), 111–15. This editorial is dated July 21, 1936. Several other pieces published in the 1930s would have angered the Germans. They repay close attention and yield interesting comparisons with Blanchot's political journalism of the time.

26. Blanchot, "La seule manière d'être français," *L'Insurgé* 23, June 16, 1937, 4; "Nous, les complices de Blum . . .," *L'Insurgé* 2, January 20, 1937, 4.

27. Blanchot, "La France, nation à venir," *Combat* 19, November 1937, 132.

28. Blanchot, "On demande des dissidents," *Combat* 20, December 1937, 155.

29. Attention should be drawn to Blanchot's article "La politique de Sainte-Beuve," *Journal des débats*, March 10, 1942, 1–2. The article is examined by Jeffrey Mehlman, "Pour Sainte-Beuve: Maurice Blanchot, 10 March

1942," in *Maurice Blanchot: The Demand of Writing*, ed. Carolyn Bailey Gill (London: Routledge, 1996), 212–31. The essay comes after a letter by Blanchot addressed to Roger Laporte, in which Blanchot castigates himself very severely for even mentioning the name of Maurras at this time. Mehlman reprinted his essay in his collection *Genealogies of the Text: Literature, Psychoanalysis, and Politics in Modern France* (Cambridge: Cambridge University Press, 1995), 174–94. Also see his essay "Blanchot at *Combat*: Of Literature and Terror," in *Legacies: Of Anti-Semitism in France* (Minneapolis: University of Minnesota Press, 1983). See Blanchot's comment in his *Lettres à Vadim Kozovoï suivi de La parole ascendante*, ed. Denis Aucouturier (Houilles: Éditions Manucius, 2009), 74.

30. See Blanchot, "Un essai sur Gérard de Nerval," *Journal des débats*, June 22, 1939, 2.

31. See Blanchot, *Chroniques littéraires du "Journal des débats": Avril 1941–août 1944*, ed. Christophe Bident (Paris: Gallimard, 2007). An English translation, prepared by Michael Holland, is forthcoming from Fordham University Press.

32. Blanchot, *Death Sentence*, trans. Lydia Davis (Barrytown, N.Y.: Station Hill Press, 1978), 1.

33. See Christophe Bident, *Maurice Blanchot: Partenaire invisible* (Seyssel: Champ Vallon, 1998), 106n. Bident explores the hypothesis that the first part of *Death Sentence* is a double narrative, personal events of 1937 and public events of 1938.

34. Blanchot, *Death Sentence*, 4.

35. See Blanchot, "La France, nation à venir."

36. Blanchot, "*Days of Hope* by André Malraux," trans. Michael Holland, *Paragraph* 30, no. 3 (2007): 11.

37. Aliette Armel, "Un itinéraire politique," *Magazine littéraire* 278 (June 1990), 40. Also see Blanchot, "For Friendship," in this volume, and Mascolo, *Entêtements* (Paris: Benoît Jacob, 2004). One can get an idea of what it would be to agree with Mascolo by reading his piece in Jean-Paul Sartre, Bernard Pingaud, and Dionys Mascolo, *Du rôle de l'intellectuel dans le mouvement révolutionnaire* (Paris: Eric Losfeld, 1971), 41–50, reprinted in *Entêtements*, 165–75. Also see the two DVDs *Autour du Groupe de la rue Saint-Benoît de 1942 à 1964: L'Esprit d'insoumission*, produced by Jean Mascolo and Jean-Marc Turine (Benoît Jacob Vidéo, 2002).

38. See Blanchot, "Dionys Mascolo: *Le communisme*," *La nouvelle revue française* 12, December 1953, 1064–71. Blanchot reprinted the review with slight changes in *L'Amitié* (Paris: Gallimard, 1971).

39. See Blanchot's letter to Vadim Kozovoï of May 28, 1982, in his *Lettres à Vadim Kozovoï*, 73, and Jacques Derrida, "A Witness Forever," trans. Charlotte Mandell, in *Nowhere Without No*, ed. Kevin Hart (Sydney: Vagabond Press, 2003), 47.

40. Blanchot, *The Instant of My Death*, together with Jacques Derrida, *Demeure: Fiction and Testimony*, trans. Elizabeth Rottenberg (Stanford: Stanford University Press, 2000), 5.

41. Ibid., 7.

42. Blanchot, "Two Letters to Maurice Nadeau," 19.

43. Ibid. Later in his life, Blanchot was sharply critical of his earlier political self. See "A Letter," trans. Leslie Hill, *Maurice Blanchot: The Demand of Writing*, ed. Carolyn Bailey Gill, 209–10. Also see the letter quoted by Bernard-Henri Lévy, *Adventures on the Freedom Road: The French Intellectuals in the Twentieth Century*, trans. and ed. Richard Veasey (London: The Harvill Press, 1995), 318.

44. Blanchot, "For Friendship," in this volume. In a letter to William Flesch dated December 10, 1988, Blanchot adds a detail to this story, that Drieu said Blanchot could have a free hand as editor so long as he published only purely literary texts. To which Blanchot says that he responded, "But there are no purely literary texts." Yet see Pascal Fouché's counter claim in his *L'Edition française sous l'Occupation, 1940–1944*, 2 vols. (Paris: Bibliothèque de Littérature Contemporaine, 1987), 2:80. Also see Jean Paulhan, *Choix de lettres*, vol. 2, *1937–1945* (Paris: Gallimard, 1992), 280. These are the basis of Melhman's case against Blanchot, which Blanchot consistently rejects. He was secretary for a brief period, not editor. Also see in this regard Steven Ungar, *Scandal and Aftereffect: Blanchot and France since 1930* (Minneapolis: University of Minnesota Press, 1995), chap. 5, esp. 116.

45. Blanchot gives the starting date of 1932 in his note to the *récit* version of *Thomas l'obscur*, published by Gallimard in 1950. In his letter to Laporte he says "without a doubt" that he had started to write narrative prose since 1930.

46. Blanchot, "After the Fact," *Vicious Circles: Two Fictions and "After the Fact,"* trans. Paul Auster (Barrytown, N.Y.: Station Hill Press, 1985), 64.

47. Ibid., 64–65.

48. Blanchot, "The Inquisition Destroyed the Catholic Religion . . . ," trans. Michael Holland, *Paragraph* 30, no. 3 (2007): 43; also in this volume.

49. For a full discussion of this view, see my *The Dark Gaze: Maurice Blanchot and the Sacred* (Chicago: University of Chicago Press, 2004), chap. 4.

50. See Blanchot, "The Relation of the Third Kind (*Man Without Horizon*)," *The Infinite Conversation*, trans. Susan Hanson (Minneapolis: University of Minnesota Press, 1993), esp. 66–67.

51. Blanchot, "Note," *The Infinite Conversation*, xii. Also see Blanchot's remarks on narrative writing in relation to journalistic writing in *The Step Not Beyond*, trans. Lycette Nelson (Albany: State University of New York Press, 1992), 2. Blanchot makes the same point toward the end of his letter to Laporte.

52. Blanchot, "Note," *The Infinite Conversation*, xii.

53. See on this Jacques Derrida, *Resistances of Psychoanalysis*, trans. Peggy Kamuf, Pascale-Anne Brault, and Michael Naas (Stanford: Stanford University Press, 1998), 61.

54. For a late instance of Blanchot holding this view, see his "Our Responsibility," in this volume.

55. Blanchot, "Intellectuals Are Always Guilty," trans. Michael Holland, *Paragraph* 30, no. 3 (2007): 12.

56. Blanchot, *The Step Not Beyond*, 53. It is worth noting that Laporte wrote an essay on Blanchot entitled "Tout doit s'effacer, tout s'effacera," *Études* (Paris: P.O.L., 1990), 51–62.

57. Blanchot, *The Space of Literature*, trans. Ann Smock (Lincoln: University of Nebraska Press, 1982), 187.

58. See "Correspondance D. Mascolo—M. Blanchot," *Lignes* 33 (1998): 210. The book that resulted from the correspondence is Mascolo, *Autour d'un effort de mémoire: Sur une lettre de Robert Antelme* (Paris: M. Nadeau, 1987).

59. On the various senses of *la contestation*, see Kevin Hart and Geoffrey Hartman, eds., *The Power of Contestation: Perspectives on Maurice Blanchot* (Baltimore: Johns Hopkins University Press, 2004).

60. Blanchot, "The Great Reducers," *Friendship*, trans. Elizabeth Rottenberg (Stanford: Stanford University Press, 1997), 67.

61. See, e.g., Blanchot, "What Is the Purpose of Criticism?" *Lautréamont and Sade*, trans. Stuart Kendall and Michelle Kendall (Stanford: Stanford University Press, 2004), 5; "Inner Experience," *Faux Pas*, trans. Charlotte Mandell (Stanford: Stanford University Press, 2001), 39–40.

62. See Blanchot, "Intellectuals under Scrutiny," *The Blanchot Reader*, ed. Michael Holland (Oxford: Basil Blackwell, 1995), 206–27.

63. Ibid., 224; trans. modified. Also see his remarks in *Michel Foucault as I Imagine Him*, together with Foucault, *Maurice Blanchot: The Thought from Outside*, trans. Jeffrey Mehlman and Brian Massumi (New York: Zone Books, 1990), 63.

64. The present book is a translation of an expanded version of *Écrits politiques: 1958–1993* (Paris: Léo Scheer, 2003). It is not to be confused with *Écrits politiques, 1953–1993*, ed. Eric Hoppenot (Paris: Gallimard, 2008). The latter edition includes some further relevant texts by Blanchot but unfortunately is riddled with errors.

65. Blanchot, *The Infinite Conversation*, 156, 8.

66. Kristin Ross observes that "the political subjectivity that emerged in May was a *relational* one, built around the polemics of equality: a day-to-day experience of identifications, aspirations, encounters and missed encounters, meetings, deceptions, and disappointments" (*May '68 and Its Afterlives* [Chicago: University of Chicago Press, 2002], 11).

67. See Blanchot, *The Writing of the Disaster*, 134.

68. See Blanchot, *The Unavowable Community*, trans. Pierre Joris (Barrytown, N.Y.: Station Hill Press, 1988), 29–31.

69. See Blanchot, "[I think it suits a writer better]," in this volume. Also see *Lettres à Vadim Kozovoï*, 122.

70. For a discussion of this appeal and Blanchot's part in it, see Leslie Hill, " 'Not in Our Name': Blanchot, Politics, the Neuter," *Paragraph* 30, no. 3 (2007): 141–59.

71. On the two languages in general, see: Blanchot, *The Writing of the Disaster*, 20; *The Infinite Conversation*, 48; and Blanchot's letter to Bataille of January 24, 1962, in Georges Bataille, *Choix de lettres, 1917–1962*, ed. Michel Surya (Paris: Gallimard, 1997), 595–96. On the differences between *le politique* and *la politique*, see Philippe Lacoue-Labarthe and Jean-Luc Nancy, *Retreating the Political*, ed. Simon Sparks (London: Routledge, 1997).

72. Jacques Derrida, *The Politics of Friendship*, trans. George Collins (London: Verso, 1997), 47–48.

73. Blanchot, *The Unavowable Community*, 30. Also see his remarks on communication in *The Space of Literature*, chap. 6. Yet see Jacques Derrida, *Of Grammatology*, corrected ed., trans. Gayatri Chakravorty Spivak (Baltimore: Johns Hopkins University Press, 1997), 5.

74. See Philippe Lacoue-Labarthe, *Heidegger, Art and Politics*, trans. Chris Turner (Oxford: Basil Blackwell, 1990), chap. 1. Yet toward the end of *The Order of Things*, Michel Foucault writes in bold terms about the change at hand and credits Blanchot, among others, with being an index of its coming. See Foucault, *The Order of Things: An Archeology of the Human Sciences* (New York: Vintage Books, 1970), chap. 10, esp. 384.

75. See, e.g., Jean-Luc Nancy, *The Inoperative Community*, ed. Peter Connor, trans. Peter Connor et al. (Minneapolis: University of Minnesota Press, 1991), and Derrida, *Politics of Friendship*.

76. Levinas quotes this letter, not giving Blanchot's name but giving sufficient clues to identify him as its author, in "Judaism and Revolution," *Nine Talmudic Readings*, trans. and introd. Annette Aronowicz (Bloomington: Indiana University Press, 1990), 115–16. Also see Blanchot, "Do Not Forget," in this volume.

77. Blanchot, "Intellectuals under Scrutiny," 223.

78. Quoted by Lévy, *Adventures on the Freedom Road*, 318. Also see Blanchot's "What Is Closest to Me," in this volume.

79. Blanchot, "Intellectuals under Scrutiny," 217.

INTRODUCTION: "AFFIRMING THE RUPTURE,"
BY ZAKIR PAUL

1. Georges Bataille, *Choix de lettres: 1917–1962*, ed. Michel Surya (Paris: Gallimard, 1997), 595–96.

2. Christophe Bident lists the following petitions to indicate the kinds of issues that would continue to draw Blanchot's attention after he stopped publishing his own work as such: for the foundation of an international writers' parliament in 1993, for the legal recognition of homosexual couples in 1996, and for civil disobedience against the Debré immigration laws in 1997. The last political manifesto Blanchot signed was the "Not in Our Name" appeal against the war in Iraq in 2002. See Bident, *Maurice Blanchot: Partenaire Invisible* (Seyssel: Champ Vallon, 1998), 573. A definitive list of these texts is available on the website of the Espace Maurice Blanchot: www.blanchot.fr.

3. Maurice Blanchot, *Chroniques littéraires au Journal des Débats, 1941–1944*, ed. Christophe Bident (Paris: Gallimard, 2008).

4. *Gramma*, no. 3–4, *Lire Blanchot, I* (1976) and no. 5 *Lire Blanchot, II* (1976).

5. Maurice Blanchot, "Des violences antisémites à l'apothéose du travail," *Le rempart* 10, May 1, 1933, 3.

6. Leslie Hill, "La pensée politique," in *L'Enigme Blanchot, Magazine littéraire* 424, October 2003, 35–38.

7. Cited by Hill in ibid., 36.

8. Maurice Blanchot, "Quand l'État est révolutionnaire," *Le rempart*, no. 8, April 29, 1933; cited in Hill, "La pensée politique," 36.

9. Leslie Hill, *Blanchot: Extreme Contemporary* (London: Routledge, 1997), 43.

10. Maurice Blanchot, *Après-Coup* (Paris: Minuit, 1983), 96; *Vicious Circles: Two Fictions and "After the Fact,"* trans. Paul Auster (Barrytown, N.Y.: Station Hill Press, 1985), 67.

11. Maurice Blanchot, letter to Maurice Nadeau, April 17, 1977, in *Blanchot's Epoch, Paragraph* 30, no. 3 (2007): 19.

12. Maurice Blanchot, "On demande des dissidents," *Combat* 20 (December 1937): 155. See Bident, *Maurice Blanchot*, 381.

13. In an interview in Jean Mascolo's documentary *Autour du Groupe de la rue Saint-Benoît de 1942 à 1962* (Benoît Jacob Vidéo, 2002), Gérard Legrand recalls a footnote to a text on Proust published in the September 1958 issue of *NNRF*—the text in question, "Passage de la ligne," actually deals with Nietzsche—in which Blanchot declares his disagreement with everything said about politics in Jean Paulhan's pro-Gaullist review. Legrand describes the surprise and joy this declaration provoked in André Breton and the Surrealists, who had found themselves in a political impasse. This memory is significant, since Paulhan and Blanchot would soon part ways over de Gaulle's return to power. Leslie Hill believes that Blanchot was responding to an anonymous note of support for de Gaulle by Paulhan when he wrote: "In my opinion, it would be to despair of a people and this nation to place hope only in an incidental man." See Leslie Hill, "Le tournant du fragmentaire," in *Europe*, no.

940–41 (August–September 2007): 74–83. For an account of the relation between Paulhan and Blanchot, see Laurent Jenny, "Paulhan, Blanchot, and 'Le 14 juillet,'" trans. Anna-Louise Milner, in *The Power of Rhetoric, the Rhetoric of Power: Jean Paulhan's Criticism and Editorial Activity*, *Yale French Studies*, no. 106 (2004): 125–39.

14. Maurice Blanchot, *Après Coup*, 99; *Vicious Circles: Two Fictions and "After the Fact,"* 69.

15. Maurice Blanchot, *The Space of Literature*, trans. Ann Smock. (Nebraska: University of Nebraska Press), 187; see *Lignes* 33 (Paris: Editions Hazan), 210.

16. Michel Foucault, Georges Préli, and Leslie Hill have all offered readings of *The Most High* in relation to these political concerns.

17. Paul de Man, "Impersonality in Blanchot," in *Blindness and Insight*, 2nd ed. (Minneapolis: University of Minnesota Press, 1983), 78. See Denis Hollier, "The Pure and the Impure," in *Literary Debate: Texts and Contexts: Postwar French Thought*, ed. Jeffrey Mehlman and Denis Hollier, trans. Arthur Goldhammer et. al. (New York: The New Press, 1999), 2:22.

18. Maurice Blanchot, *The Book to Come*, trans. Charlotte Mandell (Stanford: Stanford University Press, 2000), 199–200.

19. Michael Holland, ed., *The Blanchot Reader* (Cambridge: Blackwell, 1996), 107.

20. Dionys Mascolo, *Entêtements* (Paris: Benoît Jacob, 2004), 83; 120.

21. Bident, *Maurice Blanchot*, 377.

22. Cornelius Castoriadis (with Claude Chabrol), "La jeunesse étudiante," *Socialisme ou Barbarie*, no. 34 (March 1963): 56. Cited in Kristin Ross, *May 68 and Its Afterlives* (Chicago: University of Chicago Press, 2002), 39.

23. Werner Hamacher, "Journals, Politics," in *Responses: On Paul de Man's Wartime Journalism*, ed. Werner Hamacher, Neil Hertz, and Thomas Keenan (Nebraska: University of Nebraska Press, 1989), 448.

24. Blanchot, "Intellectuals under Scrutiny," in *The Blanchot Reader*, ed. Holland, 207–8.

25. Bident, *Maurice Blanchot*, 353.

26. Maurice Blanchot, *The Infinite Conversation*, trans. Susan Hanson (Minneapolis: University of Minnesota Press), 118.

27. Bident, *Maurice Blanchot*, 353.

28. In *Autour du Groupe de la rue Saint-Benoît de 1942 à 1962* (Paris: Benoît Jacob Video, 2002), Gérard Legrand recalls the negative Hegelian formulation "The coup d'état is a nothingness against which we much oppose our own nothingness."

29. Among those who refrained were Edgar Morin, Gilles Martinet, and Maurice Merleau-Ponty.

30. Alain Robbe-Grillet recalls that the examining magistrate who interrogated Blanchot about the Manifesto of the 121 eventually had to request sick leave on the grounds of moral exhaustion. See Alain Robbe-Grillet, *Angélique ou l'enchantement* (Paris: Editions de Minuit, 1987), 204, and Holland, ed., *The Blanchot Reader*, 194n.17.

31. On Sartre's return from South America, de Gaulle famously quipped: "One does not imprison Voltaire." Ironically, in fact Voltaire was imprisoned several times, including a period of eleven months in the Bastille in 1717.

32. The list of writers involved in the project included: Robert Antelme, Michel Butor, Roland Barthes, Louis-René des Forêts, Marguerite Duras, Michel Leiris, Elio Vittorini, Italo Calvino, Francesco Leonetti, Pier Paolo Pasolini, Hans-Magnus Enzensberger, Uwe Johnson, Ingeborg Bachmann, Günter Grass, Robert Walser, and Iris Murdoch.

33. In addition to *Lignes*, no. 11, ed. Michel Surya (Paris: Léo Scheer, 1990), readers interested in the review can also consult Roman Schmidt, *Die unmögliche Gemeinschaft: Maurice Blanchot, die Gruppe der rue Saint Benoît und die Idee einer internationalen Zeitschrift um 1960* (Berlin: Kadmos Verlag, 2009), and Anna Panicali, ed., *Gulliver: Progetto di una rivista internazionale* (Milan: Marcos y Marcos, 2003). Notes on the final meeting of the French, German, and Italian groups can be found in "Anhang Gulliver—Die *Internationale Zeitschrift*," in Uwe Johnson and Siegfried Unseld, *Der Briefwechsel* (Frankfurt am Main: Suhrkamp, 1999), 1094–136. I borrow the last two references from Marcus Coelen, translator of the German edition of the present volume, Maurice Blanchot, *Politische Schriften* (Zurich: Diaphanes, 2007).

34. Bident, *Maurice Blanchot*, 411.

35. René Char, *Recherche de la base et du sommet* (Paris: Gallimard, 1971).

36. Maurice Blanchot, letter to Dionys Mascolo, June 29, 1961; cited in Bident, *Maurice Blanchot*, 406.

37. Mehlman and Hollier, eds., *Literary Debate*, 380.

38. Ross, *May 68 and Its Afterlives*, 31.

39. Jean-Claude Milner, *L'Arrogance du présent: Regards sur une décennie 1965–1975* (Paris: Grasset, 2009).

40. Denis Hollier, *Absent Without Leave: French Literature under the Threat of War*, trans. Catherine Porter (Cambridge: Harvard University Press, 1997), 8.

41. Maurice Blanchot, *The Unavowable Community*, trans. Pierre Joris (Barrytown, N.Y.: Station Hill Press, 1988), 30.

42. For an analysis of the larger linguistic framework of the events of May, see Denis Hollier, "1968 May: 'Actions, No! Words, Yes!'" in *A New History of French Literature*, ed. Denis Hollier (Cambridge: Harvard University Press, 1989), 1034–40. As Hollier points out, thinkers as diverse as Michel de Certeau, Oswald Ducrot, Gilles Deleuze, Michel Foucault, and Jacques Derrida

saw the events of May as an occasion to question the relations of force inscribed in institutional frames and premises of discourse.

43. Maurice Blanchot, *The Unavowable Community*, 30. This primacy of the saying over the said could also be read as a reference to Heidegger and to the priority of the *Sage(n)* to the said.

44. Bident, *Maurice Blanchot*, 474.

45. Herbert Marcuse, *One Dimensional Man* (Boston: Beacon Press Books, 1964, 1991), 255. I'd like to thank Samuel Weber for pointing out the connection to Marcuse.

46. Ibid., 256.

47. Milner, *L'Arrogance du présent*, 171–91.

48. Ethan Kleinberg, *Generation Existential: Heidegger's Philosophy in France 1927–1961* (Ithaca, N.Y.: Cornell University Press, 2005).

49. Philippe Lacoue-Labarthe, *La fiction du politique: Heidegger, l'art et la politique* (Paris: Christian Bourgois, 1987); *Heidegger, Art and Politics*, trans. Chris Turner (Oxford: Basil Blackwell, 1990).

50. Emmanuel Levinas, "The Poet's Vision," in "On Maurice Blanchot," *Proper Names*, trans. Michael B. Smith (Stanford: Stanford University Press, 1996), 139.

51. Eleanor Kaufman, *The Delirium of Praise: Bataille, Blanchot, Deleuze, Foucault, Klossowski* (Baltimore: Johns Hopkins University Press, 2001).

52. Jean-Luc Nancy, "Maurice Blanchot (1907–2003)," trans. Leslie Hill, *Paragraph* 3, no. 30 (2007): 3.

AN APPROACH TO COMMUNISM (NEEDS, VALUES)

NOTE: First published as "Dionys Masocolo: *La Communisme*," in the *Nouvelle nouvelle revue française*, no. 12, December 1953, 1096–99; reprinted later under the current title in *L'Amitié* (Paris: Gallimard, 1971), 109–14.

REFUSAL

NOTE: In 1958, Dionys Mascolo and Jean Schuster founded the review *Le 14 juillet* with the aim of opposing the manner in which Charles de Gaulle had taken power. Three issues of the anti-Gaullist review *Le 14 juillet* appeared in 1958 and 1959; these were later reprinted by *Lignes* (special edition, Paris: Séguier, 1990). Blanchot contributed to the second and the third issues. The text published in the second issue is called "Refusal" and was preceded by excerpts from a letter to Dionys Mascolo: "This little text is above all meant to affirm my agreement with you. . . . The refusal I am talking about is easily lulled to sleep, and we must be bound by a decision that will no longer yield. The task is above all to bring the intellectuals, who are not particularly involved, to regain respect for what they are, which would allow them neither consent nor indifference: something has happened. This difficulty will doubtless keep them from being themselves, as sometimes happens when they are led to take part in public events. . . . It remains most necessary to understand what has happened, as well as the movement that ineluctably results. The past does not enlighten us very much; there is something different here, the promise of a new oppression. We risk heading down strange paths toward the worst, but since all roads are closed off to us for now, it depends on us to find an exit, precisely from here, by refusing to yield at every moment and in every way." This text was later published in *L'Amitié*.

THE ESSENTIAL PERVERSION

NOTE: "La perversion essentielle," *Le 14 juillet*, no. 3, June 18, 1959, 18–20; republished in *Gramma*, no. 3–4, 1976, 19–27; *Lignes*, n.s., "Le 14 juillet" (Paris: Séguier, 1989).

1. De Gaulle's phrase could be translated as "I have understood you," but Blanchot is playing on the double sense of *comprendre* in French, meaning both "to comprehend" and "to comprise."

2. Michel Debré (1912–96) was a pro-Gaullist politician and the prime minister of the Fifth Republic.

DECLARATION OF THE RIGHT TO INSUBORDINATION IN THE ALGERIAN WAR

NOTE: Early in 1960, shortly before the Jeanson trial for aiding the Algerian National Liberation Front (the FLN) took place, the editors of the review *Le 14 juillet* (essentially Dionys Mascolo and Jean Schuster) decided to intervene once again. They did so in a declaration titled "An Address to International Opinion." This text exists in at least fifteen different versions, to which various authors contributed before reaching the definitive version printed here. Commonly referred to as the Manifesto of the 121, this text was distributed secretly for the most part. It was also published, however, in: *Vérité-Liberté: Cahiers d'information sur la guerre d'Algérie*, no. 4, September–October 1960; and *La voie communiste*, September 1960.

UPDATE

1. Michel Cournot (1922–2000) was a French writer, journalist, and film critic.

2. *L'Humanité* is a daily French communist newspaper, founded in 1904 by Jean Jaurès.

3. Maurice Thorez (1900–64) was the general secretary of the French Communist Party from 1930 to 1964.

4. Unité Nationale des Etudiants de France, i.e. the French National Student Council.

[FOR US THE FIRST FACT]

1. Members of the *Académie française*.

[IT IS AS A WRITER]

NOTE: An unsigned, undated document found among Blanchot's papers, this text shares many similarities with the interview given to Madeleine Chapsal. The interview was intended for publication in the weekly magazine *L'Express*, which refused to print it. It was finally published, along with other interviews with the signatories of the "Declaration," in "Le droit à l'insoumission (le dossier des '121')," *Cahiers libres*, ed. François Maspero, no. 14, January 1961.

[INTERROGATION WITH THE JUDGE]

NOTE: Along with many other signatories of the "Declaration," Blanchot was first charged with "inciting insubordination and desertion," then a few days later was charged with "provoking soldiers to disobedience." This previously unpublished text is Blanchot's transcription of his questioning by the judge. All charges against him were dropped. This text was supposed to be printed in *Le Monde*, but the newspaper published only a short excerpt.

1. "S.I." abbreviates *sur interpellation*, Blanchot's phrase meaning roughly "the questioner."

[QUESTIONED BY THE JUDGE]

NOTE: This short text, previously unpublished, was found signed by Blanchot without a date among his papers.

[FIRST I WOULD LIKE TO SAY]

NOTE: This text is a transcript of an interview with Madeleine Chapsal intended for publication in the weekly magazine *L'Express*; see the explanatory note above.

[MAURICE BLANCHOT TO JEAN-PAUL SARTRE]

NOTE: This, the only letter Blanchot ever wrote to Sartre, was meant to inaugurate the *Revue internationale* project, on the heels of *14 juillet* and the Manifesto of the 121. All the preparatory materials concerning this project were published in a special issue of *Lignes*, no. 11, September 1990.

LETTERS FROM THE *REVUE INTERNATIONALE*

NOTE: The following letters concerning the *Revue internationale* project were first published in *Lignes*, no. 11, September 1990.

1. Hans Magnus Enzensberger (b. 1929) is a German author, poet, editor, and translator. He was affiliated with the post-war literary association Gruppe 47.

2. Peter Suhrkamp (1891–1959), German editor, author, and translator, founded the major publishing house Suhrkamp Verlag in Frankfurt am Main in 1950.

3. The German committee's principle objections seem to have been to the international perspective on national, social, and political issues, as well as to the fragmentary form of the review.

4. Walter Boehlich (1921–2006) was a journalist, literary critic, translator, and editor at Suhrkamp Verlag.

[THE GRAVITY OF THE PROJECT]

NOTE: This unpublished text was a working document meant to describe for an international audience of writers and editors the form and the direction that the new review was meant to take.

1. In October 1962, after publishing an article concerning the state of the West German military, the German weekly *Der Spiegel* was accused of treason and of leaking state secrets. Ensuing government censure led to a scandal.

2. The quote from Warburg should read, "Der liebe Gott selbst steckt im Detail," that is, "The good God himself is hidden in the detail."

3. Pierre Leyris (1907–2001) and Yves Bonnefoy (b. 1923), both French poets known for their translations of Shakespeare.

4. Jean Laplanche (b. 1924), French author, psychoanalyst, and the general editor of the French critical edition of Freud's writings.

5. Jean-Émile Charon (1920–88), French physician and philosopher; Marie-Joseph Pierre Teilhard de Chardin (1881–1955), French philosopher and Jesuit priest.

6. Claude Lévi-Strauss, *La pensée sauvage* (Paris: Plon, 1962); Régine Pernoud, *Histoire de la France bourgeoise*, 2 vols. (Paris: Seuil, 1960–62); Jacques Ellul, *Propaganda*, trans. K. Kellen and J. Lerner (New York: Knopf, 1965); André Leroi-Gourhan, *Le geste et la parole*, 2. vols. (Paris: Albin Michel, 1964); Frantz Fanon, *Les damnés de la terre*, preface by Jean-Paul Sartre (Paris: Maspéro, 1961).

THE COURSE OF THE WORLD

NOTE: This undated, unsigned text outlines a section of the *Revue internationale* project and was found with handwritten corrections in Blanchot's archives.

THE CONQUEST OF SPACE

NOTE: This text appeared in an Italian translation, by Guido Neri, in *Il menabò*, no. 7 (1964): 10–13. The French original was first published in the Gallimard edition of the political writings. The manuscript shows a first title, which has been crossed out: "Locus solus."

BERLIN

NOTE: Written for the *Revue internationale* and published in *Il menabò*, no. 7 (1964), this text existed only in translation (in Italian by Guido Neri, in English by James Cascaito, in German by Isolde Eckle, and, finally, in French by Hélène and Jean-Luc Nancy) until the manuscript was found and published in *Lignes*, no. 3 (October 2000), eleven years after the fall of the Berlin wall.

1. Blanchot is probably alluding to Uwe Johnson's first two novels, *Mutmassungen über Jakob* (*Speculations about Jakob*, 1959) and *Das dritte Buch über Achim* (*The Third Book about Achim*, 1961).

TRACTS OF THE STUDENT-WRITER ACTION COMMITTEE (SORBONNE-CENSIER)

NOTE: "[The solidarity that we assert here]" was first published in *Le Monde* on May 9, 1968, under the title "Il est capital que le mouvement des étudiants oppose et maintienne une puissance de refus, déclarent MM. Jean-Paul Sartre, Henri Lefebvre et un groupe d'écrivains et de philosophes" ("It is of capital importance that the student movement oppose and maintain a power of refusal, declare Jean-Paul Sartre, Henri Lefebvre, and a group of writers and philosophers"). Among the signatories were: Robert Antelme, Maurice Blanchot, Roger Blin, Vincent Bounoure, François Châtelet, Marguerite Duras, Louis-René des Forêts, Michel Fouchet, André Gorz, Pierre Klossowski, Jacques Lacan, Henri Lefebvre, Michel Leiris, Dionys Mascolo, Maurice Nadeau, Jérôme Peignot, André Pieyre de Mandiargues, Jean Ricardou, Michel Robert, Claude Roy, Nathalie Sarraute, Jean-Paul Sartre, Jean Schuster, Geneviève Serreau, and Monique Wittig.

"[By the power of refusal]" first appeared with the signatures of over a hundred artists and writers in *Le Monde* on June 18, 1968. Among others, the signatories included Jean-Paul Sartre, Simone de Beauvoir, Laurent Schwartz, Jean Hélion, Robert Bresson, Jean-Luc Godard, Achille Lebrun, Jacques Dupin, Louis Malle, Jacques Rivette, Roger Enrico, René Allio, Sylviane Agacinski, Jean-Noël Vuarnet, Bernard Dort, Robert Abirached, Françoise d'Eaubonne, Claude Roy, Roland Topor, Jean Degottex, Claude Lanzmann, and François Truffaut. This appeal gave rise to a further list, on which appeared the names of Alexandre Astruc, Mathieu Bénézet, Roger Blin, Jean Duvignaud, André Gorz, Jean Ipoustéguy, Jean Laplanche, Charles Malamoud, Octave and Maude Mannoni, Jean-Bertrand Pontalis, Alain Resnais, Nathalie Sarraute, Pierre Soulages, Pierre Vidal-Naquet, and Christian Zervos.

"Crime" was published in a different version, signed "The Student-Writer Action Committee," in the *Nouvel Observateur*, July 29, 1968. Passages that appeared in the *Nouvel Observateur* but not in the initial tract are given within brackets. The first lines appeared again in *Comité*, in an article entitled "La rue" ("The Streets").

[A government does not govern]

1. The Châtelet negotiations, also known as the Grenelle agreements, were an important step in the government's efforts to quell the mass movement by yielding to the minimal demands of the workers, that is, a re-evaluation of the minimum wage, a forty-hour work week, and the extension of union rights into factories.

[By the power of refusal]

1. The "statute of dissolution" referred to here is the June 12, 1968, decree concerning groups and organizations. After the events of May 1968, de Gaulle dissolved various political organizations by presidential decree, while modifying laws from November 5, 1870, and January 10, 1936, concerning "combat groups and private militias." The eleven groups targeted were: the Jeunesse communiste révolutionnaire (JCR); Voix ouvrière; Groupes "Révoltes"; Fédération des étudiants révolutionnaires (FER); Comité de liaison des étudiants révolutionnaires (CLER); Union des jeunesses communistes marxistes-léninistes (UJC [ml]); Parti communiste internationaliste (PCI); Parti communiste marxiste-léniniste de France (PCMLF); Fédération de la jeunesse révolutionnaire; Organisation communiste internationaliste (OCI); and Mouvement du 22-Mars. Some of these groups reorganized and continued to operate despite the presidential order.

[LETTER TO A REPRESENTATIVE OF YUGOSLAV RADIO-TELEVISION]

NOTE: The letter to Ilija Bojovic was published with a few modifications in *Comité 1*. The postscript, not published in the *Lignes* text, was published in the Gallimard edition of the *Political Writings*. The two texts also contain minor variants not indicated here.

1. "[The solidarity that we assert here]" and "[By the power of refusal]."

COMITÉ: THE FIRST ISSUE

NOTE: Only one issue of the review *Comité* appeared, in October 1968. Although these texts were not written collectively, they were published anonymously. The entirety of the issue can be found in *Lignes*, no. 33 (March 1998); here we reproduce only the texts authored by Blanchot. The texts attributed to Mascolo were reproduced in Dionys Mascolo, *À la recherche d'un communisme de pensée* (Paris: Fourbis, 1993) and *Entêtements* (Paris: Benoît Jacob, 2004). "Affirming the Rupture," "[Today]," "[Political Death]," "[The streets]," "[Communism without heirs]," "[Tracts, posters, bulletins]," "[That the immense constraint]," "[Exemplary acts]," "[Two characteristic innovations]," "[A rupture in time: revolution]," "[For Comrade Castro]," "[Ideological surrender]," and "[Clandestine resistance out in the open]" are all anonymous texts attributed to Blanchot by Mascolo. "Letter to Ilija Bojovic" was published in the journal *Europe*, August–September 2007. "[Reading Marx]" is the only text written for *Comité* that Blanchot included, under the title "Marx's Three Voices," in *L'Amitié* (Paris: Gallimard, 1971; *Friendship*, trans. Elizabeth Rottenberg [Stanford: Stanford University Press, 2003]).

[Communism without heirs]

1. At their very first meeting, André Malraux declared to de Gaulle that he had "married France." See André Malraux, *Antimémoires* (Paris: Gallimard, 1967).

[Tracts, posters, bulletins]

1. *Mots de désordre*: This phrase plays on the expression *mots d'ordre*, "watchwords" or "slogans."

[Exemplary acts]

1. On May 16, 1968, the Odéon Theater in the Latin Quarter was occupied by students and became a meeting place for workers and activists. On the evening of May 24, when the most intense street fighting of the crisis took place in Paris, revolutionary students temporarily seized the Bourse (the Paris Stock Exchange), raised a communist flag over the building, and then tried to set it on fire. One policeman was killed during the night's violence.

2. Flins sur Seine is a French commune situated in the Yvelines *département* and the Ile-de-France region. In May and June 1968, violent demonstrations occurred in the area surrounding the Renault factory. On June 10, 1968, a young student died in the Seine trying to flee the police.

3. A Franco-German student leader, Daniel Cohn-Bendit became a public face for the mass movements of May 1968. Rumors that he would be expelled from the university in 1967 led to student protests, during which xenophobic utterances were countered with the cry, "We are all German Jews."

[Two characteristic innovations]

1. Parti Communiste Français, that is, the French Communist Party.

[A rupture in time: revolution]

1. The "July Revolution" refers to the three-day insurrection from July 27 to July 29, 1830, that put an end to the reign of Charles X and cleared a path

for the bourgeois monarchy of Louis-Phillipe, referred to as the July monarchy.

2. Walter Benjamin, "On the Concept of History," in *Selected Writings*, vol. 4, *1938–1940*, ed. Howard Eiland and Michael W. Jennings, trans. Edmund Jephcott (Cambridge: Harvard University Press, 2003), 395. We have translated the quotation from Blanchot's French paraphrase.

[For Comrade Castro]

1. On August 21, 1968, the armies of four Eastern Bloc countries—the USSR, Bulgaria, Poland, and Hungary—invaded Czechoslovakia, putting an end to the reforms that had been taking place under the newly elected government of Alexander Dubček. The suppression of the Prague Spring was a first instance of the Brezhnev Doctrine, namely, the Soviet Union's policy of constraining satellite states through military force.

2. On August 23, 1968, two days after the invasion of Prague, Castro took to the airwaves and publicly denounced the Czech rebellion. Castro warned the Cuban people about the Czechoslovakian "counterrevolutionaries," who "were moving Czechoslovakia towards capitalism and into the arms of imperialists." In exchange for his public backing of the invasion, Moscow continued to support the Cuban economy. For a transcript of this speech, see "Castro Comments on the Czechoslovak Crisis," Havana Domestic TV, Latin America Network Information Center archive, hosted online by the University of Texas.

3. Blanchot is referring to Hegel's remark about Napoleon in his October 13, 1806, letter to Niethammer. (See Terry Pinkard, *Hegel* [Cambridge: Cambridge University Press, 2001], 228.)

[Clandestine resistance out in the open]

1. The author of this manifesto was Ludvick Vaculik, a Czech writer, journalist, and member of the opposition.

[Reading Marx]

1. This phrase—"Ce jeu insensé d'écrire"—borrowed from Mallarmé's homage to Villiers de l'Isle Adam, is a repeated reference throughout Blanchot's writing.

ON THE MOVEMENT

NOTE: Following the dissolution of the Student-Writer Action Committee, Maurice Nadeau and *Lettres nouvelles* published five anonymous texts under the heading "A Year Later, the Student-Writer Action Committee" ("Un an après, le Comité d'action écrivains-étudiants," June–July 1969). One of these texts was by Marguerite Duras; three others were by Dionys Mascolo. The latter were later published in D. Mascolo, *À la recherche d'un communisme de pensée* (Paris: Fourbis, 1993), 324–63. The last was by Blanchot. Although published in 1969, Blanchot dates it as having been written in December 1968.

1. Frederick Barbarossa (1122–90) was crowned Holy Roman Emperor in 1155. According to legend, he is not dead but sleeps in a cave with his knights, waiting for a propitious moment to restore Germany to its ancient greatness.

2. Edgar Faure (1908–88), French politician, minister, and president of the National Assembly, was nominated minister of national education in 1968. He proposed a law in November 1968, which was passed with the approval of the moderate right and the left (while the Communists abstained). Considered the most important revision of the French national educational system since its inception by Napoleon in 1808, Faure's reform claimed to take into account many of the student demands of May 1968, especially increased participation on an institutional level, less bureaucracy and centralization, and easier access to interdisciplinary curricula. Raymond Aron criticized the measures, declaring that they prepared the way not for reform but for ruin.

PARANOIA IN POWER (THE DIALECTICS OF REPRESSION: A SMALL CONTRIBUTION TO RESEARCH)

NOTE: First published anonymously in *Lignes*, no. 33, this text was found among Blanchot's papers in an unsigned typed copy, with handwritten corrections suggesting that it was meant to be his contribution to the unpublished second issue of *Comité*.

1. The word *chienlit*, which could be translated as "disorder," was made famous by one of de Gaulle's few pronouncements on the mass movements in France. He said, "La réforme, oui; la chienlit, non." The term was quickly used against him in the popular slogan "La chienlit, c'est lui," implying that the general was himself the source of chaos. As Kristin Ross points out in her *May 68 and Its Afterlives* (Chicago: University of Chicago Press, 2002), 65, this sixteenth-century word, which referred to a carnival mask and literally invoked the idea of "fouling one's own nest," was first evoked in the context of May by the neo-fascist newspaper *Minute*. Pierre Poujade (1920–2003) was a French politician associated with Poujadisme, a policy of protecting the interests of small business owners and craftsmen. Alain Vivien (b. 1938) is a French socialist politician; André Fanton (b. 1928) and Christian Fouchet (1911–79) were pro-Gaullist French politicians.

2. Maurice Grimaud (1912–2009), a high-ranking civil servant, served as the chief of police during the events of May 1968. Georges Pompidou (1911–74), a French politician, was prime minister from 1962 to 1968 and president from 1969 to 1979. Addressing the National Assembly on May 15, 1968, Pompidou expressed the conspiracy theory according to which subversive forces in

France were receiving financial support and training from Cuba, Berlin, Prague, Moscow, and Beijing.

3. A faction of the security service of the students occupying the Sorbonne dubbed themselves the *Kantangais*, because some of them were ex-legionnaires who claimed to have served in Kantanga in the Congo.

4. Jacques Baumel (1918–2006), pro-Gaullist French politician.

5. Raymond Marcellin (1914–2004), French politician, nominated interior minister after May 1968, was nicknamed "Raymond la matraque" ("Raymond the club") for his repressive policies against the left.

6. Pierre Frank (1905–84) was a French Trotskyist leader.

7. Alain Krevine (1941) is a French politician, a leader of the French Trotskyist movement, and served as a student leader in 1968.

8. Civic action committees formed by pro-Gaullists expressed their support for the regime by compiling black lists of strike leaders and activists.

9. SAC is an acronym for Service d'action civique (Civic Action Service), a pro-Gaullist association that existed between 1960 and 1981. CDR stands for the Comités pour la défense de la République (Committees for the Defense of the Republic), founded in May 1968.

REFUSING THE ESTABLISHED ORDER

NOTE: "Refusing the Established Order" is Maurice Blanchot's response to a questionnaire from the *Nouvel observateur* on committed literature (special issue, *Literature*, May 1981). The questions, asked by Catherine David, were: (1) Can a writer today still believe in the virtues of committed literature? (2) What is the best that this genre has produced, in your opinion? (3) Would you be prepared, under certain circumstances, to write in the service of a cause? If so, which one?

THINKING THE APOCALYPSE

NOTE: "Thinking the Apocalypse" is the title given by the editorial committee to an epistolary text, addressed to Catherine David, that was published in the *Nouvel observateur* (January 22–28, 1988) in a section entitled "Heidegger and Nazi Thought." Emmanuel Levinas, François Fédier, and Philippe Lacoue-Labarthe also contributed. The issue was published in response to the appearance of Victor Farias's book *Heidegger et le nazisme* (Paris: Verdier, 1987).

1. The letters "H. & H." here stand for Heidegger and Hitler.

2. The "Luchaire affair" refers to the French arms dealership, directed by Daniel Dewavrin, that illegally exported 450,000 explosive shells to Iran between 1982 and 1986. This traffic was covered up by the defense minister, Charles Hernu. The "Chaumet affair," a financial scandal involving the fraudulent bankruptcy of the luxury jeweler and watchmaker The House of Chaumet, was exposed by the satirical newspaper *Le canard enchaîné* in 1987.

3. Julius Streicher (1885–1946) was the founder and publisher of the Nazi propaganda newspaper *Der Stürmer*.

4. Ernst Kriek (1882–1947), a German teacher, professor, and writer, was one of the leading pedagogues of National Socialism. In 1933, he was named rector of the Goethe-University at Frankfurt, and he was given a chair in pedagogy at the University of Heidelberg the following year. Alfred Rosenberg (1893–1946), an influential member of the Nazi party, was held to be one the main authors of its racist ideologies; he was sentenced to death as a war criminal at Nuremberg.

5. This statement is taken from a 1949 Bremen lecture, published in Wolfgang Schirmacher, *Technik und Gelassenheit* (Freiburg: Karl Alber, 1984).

6. Philippe Lacoue-Labarthe, *La fiction du politique* (Paris: Christian Bourgois, 1987); *Heidegger, Art, and Politics*, trans. Chris Turner (Oxford: Basil Blackwell, 1990).

7. Albert Leo Schlageter (1894–1923) was a member of the German Freikorps volunteer army who was tried for sabotage and executed by the French during the occupation of the Ruhr in 1923. He later became a martyr figure for the Nazis.

DO NOT FORGET

NOTE: Blanchot wrote this text as a letter addressed to Salomon Malka. It was published in *L'Arche*, no. 373, May 1988.

1. Sabbatai Zevi (1626–76), a renowned rabbi and Kabbalist who claimed to be the Messiah but later converted to Islam. Gerschom Scholem devoted a monumental study to this figure in his *Sabbatai Sevi: The Mystical Messiah, 1626–1676*, trans. R. J. Zwi Werblowsky (Princeton: Princeton University Press, 1973).

2. Jean Halpérin is Professor Jewish thought at the University of Fribourg and the president of the Colloques des intellectuels juifs de langue française.

3. See *L'Écriture du désastre* (Paris: Gallimard, 1980), 80; *The Writing of the Disaster*, trans. Ann Smock (Nebraska: University of Nebraska Press, 1995), 47, trans. modifier.

4. Pierre Bourdieu, *L'Ontologie politique de Martin Heidegger* (Paris: Minuit, 1988); *The Political Ontology of Martin Heidegger*, trans. Peter Collier (Stanford: Stanford University Press, 1991), 105. The quote is translated as Blanchot reproduces it.

5. Gérard Granel (1930–2000) was a French philosopher and translator, notably of Wittgenstein, Gramsci, and Heidegger.

YES, SILENCE IS NECESSARY FOR WRITING

NOTE: This text first appeared as a handwritten letter in *Globe*, no. 44, February 1990, 72.

"FACTORY-EXCESS," OR INFINITY IN PIECES

NOTE: This text was first published in the German review *Schreibheft*, no. 27, April 1986, then in *Libération*, February 24, 1987, on the occasion of the reprinting of Leslie Kaplan's book *L'Excès-l'usine* (*Factory-Excess*), by Editions P.O.L.

1. "L'univers concentrationnaire," a reference to the 1946 book with this title by David Rousset.

IN THE NIGHT THAT IS WATCHED OVER

NOTE: "In the Night That Is Watched Over" was written for the issue of *Lignes* (no. 21, January 1994) dedicated to Antelme. The text was later published in a volume edited by Daniel Dobbels: Robert Antelme, *Textes inédits sur l'Espèce humaine* (Paris: Gallimard, 1996); *On Robert Antelme's Human Race*, trans. Jeffrey Haight (Evanston, Ill.: Northwestern University Press, 2003).

FOR FRIENDSHIP

NOTE: This piece was published as an offprint, *Pour l'amitié* (Paris: Fourbis, 1996). It was published in English translation by Leslie Hill in "Three Texts," *The Oxford Literary Review* 22, special issue *Disastrous Blanchot*, 2000.

1. *Jeune France* was a cultural organization founded by the Vichy government in December 1940 in order to draw French youth into the folds of the "national revolution." The group was dissolved in March 1942, after having been infiltrated by anti-Vichy artists and intellectuals intent on using it as a platform against the government.

2. In 1964 Char wrote a brief prose fragment on "The Essential Perversion" ("Note à propos d'une deuxième lecture de 'La perversion essentielle' in *Le 14 juillet* 1959"), later published in his collection *Recherche de la base et du sommet* (Paris: Gallimard, 1971).

3. This is a reference to the *porteurs de valise* ("suitcase carriers") who worked as part of the clandestine "Jeanson network" to deliver false papers and money to the National Liberation Front (FLN) during the Algerian War.

4. Pierre Mendès-France (1907–82) was a French politician who served as prime minister from 1954 to 1955. After years of working alongside de Gaulle, Mendès-France founded the anti-Gaullist group Union of Democratic Forces and lent his moral support to the mass movements of 1968.

OUR CLANDESTINE COMPANION

NOTE: This text was first published as "Notre compagne clandestine" in Maurice Blanchot et al., *Textes pour Emmanuel Levinas* (Paris: Jean-Michel Place, 1980), 79–87.

1. The exact quote reads: "Everyone seems to think this century is the end of philosophy!" "Le regard du poète," in *Sur Maurice Blanchot* (Paris: Fata

Morgana, 1975); "The Poet's Vision," in *Proper Names*, trans. Michael B. Smith (Stanford: Stanford University Press, 1996), 127.

2. Emmanuel Levinas, "Le Dire et le Dit," in *Autrement qu'être ou au-delà de l'essence* (The Hague: Martinus Nijhoff, 1974), 6–9; "The Said and the Saying," in *Otherwise than Being, or Beyond Essence*, trans. Alphonso Lingis (The Hague: Martinus Nijhoff, 1981), 5–7. (In references to this work hereafter, the French page number will follow that of the English translation.)

3. Ibid., 7/8.

4. Ibid., 181/228.

5. Ibid., 170/216.

THE ASCENDANT WORD, OR ARE WE STILL WORTHY OF POETRY? (SCATTERED NOTES)

NOTE: This text was first published as "La parole ascendante, ou Sommes-nous encores dignes de la poésie?" in Vadim Kozovoï, *Hors de la Colline* (Paris: Hermann, 1984), 119–27. Vadim Kozovoi (1937–99) was a Russian poet and translator who engaged in a lengthy correspondence with Blanchot, which has been partially published in Maurice Blanchot, *Lettres à Vadim Kozovoï, suivi de La parole ascendante* (Paris: Manucius, 2009). Throughout this highly allusive text, Blanchot does not provide any references or use exact quotations, thus the notes provided here are merely indicative.

1. In a letter to Léo d'Orfer written in June 1884, Mallarmé would express a similar thought: "Poetry is the expression, by human language brought back to its essential rhythm, of the mysterious meaning of existence: it thus endows our existence with authenticity and constitutes the only spiritual task." The quote from Paul Valéry is taken from *Cahiers* (Paris: Gallimard, 1974), 2:987.

2. Vadim Kozovoï, *Hors de la Colline* (Paris: Hermann, 1984).

3. Jules Renard, *The Journal of Jules Renard*, ed and trans. Louise Bogan and Elizabeth Roget (Portland, Or.: Tin House Books, 2008), 124.

4. Stéphane Mallarmé, *Oeuvres complètes*, 2 vols. (Paris: Gallimard, 1998–2003), 2:141.

5. Ibid., 2:211.

6. René Char, *Les Matinaux* (Paris: Gallimard, 1984), 80.

7. Stéphane Mallarmé, "La musique et les Lettres," *Oeuvres complètes* 2:64. During his Oxford and Cambridge lectures in 1894, Mallarmé announced: "I am truly bringing news. Astonishing news. And never seen before—We have been meddling with verse" (trans. Lawrence Lipking, cited in "Poet-critics," in *The Cambridge History of Literary Criticism*, vol. 7, ed. A. Walton Litz, Louis Menand, and Lawrence Rainey [Cambridge: Cambridge University Press, 1989]; an alternative translation by Rosemary Lloyd reads: "Poetry has been under attack" ["Music and Letters," in *Mallarmé in Prose*, ed. Mary Ann Caws (New York: New Directions, 2001), 32]).

8. Stéphane Mallarmé, "Enquête sur l'évolution littéraire," *Oeuvres Complètes*, 2:698.

9. André Fontainas, *De Stéphane Mallarmé à Paul Valéry: Notes d'un témoin 1894–1922* (Paris: Edmond Bernard, 1928).

10. Arthur Rimbaud, letter to Paul Demeny, Charleville, May 15, 1871.

11. Arthur Rimbaud, "Qu'est-ce pour nous mon coeur," in *Oeuvres* (Paris: Classiques Garnier, 1991), 171; "What do we care, my heart," in *Complete Works*, (New York: Harper, 2008), 96.

12. Rimbaud, "Vies," in *Oeuvres*, 264; "Lives," in *Complete Works*, 256.

13. Rimbaud, "Enfance," in *Oeuvres*, 255; "Childhood," in *Complete Works*, 173.

14. Rimbaud, *Une Saison en Enfer*, "Délires I," in *Oeuvres*, 220; *A Season in Hell*, "First Delirium: The Foolish Virgin," in *Complete Works*, 227.

15. Henri Michaux, *Misérable Miracle* (Paris: Gallimard, 1991); *Miserable Miracle*, trans. L. Varese (New York: NYRB Classics, 2002).

16. Stéphane Mallarmé, "Crise de vers," in *Oeuvres complètes*, 2:211; "Crisis of Verse," in *Divagations*, trans. Barbara Johnson (Cambridge: Harvard University Press, 2009).

17. René Char, *Oeuvres complètes* (Paris: Gallimard, 1983), 743.

ENCOUNTERS (ON THE RESISTANCE AND MAY 68)

NOTE: This text was published as "Les rencontres," *Le nouvel observateur*, no. 1045 (special issue), November 1984, 84.

PEACE, PEACE FAR AND NEAR

NOTE: Published as "Paix, paix au lointain et au proche," *De la Bible à nos jours: 3000 ans d'art*, exhibition catalogue, Grand Palais–Paris, Salon des indépendants, June 6 to July 28, 1985 (Paris: Société des artistes indépendants, 1985), 51–54.

1. In the King James Bible, Genesis 18:1 reads: "And the Lord appeared unto him in the plains of Mamre: and he sat in the tent door in the heat of the day."

LETTER TO BLANDINE JEANSON

NOTE: Published in *Photographies en quête d'auteurs* (Paris: Agence VU, 1986), 49, a collection of photographs of contemporary French writers. Since Blanchot refused to have his photograph taken, the editors published a photograph of his letter instead.

OUR RESPONSIBILITY (ON NELSON MANDELA)

NOTE: Published as "Notre responsabilité," in Jacques Derrida et al., *Pour Nelson Mandela* (Paris: Gallimard, 1986), 213–17.

1. G. W. F. Hegel, *The Philosophy of History* (New York: Dover, 1956), 99.

2. Breyten Breytenbach, "Lettre à Winnie Mandela," preface to Nelson Mandela, *L'Apartheid* (Paris: Minuit, 1985); "A Letter to Winnie Mandela", in *End Papers* (London: Faber & Faber, 1986), 213–15.

WHAT IS CLOSEST TO ME

NOTE: These lines were originally requested by Salomon Malka as a contribution to a special issue of *Globe* dedicated to the fortieth anniversary of Israel. They arrived too late to be published in that volume and appeared instead as "Ce qui m'est le plus proche," *Globe* 30 (July–August 1988): 56.

1. Menahem Begin (1913–92), Israeli politician and member of the Likud Party. While he was the sixth prime minister of Israel, from 1977 to 1983, he carried out an expansion of Jewish settlements in the occupied territories. According to the Israeli Bureau of Statistics, the period witnessed a fourfold increase in Jewish population of the West Bank and Gaza.

WRITING COMMITTED TO SILENCE

NOTE: Published as "L'Écriture consacrée au silence," *Instants* 1 (1989): 239–41.

1. Emmanuel Levinas, "Au-delà du souvenir," in *À l'heure des Nations* (Paris: Minuit, 1998), 89; "Beyond Memory," in *In the Time of Nations*, trans. Michael B. Smith (London: Athlone Press, 1994), 76.

2. Claude Lanzmann, "Hier ist kein Warum," in *Au sujet de Shoah: Le film de Claude Lanzmann* (Paris: Belin, 1990). This phrase alludes to an episode in Primo Levi's *If This Is a Man*.

[I THINK IT SUITS A WRITER BETTER] (ON NATIONALISM AND INTERNATIONALISM)

NOTE: Published as "Je crois qu'il convient mieux à un écrivain" in *La règle du jeu*, January 1991, 221–22. This is Blanchot's response to a "New Enquiry into the National Question." Among the questions addressed to him, the only one he answers is: "According to you, is there such a thing as a 'good' and a 'bad' nationalism?"

[THE INQUISITION DESTROYED THE CATHOLIC RELIGION] (ON SALMAN RUSHDIE)

NOTE: This text first appeared in *La règle du jeu*, no. 10, May 1993, 206. It was written following the *fatwa* against Salman Rushdie by the Ayatollah Khomeini, on February 14, 1989, for the publication of *The Satanic Verses*.

INDEX OF NAMES

Library of Congress Cataloging-in-Publication Data

Blanchot, Maurice.
[Écrits politiques, 1953–1993. English]
Political writings, 1953–1993 / Maurice Blanchot ;
translated, with an introduction by Zakir Paul.
p. cm.
Includes bibliographical references and index.
ISBN 978-0-8232-2997-0 (cloth)
ISBN 978-0-8232-2998-7 (pbk.)
1. Blanchot, Maurice—Political and social views. I. Paul,
Zakir. II. Title.
PQ2603.L3343E2613 2010
848'.912—dc22
2010011591

www.ingramcontent.com/pod-product-compliance
Lightning Source LLC
Chambersburg PA
CBHW050245110726
47898CB00007B/2289

* 9 7 8 0 8 2 3 2 2 9 9 8 7 *